DogLife 🐾 Lifelong Care for Your Dog™

BOSTON
TERRIER

tfh

Elaine Waldorf Gewirtz

BOSTON TERRIER

Project Team
Editor: Stephanie Fornino, Mary E. Grangeia
Indexer: Elizabeth Walker
Designer: Angela Stanford
Series Design: Mary Ann Kahn, Angela Stanford

T.F.H. Publications
President/CEO: Glen S. Axelrod
Executive Vice President: Mark E. Johnson
Publisher: Christopher T. Reggio
Production Manager: Kathy Bontz

T.F.H. Publications, Inc.
One TFH Plaza
Third and Union Avenues
Neptune City, NJ 07753

Printed and bound in China

10 11 12 13 14   3 5 7 9 8 6 4 2

Library of Congress Cataloging-in-Publication Data
Gewirtz, Elaine Waldorf.
  Boston terrier / Elaine Waldorf Gewirtz.
    p. cm.
  Includes index.
  ISBN 978-0-7938-3601-7 (alk. paper)
  1. Boston terrier. I. Title.
  SF429.B7G493 2010
  636.72--dc22

                    2010013176

This book has been published with the intent to provide accurate and authoritative information in regard to the subject matter within. While every reasonable precaution has been taken in preparation of this book, the author and publisher expressly disclaim responsibility for any errors, omissions, or adverse effects arising from the use or application of the information contained herein. The techniques and suggestions are used at the reader's discretion and are not to be considered a substitute for veterinary care. If you suspect a medical problem consult your veterinarian.

Note: In the interest of concise writing, "he" is used when referring to puppies and dogs unless the text is specifically referring to females or males. "She" is used when referring to people. However, the information contained herein is equally applicable to both sexes.

The Leader In Responsible Animal Care for Over 50 Years!®
www.tfh.com

CONTENTS

INTRODUCTION

INTRODUCING THE BOSTON TERRIER

D apper and distinguished, the Boston Terrier is the quintessential all-American breed. From the canine's roots in the wolf family to the breed's creation in Boston, Massachusetts, it's no surprise that this Yankee Doodle dog is everyone's favorite gentleman. The Boston owes his popularity to many dedicated caretakers over the years, both in the show ring and at home.

DOMESTICATION OF THE DOG

When your devoted Boston Terrier follows you from room to room, it's easy to imagine the first partnership between man and dog more than 20,000 years ago. Just when the dog became a part of our lives is not clear, and we may never know precisely how early humans and canines came together. Archaeological evidence shows, however, that the wild canid, a smallish wolf subspecies, was the principal ancestor of our domestic dog. The dog is part of a family of similar animals that includes wolves, coyotes, foxes, jackals, and wild hunting dogs such as the Dingo and African Wild Hunting Dog, who all share common traits.

While historians once believed that man shared a relationship with dogs in East

Asia, recent genetic studies prove otherwise. Mutations in the DNA of wolves reveal a Eurasian and possibly North African origin. The earliest traces of their bones—a jawbone found in a cave in Iraq—dates back 12,000 years ago. Other sites from the same period have been discovered scattered around Iraq and Israel. One Israeli site included a tomb that held the skeleton of an aged woman whose hand was placed over the chest of the skeleton of a puppy, indicating an affectionate relationship.

The territories of prehistoric man and the dog's ancestors overlapped 10,000 to 14,000 years ago when the animals scavenged for food scraps and garbage in and around early human gatherings. Humans became accustomed to the presence of these creatures and discovered that they could help with hunting and protection tasks. Perhaps they recognized the animals' superior scenting ability and speed in locating and tracking prospective kills and relied on their ability to use their keen senses at night to warn them of approaching danger.

Wild orphaned wolf cubs were soon adopted and nursed alongside human babies. Once these cubs began breeding amongst themselves, taming the offspring became

Dapper and distinguished, the Boston Terrier is the quintessential all-American breed.

an important custom of the culture. These wolf-like animals evolved over generations to become domesticated and similar to the dogs we are familiar with. DNA research reveals that the bond between humans and dogs could be almost as old as modern man. The dog was probably the first and only domesticated animal to accompany humans to different continents in ancient times.

Domesticated dogs became important allies in human survival. They served as guard animals, sources of food and fur, and as beasts of burden. Regardless of where they lived, dogs and man have always relied on one another. The Greeks thought that dogs could help ward off death and kept them as therapists in their healing temples. Assyrian artwork of ancient civilizations depicts large heavy dogs resembling Mastiffs fighting in battles and serving as guard dogs and hunters. North American Indians used dogs to help transport their possessions, and Inuit communities relied on Huskies to pull their sleds.

Today, dogs—and especially Boston Terriers—share their owners' lives and provide companionship in myriad ways.

EARLY DEVELOPMENT OF THE BREED

The Boston Terrier's short-backed physique and stately charm come from crosses between the Bull Terrier, the Bulldog, and their White English Terrier ancestors. In the early years, crosses were made to the French Bulldog as well.

Originally developed as fighting and guard dogs descended from Mastiff types, the Boston's early ancestors were 100-pound (45-kg) plus canines who used their brains and brawn to rule their territories. Some were assigned to butchers' quarters to control bulls before slaughter. At the time, people believed that the best and most tender cuts of meat came from animals who were harassed before slaughter.

These dogs' exposure to the bulls evolved into their next job as bull baiters. In this sport, the dog grabbed onto the bull's nose with his jaw, trying to suffocate him while the crowd cheered. Bull baiting was banned in England in 1835, but the dogs' tenacity and formidable physical characteristics, such as the undershot jaw, big bones, and short legs, remained. The aggressive temperament and massive size has long since been bred out of the Boston Terrier. In its place is today's compact little dog, with flashy markings and a blocky head with a slightly undershot jaw.

Adding to the Boston Terrier's Bulldog ancestry is the high-spiritedness of the terrier. Known as ratters, terriers hunt and kill vermin and need agility, speed, and intelligence to perform their job. The Boston is linked to the White English Terrier, who later evolved into Fox Terriers and Jack Russell Terriers but became extinct in the 1870s. Besides its name, the energetic and lively Boston Terrier has retained classic terrier traits.

BREED HISTORY IN THE UNITED STATES

Boston Terrier history stretches back to the latter half of the 19th century. Nicknamed the "American Gentleman," the Boston was the first American-bred and the first non-sporting breed recognized by the American Kennel Club (AKC), the largest and oldest multi-breed registry in the United States, formed in 1884 to register purebred dogs and maintain a Stud Book registry.

Breed Ancestry

The breed traces its ancestry to an imported Bulldog–terrier cross named Judge, who was purchased by Robert C. Hooper in Boston, Massachusetts around 1870. At 32 pounds (15 kg), Judge was more Bulldog than terrier.

When noted dog fancier Edward Burnett saw Judge, he was so impressed with him that he bred his 20-pound (9 kg) female dog Gyp to him. The breeding produced only one puppy, Well's Eph, who went on to produce attractive progeny, including Barnard's Tom, who closely resembled today's Boston Terrier.

Other breeders bred their bitches to Tom and further refined the look, calling their new breed the American Bull Terrier, much to the objection of some who believed that this new little terrier dog no longer looked anything like a Bull Terrier.

Several years later, about 30 fanciers in the Boston area were showing dogs they called Round Heads or American Bull Terriers. They applied for membership in the AKC, but Bull Terrier and Bulldog fanciers complained by saying the breed's name was too much like their own. One requirement for AKC membership is that the breed must consistently reproduce the same look, or type. Not wanting to give up, the new breed's advocates changed the name of the breed from Round Heads or Bull Terriers to Boston Terriers. In 1891, after renaming the breed after the city in which it originated, the Boston Terrier Club of America was established. Because the new breed was just getting started, it took the AKC two years to accept it, and it was finally recognized in 1893.

Modern-Day Bostons

The Boston ruled in the early 20th century as one of the most popular breeds in America, among many other notable achievements. The Brown shoe company created comic-strip

Unlike most breeds, the Boston Terrier's ancestry is well known.

characters to sell its Buster Brown shoes, one of which was a Boston Terrier named Tige, thought to be the first talking pet to appear in American comics. Between 1920 and 1970, the Boston ranked continuously in the top-ten most popular breeds, and for a few years it was ranked either number one or number two. President Warren G. Harding, Bing Crosby, and jazzman Louis Armstrong each had a Boston. Silent-film star Pola Negri took her Boston, Patsy, with her everywhere—that's probably where Paris Hilton got the idea to carry around a Chihuahua in her purse.

RECOGNITION OF THE BREED BY MAJOR CLUBS

The Boston Terrier breed was officially recognized by the American Kennel Club (AKC) in 1893. Seventy-five Bostons were approved for the AKC Stud Book. They were certified to have been bred pure for at least three generations, and they formed the foundation of the purebred Boston Terrier stock. When the AKC separated the breeds into five groups in 1923, the Boston was assigned to the Non-Sporting Group.

The United Kennel Club (UKC) is the second-largest registry in the United States. This club recognized the Boston Terrier in 1914 and placed the breed into the Companion Dog Group.

Boston Terrier historians believe the first Boston was imported into England in 1901; the breed was registered in the Kennel Club in 1937. Perhaps because the Boston is an all-American breed, records of these dogs are sketchy in Europe. Bostons are shown today in the Utility Group at dog shows in England.

The first Boston Terrier was registered in the Canadian Kennel Club in 1899, just a year after the club was established. In Canada, the breed belongs to the Non-Sporting Group.

All of these clubs maintain slightly different breed standards for the Boston Terrier.

INFLUENTIAL PEOPLE IN THE BREED

In the late 1800s, Dwight Baldwin was nominated the first President of the Boston Terrier Club of America (BCTA). After the breed was recognized by the AKC, J. Varnum Mott, M.D., became the editor of the club's first publication, *The Boston Terrier*, in 1903. Mott chronicled the origin and history of the breed, the purposes and objectives of the Club, and the first standard adopted by the BTCA and the AKC.

From 1930 to 1970, as the breed grew in status and popularity, other Boston Terrier fanciers made significant contributions to the breed. Mr. Alva Rosenberg was a highly respected all-breed judge who owned and bred Bostons in his Ravenroyd Kennels. He also served as the Secretary of the Boston Terrier Club of New York.

Another judge, Vincent Perry, made many friends for the breed as a prolific writer of breed books and dog stories in general. His kennel, Globe, may be found several generations back in the pedigrees of today's winners.

Joseph Faigel was an astute and well-admired judge and breeder. His kennel, under the Magnificient prefix, produced outstanding Boston Terriers. For nearly six decades, from 1906 until his death in 1975, Harry Clasen

The Boston Terrier's short-backed physique and stately charm come from crosses between the Bull Terrier, the Bulldog, and their White English Terrier ancestors.

Nicknamed the "American Gentleman," the Boston Terrier was the first Non-Sporting Group breed recognized by the American Kennel Club.

was a professional handler and judge at a time when the AKC permitted professional handlers to judge specialty shows only. He bred several outstanding Boston Terriers, including Ch. Clasen's Bit O'Honey and Clasen's Syncopation. He handled Ch. Star Q's Brass Buttons, the last Boston Terrier to win the Non-Sporting Group at the Westminster Kennel Club Show, in 1970. He was also a former president of the BTCA.

Owner-handler and judge Emory Wheeler excelled in all aspects of breeding and showing dogs. Breeder-owner-handler Florence Dancer added great prominence to the breed with her outstanding bitch Ch. Iowanna's Velvet Coquette. Mrs. Signe Carlson had a keen eye and was quite knowledgeable as a breeder. She ran the highly successful Kingway breeding program, which Leonard

Myers continued, making him revered by many as a living legend.

Mrs. E. P. Anders, founder of the Royal Kennels, bred Ch. Royal Kid, the sire of 23 champions, including Ch. Royal Kid Regards, who sired 18 champions and won four Bests in Show.

Mrs. Madeleine McGlone maintained up to 90 dogs at a time at her Mosholu Kennels and owned more than 30 champions. Partnered with Alva Rosenberg, she produced Boston Terriers who dominated the mid 1900s.

All these individuals laid a solid foundation for decades to come, stabilizing the type, balance, and soundness of the breed.

MEMORABLE DOGS

Although recognized by the American Kennel Club in 1893, it wasn't until the middle of the

1920's that the Boston Terrier began to register some notable wins in All Breed competition. In 1925, Million Dollar King, owned by Emma Fox, became the first Boston Terrier to win the Non-Sporting Group at the Westminster Kennel Club Show. Four years later, Ch. Reigh Count, owned by Mrs. L. Daley, claimed the same honor.

In 1931, Imogene V, owned by William Cornbill, won the Non-Sporting Group at Westminster. Ch. Million Dollar Kid Boots, owned by Mrs. Jesse Thornton, nabbed the title in 1932. It wasn't until the 1940s that the breed regained some momentum, with three Group I wins in a row at Westminster: Ch. Emperor's Ace, owned by Fred Lucas, in 1946, and Ch. Mighty Sweet Regardless, owned by Mrs. Claude Fitzgerald, with back-to-back wins in 1947 and 1948.

Ch. Mighty Sweet Regardless is still considered one of the best Boston Terriers in breed history. She won countless All Breed Bests in Show and captured the attention of Boston fanciers around the United States. During the next decade, there were a number of top show dogs, such as Ch. Chappie's Little Man, owned by Mrs. Charles Cline, Ch. Clasen's Syncopation, owned by Mrs. H. Peru, and Ch. Grant's Royal Command, owned by Mrs. Parker Grant, who passed on many of his excellent traits to his progeny. The dog of the 1950s was the showy Ch. Sovereign's Escort, owned by Mrs. Dorothy F. Drury.

During the 1960s Ch. B-B's Kim of Fellow, owned by Mrs. Celeste Schulte, and Ch. Personality's Bold Ruler, owned by Mrs. L. B. Hunt, were the top Bostons of the decade. Then along came Ch. Montecalvo's Little Whiz II, owned by Frank Montecalvo; Little Whiz was a truly exceptional dog, who after a repeat win at the New York Specialty was furiously sought after and ultimately sold to a British exhibitor and exported to England.

Ch. Dynamic Doll, owned by Leonard Myers, was a fantastic bitch and the gem of the breed toward the end of the decade.

In 1970 Ch. Star Q's Brass Buttons, owned by Dr. K. Eileen Hite, became the last Boston Terrier to win the Non-Sporting Group at the prestigious Westminster Kennel Club Show. A repeat breeding produced his brother, Ch. Star Q's Pease Knutu, who had a stellar show record.

During the first half of the 1980s, Eleanor and Bob Candland's Ch. Rudy Is a Dandy won a Group II at Westminster in 1982 and several All Breed Bests in Show and produced countless champions. He reproduced his elegant style and class in many of his offspring.

Multiple Best in Show and Boston Terrier Club of America's National Specialty Winner Ch. Staley's El-Bo's Showman still holds the record today as the breed's all-time top producer, surpassing his sire and runner-up, Ch. El-Bo's Rudy.

The Boston Terrier has registered numerous notable wins both in its group and in All Breed competition.

PART I

PUPPYHOOD

CHAPTER 1

IS THE BOSTON TERRIER RIGHT FOR YOU?

Dressed to the nines in a dapper black and white tuxedo, the Boston Terrier appears on the scene with flash and panache. With his charming good looks and debonair attitude, all that's missing is a top hat and tails. But despite this flashy exterior, the Boston sports the nickname "American Gentleman" for a reason.

A courteous and honorable dog, the Boston arrives focused, attentive, and sensitive. Then again, he's always up for fun and games and shows off the pluck of his terrier ancestors with pride and distinction. While a Boston may reach his full growth between nine months and a year, he remains a puppy at heart until 18 months of age.

When you consider adding a Boston to your life, plan on keeping him for life. The breed's winning personality, small size, high trainability, and minimal exercise and grooming requirements make him a joy with which to share your couch. Those assets, coupled with only a few health issues to manage, make the Boston Terrier an ideal canine companion.

BREED CHARACTERISTICS

The quintessential Boston Terrier never runs out of kisses and adores children and adults.

However, this dapper dog's energetic, in-your-face attitude may build a bond but sometimes goes over the top. Behind those perky ears and big brown eyes is a small breed with a big-dog personality. Here's a look into whether a Boston Terrier is all that you're hoping for.

Temperament

The official breed standard describes the Boston's temperament as friendly and lively, with an excellent disposition and a high degree of intelligence, qualities that certainly make this dog an excellent companion. But this description barely scratches the surface. Classic Boston temperament more closely resembles that of a good-natured, spunky little fireball who has little concept of his size. He imagines himself as a giant breed ready to take on the world. Perhaps this comes from the days when the Boston Terrier weighed 25 to 35 pounds (11 to 16 kg) and thought nothing of tackling a badger or hunting mice. Today, a 15-pound (7 kg) Boston has the same sassy attitude of his ancestors. With a fighting breed heritage of 60 years before his acceptance as primarily a companion, he displays a range of temperaments, from the mellow steadfastness of the Bulldog to the feisty moxie of the terrier.

The Boston Terrier is a lively, highly intelligent dog with a friendly disposition.

Eager to explore new situations, the Boston is ever curious and never fearful of new things that cross his path. It's no surprise that this alert, animated dog eagerly rushes to greet people in a friendly manner. He's only too happy to return the affection of his willing admirers. Then again, if a dog lacks discipline and has never received the right training, he may try to take control of an encounter. A strong-willed, bratty Boston may get pushy with strangers if he senses danger or someone invades his territory. But generally, this is a sharply defined dog with no emotion or flaw to disguise. Carrying his heart for all to see, the Boston conveys the message that what you see is what you get and that there's no hidden agenda. Count on the breed's enthusiasm and attentive personality to endear him to all he meets.

Common Behavioral/Personality Traits

A Boston Terrier may be everyone's favorite prom date, but he's no push-button plaything. Far from being a laid-back dog who lives to follow your every wish and command, he has a zest for life that can be overwhelming for some people. He is active but not hyperactive, and lively, just as the breed standard calls for. This delightful little dog is far from the lap dog his small size may suggest to those who don't know him.

Sociability and Playfulness

A perpetual motion machine, a Boston insists that his family take part in his activities. Playing alone is not usually an option, especially if there's a ball around. He will chomp on a toy and drop it into your lap, whether you want it or not. Throw it once and he will keep bringing it back, no matter how many times you toss it.

Bostons beg to play tug of war, too. They'll keep swatting your legs with their rope toy until you finally pick it up. In a flash, they'll shift their grip on the object to their back teeth, and no amount of pulling on your part can dislodge it. The only way a Boston will drop a toy is if you offer him a piece of food. In fact, food and toys are a Boston's best friends forever. He will do anything for either of them and may become fixated on carrying around a stuffed pillow or treasured fabric creature for months. Then suddenly, and without any apparent reason, he'll spend an hour ripping out the toy's stuffing before walking away and leaving it shredded up on the floor.

Resourceful and intelligent, a Boston can do things to keep himself entertained that may either amuse or frustrate some owners. For example, if there's something interesting stuffed inside a kitchen cabinet, he may expend any amount of energy necessary to pull everything out in order to get at it before eventually tearing it up. He doesn't do this out of anger; it's just the Boston way of having some fun. But those characteristics responsible for the Boston's playfulness and mischievousness also make him an eager participant in agility, hiking, and walking, so you can look forward to having a willing exercise partner and fun companion.

Owners who aren't into games with their dogs would likely be overwhelmed by this insistence on interaction. But while some Bostons are capable of going full-speed all day just to keep up with everything happening around the house, they also know when it's time to settle down. Happy, alert, and amusing, Bostons can play at a moment's notice, but usually plop down in your lap or beside you on the rug once the games are over.

Sensitivity

There's a sensitive side to Boston Terriers, too. Highly intelligent and tuned in to their owners, they sense what their human companions are thinking. If you're feeling down, they'll come up and encourage you to smile. If you're joyful, they'll be up and bouncing around.

Do something they don't like, however, such as leave them in a kennel or ignore them when guests come to visit, and they may carry a grudge. Because the breed is so people-oriented, separation can be difficult. Leaving them alone for long hours at home, either

Highly sociable and playful, a Boston insists that his family take part in his activities.

The Boston Terrier's small, square-shaped, and compactly built body conveys a sense of strength and determination.

confined to a dog run or a crate or boarded at a kennel, will not make them happy, and they'll sulk for hours.

Bostons are not a yappy breed, but they take pride in defending their household first. Your dog will not hesitate to go after anyone or anything attempting to gain entry to your home without permission, including your mail if it's delivered through a slot in your door. Many Bostons have been known to destroy checks and other important mail.

Intelligence

If you want a dog who really understands what you are saying, a Boston Terrier may be right up your alley. Verbal cues, gestures, and the tone of your voice add to any dog's comprehension, and most canines figure out the meaning of some basic commands such as *sit*, *stay*, and *come*. The average dog can learn more than 100 words, but a Boston can comprehend nearly 200 words without any special preparation.

Ask a Boston to go get the ball in the back bedroom, and he'll do it. Tell him to fetch the rope in the hallway, and he'll trot off after it. Wonder if he can retrieve your slipper from the bathroom? Just ask him and minutes later it's at your feet.

Enthusiastic and rambunctious, Boston Terriers bring a wonderful sense of humor to most situations, and it's easy to succumb to their charms. Once you evaluate the breed's physical attributes, making a lifelong commitment to this spectacular "American Gentleman" just naturally follows.

PHYSICAL APPEARANCE

The perfect Boston Terrier hasn't been born yet, but this doesn't prevent conscientious breeders from following the breed standard and trying to produce that flawless specimen. While the tuxedo effect contributes to the Boston's appeal, there's so much more to the breed. It possesses an overall look, or true essence, that no other breed can claim.

Breeders refer to this as the Boston Terrier's *breed type*. The qualities that make up its character respect both its Bulldog and terrier heritage in both appearance and personality. The ideal specimen is first and foremost a compact dog with a large, square head, but more than likely the consummate Boston Terrier companion is the one that you care for every day.

Size

The Boston Terrier is a small dog. More specifically, Bostons are usually no taller than 12 inches (30 cm) at the top point of the shoulder (called the withers) and no shorter than 9 inches (23 cm). The AKC breed standard lists three weight classes: under 15 pounds (7 kg), 15 pounds to under 20 pounds (7 kg to under 9 kg), and from 20 to 25 pounds (9 kg to 11 kg) .

Usually, you should be able to tell the difference between the sexes just by looking at the dog's overall size. Males are usually bigger than females and weigh 15 to 18 pounds (7 kg to 8 kg), while females weigh 12 to 14 pounds (5 kg to 6 kg). Females look slightly

more refined and delicate without appearing spindly.

Coat Type and Color

Unlike longhaired breeds that require weekly trips to the groomer to maintain their tangle-free locks, the Boston's short coat is virtually trouble-free. Fine and smooth, the black, brindle, and white hairs glisten and need minimal maintenance.

Coat colors are brindle, seal, or black, with white markings; these colors produce the sharp tuxedo effect described in the breed standard. Along with very dark eyes and deep black pigment on the nose, lips, ears, and pads, these coat shades distinguish a Boston Terrier from other breeds.

According to the breed standard, brindle and white is preferred only if all the other qualities of the dog are equal. The seal color actually looks black but exhibits a red cast when the dog is in the sun or in bright light.

General Body Structure

Regardless of color or size, the Boston Terrier's general appearance is the first characteristic mentioned in the breed standard. It represents the judge's overall impression of the dog when viewing him in the show ring. A total of 100 points is assigned to all of the features, with the overall appearance of the dog valued at 10 points.

Brindle

Brindle is a coat pattern in which layers of black hairs in regions of a lighter color produce irregular-looking stripes. This flecked shading must be evenly distributed throughout the body and shouldn't be blotchy or dull.

The correct Boston head is the hallmark of the breed. It should look flat on the top, be wrinkle free, and have a short, sloped brow.

A sturdy, sharp-looking Boston is all about the right proportion. The standard describes the Boston's body as square-shaped, compact, and well balanced, with the length of the legs in balance with the length of the body to accomplish the square look. The body should never look coarse, clumsy, blocky, or chunky.

The neck, topline (the dog's back), body, and tail constitute 15 points of the standard.

The Boston Terrier's back should be short but in proportion to the rest of his body, and the topline should be level. The croup has a slight curve over the rump and tail. Too much of a curve will interfere with the dog's rear gait and produce faulty movement. The chest should be deep and wide.

The Boston has a short tail, which should not be too long or it may throw the balance off. It may resemble the shape of a corkscrew or it may be straight, but it must not be carried above the back or curl upward off the back. The ideal tail should not exceed in length more than one-quarter the distance from the base to the hock. Docked tails are not permitted in the show ring.

The Boston is meant to give the impression of determination, strength, and activity, and the correct shaped body and desired accompanying features accomplish this.

Head and Neck

Amongst breeders, the Boston Terrier is referred to as a *head breed*. This means that great importance is assigned to how the head should look, and the standard assigns 15 points— the largest allocation of points to one feature—to the head. This includes the dog's muzzle, jaw, bite, skull, and stop (the indentation where the nose joins the skull between the eyes). The correct Boston head is the hallmark of the breed. It should look flat on the top, be wrinkle free, and have a short, sloped brow.

The Boston's muzzle is important to the overall look of the head and is also a primary characteristic of the breed. In proportion to the skull, this short, flat facial feature gives the face good balance. When the muzzle is too short or too long for the length of the skull, it throws the balance off. A muzzle that is too curved results in a dish-faced appearance, while a muzzle that slopes downward from the side results in a down-faced appearance, neither of which is acceptable.

The nose should be black and wide, with a well-defined line between the nostrils. If the nose is flesh-colored and lacks black coloration it's called a Dudley nose, which is a disqualification in the breed standard. Bostons with a Dudley nose need to be sunscreened because they're susceptible to sunburn and skin cancer.

Beyond the shape of the head, the striking markings on it tell the Boston's story of an alert, highly intelligent dog. The breed standard requires that the markings include a white area around the nose (called a nose band) and a white blaze, or large area of white color, between the eyes. The blaze should extend from the nose band up between the eyes and onto the top of the head. White markings may also extend to the collar, forechest, and on to part or all of the forelegs and hind legs below the hocks. The sharp black and white contrast markings on the head leading into the body are characteristic of the breed because they affect the dog's expression, and the Boston is all about the expression.

Expression, or the facial appearance of the dog, is a top priority and awarded a total of

The Boston has large, round, soft dark eyes that are set wide apart.

10 points out of the 100 possible points of the standard. The classic Boston does not have a harsh or unkind look. When judges look into a Boson's face, they hope to see the character of the breed—a friendly and lively dog with an excellent disposition and a high degree of intelligence, which sends the message that this dog is a wonderful companion.

Eyes

Look into a Boston's keen eyes and it's easy to imagine that he's thinking about his next move. The breed standard calls for large, round, soft, dark eyes that are set wide apart. Too much white, or haw, showing in the eyes, and small or light-colored almond-shaped eyes detract from the alert expression. Blue eyes, or any trace of blue, disqualifies the Boston in the show ring. Responsible breeders are careful not to breed Boston terriers with blue eyes, especially since veterinary researchers correlate blue eyes with deafness.

Healthy eyes do not have specks in the corneas; the pupils should be dark and the irises should constrict when light enters the eyes. No stray eyelashes directed from the lids should rub against the corneas.

Ears

When erect and set correctly in the skull, the Boston's small black ears should lie as close to the corners of the head as possible, giving the head's outline a square appearance. Although many breeders dislike ear cropping and no longer have it done, the standard allows for either natural ears or ears cropped so that they stand erect.

Cropping involves surgically removing the extra piece of earflap that prevents the ears from standing erect. Only a veterinarian skilled in ear cropping should perform this procedure because it must be done with precision, with the dog under full anesthesia. If you want a Boston with perfectly cropped ears, discuss this with your dog's breeder and veterinarian. The modification must be done between 6 and 12 weeks of age, and it requires postoperative care because there are some risks. It is also painful for the dog. Dogs experience discomfort during healing, stretching, retaping, and bandaging, as well as other manipulations of the ears after surgery. Experienced breeders can judge what position the ears will take by the time the dog is an adult. They can use special tape to reinforce the soft cartilage in the ear if it folds over.

Ear cropping is controversial and is prohibited in Britain and in many continental European countries, including Scandinavian countries, and in New Zealand. Bostons with cropped ears are prohibited from competing in United Kingdom Kennel Club events.

SUITABILITY AS A PET

A compact, showy little dog with a happy, outgoing temperament, the Boston Terrier

By the Numbers

If you look at a puppy between the ages of 12 and 18 weeks of age, you'll notice that the tops of his ears flop over and stick out slightly at the sides. This is usually a sign that he is teething. By the time he is 8 months of age, all of his adult teeth will have erupted and his ears will naturally settle into their permanent position.

Easy keepers, Bostons require only moderate daily exercise and minimal grooming.

treasures his toys and loves his people. If you think you want a Boston, be prepared to provide for all his emotional and physical needs, as well as his constant antics.

On the surface, this versatile short-coated canine companion seems low maintenance, but keeping any dog healthy and in good condition can be expensive. Besides the initial cost of buying a dog from a reputable breeder, the money spent on food, toys, grooming essentials, bedding, training, and veterinary care adds up quickly. Like keeping extra emergency funds in a bank account for yourself and family, it's not a bad idea to save up six months' worth of canine care money before bringing a dog home.

While a Boston Terrier is an attractive dog with an appealing sense of humor, it's important to choose a pet whose needs and personality match your lifestyle. If you are an avid outdoor fan looking for a biking, hunting, or fishing companion, a Boston may not be the breed for you. Or if you're a working parent who spends long hours at the office and weekends shuttling children to soccer games and dance recitals, this dog won't enjoy playing second fiddle and staying home alone much of the time. Boston Terriers thrive on human companionship.

You can't expect your children or other dogs in the family to babysit your Boston either. All dogs require and deserve individual attention. Once you make the decision to acquire a dog, he's yours for life. It's then your responsibility to put his needs ahead of your own if necessary and to make sure that he has a good-quality life with you. If you designate a family member to always

If it's raining or cold out, your Boston will need a sweater or doggy raincoat to keep him warm.

oversee daily care and to monitor the dog's health, behavior, and training, you can look forward to sharing many long years together.

Environment

As long as you provide your Boston with companionship and steady care, he'll be happy no matter where you live. With regular exercise every day, he doesn't require a lot of room to run and can thrive in the city or the country. For apartment life without a yard, though, plan on taking your Boston on regular outings several times a day. Don't forget to take along clean-up supplies, too.

Although he enjoys playing outdoors, a Boston must always sleep indoors with his family at night. It should be noted that he won't be wild about spending his days alone outside

either—or indoors for that matter. The most ideal situation gives him free access to go in and out of the house into a secure fenced-in yard. Just make sure he has a shady area to cool off in if the weather heats up, and don't let him stay outdoors for too long if it's very cold. His short coat offers no protection from extreme cold or rainy weather. Always supervise your dog when he is outdoors. Like every other dog, your Boston should never be allowed to run loose. Anyone could easily walk off with him or worse—he may be hit by a car, ingest something poisonous, or chase after a small animal and lose his way home.

Exercise

Every dog, including a small Boston Terrier, needs daily exercise to stay healthy. Exercise strengthens the immune system, builds strong bones and muscles, and stimulates the heart. Keeping your dog healthy and active spices up his day and helps him to burn off excess energy.

Chasing a ball in a long hallway indoors or running around the yard helps maintain your Boston's fitness and alleviates boredom. He'll especially enjoy going for a long walk with you once a day. Puppies tire easily and can only handle several short exercise sessions throughout the day. If you're a jogger, hold off on taking your puppy running until he's 18 months of age because his bones are still growing and too much vigorous exercise that he doesn't instigate himself can cause injury.

In hot weather, your Boston needs special protection while exercising. His unique facial structure and pushed-in nose can cause difficulty breathing during exertion. Exercise him early in the morning and late in the afternoon to avoid problems associated with the heat.

If it's raining or cold out, your dog will need a sweater or doggy raincoat to keep him warm.

Getting Along With Others

Although they are very social creatures, Bostons often choose favorites in the family. Your dog will like whoever feeds and takes care of him. Other relationships may take some nurturing. Bostons are loyal, so once a strong bond has been formed, you can look forward to a long, happy companionship.

Children

With their high interest in play, Bostons and children can become fast friends. Even an energetic parent may have trouble keeping up with a lively youngster the way a Boston can. When socialized to children at a young age, most will love kids. Maybe it's because they both can have the same interest and curiosity about toys or in playing a good game for hours on end. Kids find everyday dog chores such as brushing, bathing, and feeding treats exciting, and they have a special way of making them interesting for your dog, too. When it comes to housetraining, children relate to the responsibility and know how to heap on the praise when your dog hits the right spot. From the Boston's standpoint, a perfect day consists of tagging along with the family members to all their activities.

Kids and canines make a great match, but adults should always supervise them. Never leave them unattended—even for a few minutes—because either one can have poor judgment when reacting to sudden movements or loud noises. It's important to teach your dog and your child to respect one another. For a Boston, this means keeping all four black and white feet on the ground; no jumping up on kids or adults. Grabbing food out of a child's hand or nipping should never be allowed either. Likewise, don't allow your toddler to walk around the house carrying a small toy that your dog could swallow and choke on. Teach your child from the first day you bring your Boston home to act gently and move slowly around him. Screaming, running around the dog, sneaking up on him and scaring him, or teasing him are big no-no's.

Your dog's primal reaction might be to protect himself and snap back.

The Boston makes an excellent companion to a child who doesn't

Want to Know More?

For more detailed information on how to socialize your Boston Terrier, see Chapter 4: Training Your Boston Terrier Puppy.

While your Boston may enjoy cavorting with other dogs and competing for a stick, he won't be wild about sharing a treasured toy.

poke, pinch, or hurt him. Show your child the correct way to pet a dog, and teach her that pulling ears, jabbing at eyes, and grabbing legs are definitely off limits. When you bring your puppy home, instruct your child to sit on the floor while holding him. Never hand a puppy to a child who is standing because even an 8-pound (4 kg) Boston is too heavy for a youngster to hold safely, and the puppy can become seriously injured if he's dropped. Restrain your child from picking the puppy up on her own, too, because he can easily wriggle free and slip to the ground.

Build a positive bond between your dog and your kids by asking them to help with easy daily care tasks, such as adding water to the water dish, putting a blanket into your dog's bed, tossing the ball, and brushing his coat.

Strangers
The Boston's terrier heritage makes him naturally protective of his family. This means that strangers are not always welcome unless you give your approval first. Expect that a Boston will bark first and ask questions later. If an uninvited stranger tries to gain entrance into your home through a back door, your Boston will not welcome him in. In fact, expect aggression; your dog will surely bite the intruder.

Other Dogs and Pets
Bostons love to be the center of attention and work hard to earn their family's admiration,

often preferring human companionship to that of other dogs. While they may enjoy cavorting with other dogs and competing for a stick, they're not wild about sharing treasured items.

If you're considering getting a second dog or if you already have a dog and plan on bringing a Boston into the household, know that male Bostons don't usually get along well with other male dogs, especially if there's a female canine in the house. They do, however, make great companions for dogs of the opposite sex.

When Boston pups are introduced to cats and perhaps pet rabbits at an early age they can often live in harmony with them. After that, the Boston's territorial nature takes over and new pets are viewed as trespassers with whom they may not get along.

Trainability

All dogs need training, but the Boston willingly accepts guidance and discipline with dignity. He's an eager learner, although he does best when handled appropriately, which means using positive reinforcement rather than harsh corrections. Reward good behavior with food, praise, and toys. Create a learning environment with fun and games, and keep it moving fast. Bostons catch on quickly and don't need a lot of repeat drilling.

Teaching basic commands such as *sit, stay, down,* and *come* will prove invaluable in everyday situations, for example, if the front door or gate is accidentally left open. Unlike other breeds who take loose dogs running past them in stride, Bostons are territorial creatures who don't like trespassers on their property—they'll think nothing of chasing after them.

Grooming Needs

With his short, knot-free coat, your Boston doesn't require a lot of grooming to look his best. As with all other breeds, his skin and coat should be regularly bathed and brushed, and his nails should be trimmed once a week. Additionally, every few days, check the ears and eyes and clean them if necessary; also clean the folds around the tail. Your Boston's teeth will need daily brushing to prevent gum infection and tooth decay.

General Health Issues

Your dog's health depends on the genes he inherits from his parents and the care you provide. Once you're aware of the health issues prevalent in the breed, you can take steps to prevent them if possible or to obtain help for your dog early on.

Compared to other breeds, Bostons are a hardy and healthy breed. They may, however, be prone to patellar luxation, skin disorders, eye problems, and breathing difficulties. Buying your dog from a reputable breeder who spends the time and money necessary to screen for inherited diseases will increase your chances of obtaining a healthy dog.

◎ *Training Tidbit*

Teaching your Boston the *leave it* command could save his life. Once a Boston grabs something poisonous in his strong back jaws it's nearly impossible to yank it out of his mouth. Instead, offer your dog a yummy piece of food in trade for whatever he has in his mouth. You may need to repeat this exercise many times before your dog willingly gives up the goody.

CHAPTER 2

FINDING AND PREPPING FOR YOUR BOSTON TERRIER PUPPY

With visions of this charming breed dancing in your head, you're ready to add a new American Gentleman or Gentlewoman to the household. Perhaps you have your heart set on bringing home a puppy—well, this is the chapter for you!

WHY GET A PUPPY?

If you can't decide between a puppy and an adult dog, consider the ooh-aah factor of a pup. There's nothing quite like a Boston youngster who's eager to explore the world one minute yet cuddle in a lap the next. Scaled-down versions of their parents with double the spirit and spunk, puppies are clearly capable of melting anyone's heart. They're adorable and huggable and pack a lot of love into their compact little bodies.

The Truth About Puppies

Cuteness aside, puppies are not right for everyone. They require constant supervision, housetraining, and socialization, in addition to needing much more time and patience than an adult dog. Hopefully, your lifestyle is conducive to raising a puppy yourself and teaching him how to act appropriately. Look forward to spending extra hours training your Boston, including taking him to obedience classes. He

will also need to learn how to accept having his nails trimmed and receiving a bath, whereas an adult dog is often already comfortable with grooming sessions. Also, when you buy a puppy you're not quite sure how he will turn out, while an older dog is a known commodity.

Expect to pay more for a puppy than you would for an adult dog, as Boston pups are pricey. Most litters are born by caesarean section, and the average litter size is small—usually no more than four puppies, which raises the price of each puppy.

In addition to the purchase price and cost of feeding, training, and grooming supplies and toys, the first-year veterinary expenses add up quickly. Puppies require several visits to the veterinarian for regular checkups and vaccinations, and you'll need to pay for parasite prevention. Your veterinarian can catch health problems in the early stages and can provide advice on general issues of behavior, care, and training.

Then again, it's a joyous experience to raise your own puppy exactly the way you want and to see him develop into a confident, self-assured Boston. Not every dog grows up with the right training, and often it's harder to locate a stable adult dog raised by someone else.

But with patience and a diligent search, you'll surely find a great Boston of any age.

Show or Pet Quality?

When you interview breeders, it helps if you know whether you want a show prospect or a pet-quality companion. Finding a well-bred, healthy dog with a great temperament is the main priority, but this requires time and patience.

Perhaps you've owned a pet-quality Boston in the past and now want one who looks like the Boston Terriers you see in dog shows on television. Or maybe you think that exhibiting a dog to a championship title would be fun.

When you interview breeders, it helps if you know whether you want a show prospect or a pet-quality companion.

If so, you'll need to buy a puppy with show potential—one with correct and desired markings, sound movement, and a confident, outgoing personality. Just because a dog is purebred and American Kennel Club (AKC) registered doesn't guarantee that he's a show specimen. Go to a breeder who actively shows her dogs and who is willing to introduce you to the competition world. Show exhibitors take their hobby seriously, and it helps enormously to have a mentor teach you the ropes. Competing can be expensive and requires time, training, and patience, so find out all that's involved.

Before buying a pup with champion promise, attend a few dog shows to observe good examples of the breed and see how the dogs are presented in the conformation ring.

Consider how closely those Bostons meet the breed standard and lack disqualifying faults, such as blue eyes, a Dudley (flesh-colored) nose, or solid black, brindle, or seal color without enough white markings.

If you've never shown a dog before, it may be a little more difficult to buy the pick of the litter from a show breeder. Competitive breeders often want to keep the best for themselves and are sometimes reluctant to let a prize pup go to a novice, so you may have to wait for another litter.

Or you may choose a pet-quality Boston who fails to meet the breeder's show expectations and is available as a pet. While pet-quality pups go to their new homes at nine weeks of age, breeders often hold onto conformation candidates a few weeks longer to see how they develop. No matter how perfect a pup may appear at six weeks, he may change as he matures and not work out for the show ring. Sometimes the black markings will slightly overtake the white, or he may be too small for the under-15-pound (7-kg) class, or he may exceed the 25-pound (11.5-kg) weight limit.

An experienced breeder can estimate show potential, but it's never a guarantee. If the pup fails to meet the breeder's precise expectations—maybe he's longer than the standard allows, his eyes show too much white, or the bite isn't correct and his muzzle isn't square, he'll be sold as a pet and you may be able to purchase a quality Boston Terrier for a pet price.

Brindle, Seal, or Black?

As mentioned in Chapter 1, the breed standard for Boston Terriers does not mention any colors in the breed other than brindle, seal, or black, all with white markings. When looking for puppies, you may come across unscrupulous breeders who advertise rare-colored red, fawn, liver, brown, blue, gray, or white Boston Terriers and sell them at inflated prices. While these dogs may make fine pets, they are mixed breeds rather than purebred Bostons, and you should never have to pay a higher price for them. These incorrectly colored dogs lack the proper expression that defines the Boston Terrier as a breed.

When trying to decide between a black and a brindle champion in training, know that inside the show ring more blacks than brindles compete. That's because many owners seem to prefer the sharp tuxedo look of the black and white Boston, and according to the standard, brindles need to possess good-quality markings to gain the judge's approval.

In the pet-quality category, don't overlook Bostons who are lovingly referred to as "splashes." These

In the show ring, more blacks than brindles compete.

mismarked dogs may have a half-white head or white overlapping an eye and may pop up from time to time in even the most well-bred litters. No conscientious breeder purposely breeds splashes to sell.

Size

In the show ring, Bostons are divided by weight in these classes: under 15 pounds (7 kg); 15 pounds (7 kg) but under 20 pounds (9 kg); 20 pounds (9 kg) but not to exceed 25 pounds (11.5 kg). Although you may prefer one size to another, a breeder cannot guarantee how much

Want to Know More?

For more detailed information on what a Boston Terrier should look like, see Chapter 1: Is the Boston Terrier Right for You?

a puppy will weigh when fully grown. Don't be fooled by pet sellers who sell you a pup with the promise that he will grow up toy sized or an exact weight. Even the best breeders can't predict the size the pup will be when grown.

Whether you choose a pet or show prospect, a mismarked, or a brindle, seal, or black and white, a Boston Terrier who weighs under 15 pounds (7 kg) or more than 20 pounds (9 kg), know that these all-American couch cuddlers come ready to love in different colors and sizes.

WHERE TO FIND THE PUPPY OF YOUR DREAMS

You would think that finding a well-bred, healthy Boston with a great temperament would be easy, but that's not always the case. Although you might walk into a pet store and see a Boston pup for sale or read advertisements for puppies in the newspaper or posted on community bulletin boards, these pups miss the basics. Sure, it's easy to fall in love with the first dog that resembles a Boston, and perfect conformation may not matter to you, but good health and a stable personality are priorities.

Breeders

When breeds such as the Boston Terrier become popular, inexperienced breeders try to cash in on the craze. Commercial breeders mass produce puppies for profit with little regard for the dogs' quality or welfare. Avoid these instant Boston brokers who are solely interested in making a quick sale and aren't concerned about what happens to the puppy once the buyer takes him home. They offer no help if the new owner has a question or if the puppy has a problem later on.

These outlets do not screen the sire and dam for any hereditary problems before breeding the pair together and fail to provide any information about the parents' overall health, conformation,

or temperament. Unlike reputable breeders, commercial breeders will not take the puppy back if the owner must surrender him.

While you'll see dozens of listings for breeders on the Internet, think twice before purchasing a puppy from anyone willing to ship a puppy sight unseen. If the pup arrives in poor condition or he isn't what you were expecting, you'll need to take him to the veterinarian and think about sending him back to the breeder. This can be emotionally and physically upsetting for you and the puppy. Skip pet sellers, too, who offer "old-

Good health and a stable personality are priorities when selecting a Boston.

fashioned Boston Terriers," or "Boston Bulldogs," usually for an inflated price. These are fancy names for mixed breeds combining Boxer, Pit Bull, or Staffordshire Terrier and a poor-quality Boston. If you see dogs with long muzzles, drop ears, or odd colors, they are not purebred Boston Terriers.

For a quality Boston pup, go to a breeder who is careful about the dogs she breeds, the way they are raised, and the people who buy them. Hunting down a reputable breeder requires time and patience, as really good Boston Terrier breeders seldom live nearby, but the effort is worth it. You're going to have this dog for a dozen or more years, so spending a few weeks or months to find a conscientious breeder pays off over time.

When you buy a puppy from a conscientious breeder, you're also buying the breeder's expertise for the life of the dog. Passionate about producing quality Bostons, this person will eagerly share the newest information about their behavior, care, health, and training and will encourage you to call with any questions or problems that may arise in the future.

Before planning a litter, a reputable breeder carefully studies the pedigrees, or family trees, of the dogs and understands their physical and mental characteristics. She breeds to improve the quality of the stock, and tests for genetic problems and diseases such as slipped kneecaps, heart problems, deafness, and eye diseases. A good breeder pairs together only dogs who are free from those problems.

The breeder may breed for show or obedience competition and place health, temperament, and the breed standard foremost. Once the litter arrives, conscientious breeders handle their pups regularly and prepare them for life as adult dogs by socializing them to new sights, sounds, and experiences. Before placing the pups in their new homes, these breeders evaluate personality and

By the Numbers

Most responsible Boston breeders keep their pet-quality puppies until they are nine weeks of age before allowing them to go to their new homes. Breeders will often hold onto show candidates until they are four months of age before deciding whether to sell them.

conformation and the amount of training they'll require.

Locating a Breeder

The best way to find a reputable breeder is to contact the Boston Terrier Club of America (BTCA) (www.bostonterrierclubofamerica. org). The club can refer you to local Boston Terrier clubs and provide a list of breeders in the club. Membership in the BTCA requires the recommendation of two other members, and applicants must agree to abide by a code of ethics regarding their breeding practices.

This standard includes giving puppy buyers a health guarantee and a sales contract and promising not to sell puppies to commercial facilities, puppy brokers, or puppy mills. BTCA members pledge to breed all bitches with the intention of improving the breed; keep accurate breeding records; act responsibly for the welfare of every dog bred or sold; and refuse to sell a Boston to anyone unable to properly care for the dog.

Visit a dog show, especially a Boston Terrier specialty show, to locate breeders too, although most breeders are usually BTCA members. Specialty shows attract top breeders from around the country who bring their best dogs. Puppies are not sold at shows, but this is a great place to see breeding stock and ask breeders about upcoming litters. While you may not want to show your dog, there's satisfaction in knowing that a pet-quality puppy from a show-bred litter is raised the same as his top-winning littermates.

What to Expect

Once you've selected a few breeders you like, schedule a visit to their kennels, even if they don't have any puppies at the time. Here you'll see the conditions in which the pups are raised. The litter should live indoors so that it is accustomed to the sights and sounds of a family. This will ease the transition to your household. You'll also see the litter's mother and possibly other dogs related to the puppies, which will give you a glimpse of what your puppy might look and act like when he's full grown. The premises should appear clean, the pups well cared for, and the adult dogs outgoing and healthy.

The sire may not live at the same kennel, but the breeder will explain why the sire was chosen and what qualities he will hopefully pass on to the youngsters. The breeder will likely show off the sire's pedigree, photos, and health test results.

Expect the breeder to interview you and ask you to fill out an application with references. Boston breeders care deeply about their pups and want to verify that you will provide a healthy and happy environment for the dog throughout his life. A good breeder will explain all of your responsibilities.

On your part, feel free to ask the breeder for the names of previous puppy buyers. Give them a call to inquire about the health and temperament of the puppy they purchased. Feel free to ask the breeder how many litters are produced each year. Usually two or three

litters are more than enough for most breeders to properly care for. Avoid a breeder who always has puppies, especially unplanned litters. This usually means that the breeder is not paying close attention to the dogs.

Documents

The well-bred Boston Terrier comes with a stack of papers. This includes information about the behavior, care, health, and training of your puppy, as well as a three-generation pedigree, although many Boston breeders offer a four- or five-generation family tree and photographs of many prominent ancestors. Dogs with a "Ch" in front of their names are AKC champions. The initials "CD", "NA", or "RA" indicate performance titles—obedience, agility, or rally.

The litter should be registered with the AKC, and the breeder should give you the puppy's registration application when you

When visiting the breeder, insist on meeting your potential dog's mother and littermates.

pick up your puppy. To obtain the puppy's registration certificate, you and the breeder must sign the application and mail it to the AKC with the correct fee. Pet-quality puppies are usually sold with AKC limited registration, meaning that they cannot be shown in AKC conformation events, and any puppies they may produce will be ineligible for AKC registration. If you're lucky, your breeder has already registered your puppy with the AKC, so all you have to do is add your name to your pup's registration.

The paper trail should include a letter from the veterinarian stating that the puppy has been examined and is in good health. Verification of any immunizations and dewormings should also be included. A reputable breeder will also give you a sales contract. This specifies the health and quality of the puppy and explains the refund or replacement policy. You'll also be asked to sign an agreement that you will always care for this puppy and never abandon him. If, for any reason, you can no longer keep this dog, you are required to notify the breeder.

If you're buying a pet-quality Boston, the breeder will ask you to sign an agreement to spay or neuter the dog. When breeders sell show-potential pups, they usually require the buyer to sign an agreement to show the dog. Hopefully you and the breeder have discussed these expectations before you see this contract. Be sure to ask about anything in the contract that you do not understand.

Part of the paperwork accompanying your puppy should state that he has been examined by a vet and is in good health.

Health Guarantee

A good breeder includes a health guarantee for about a week after you take the puppy home and requires you to take the pup to your own veterinarian for a checkup. After that, no one can promise that a dog will be free from every illness for years. Choosing a litter from a family in which hereditary problems seldom crop up is the best protection you have.

The breeder should provide copies of the parents' and puppy's health certifications. For Boston Terriers, these include complete eye examinations by a veterinary ophthalmologist to detect congenital heritable eye defects and certification from the Canine Eye Registration Foundation (CERF). This foundation certifies dogs to be free of inherited eye problems.

A reputable breeder will have both the sire and dam "CERFed" before every breeding. CERF certification numbers are only good for one year because there are many late-onset diseases that can occur, such as retinal atrophy and cataracts. Ask to see the CERF number and examination forms. Puppies can be examined at eight weeks old, although they must be rechecked once a year because their eye conditions may change.

You should also receive the results of a

preliminary patella examination when the puppy is eight weeks of age, although the Orthopedic Foundation for Animals (OFA) cannot certify the results until the puppy is 12 months old. The breeder should supply you with the results of a Brainstem Auditory Evoked Response (BAER) test, which tests hearing in both ears. A veterinarian can test a puppy's hearing as early as five weeks of age.

Steer clear of any breeder who tells you that she knows the puppies can see or hear and move just fine without the exams.

Shelters and Rescues

While Boston Terrier rescue groups and shelters usually have adolescent and adult Bostons available for adoption, they may only have a purebred Boston puppy available occasionally. As you can imagine, cute Boston pups are usually rehomed quickly. If you have your heart set on adopting a puppy, the best way to obtain one from a rescue group or shelter is to keep checking in with them. If you are lucky enough to adopt a Boston pup, a pedigree, AKC registration, and background health information may or may not be available, depending upon the circumstances. A fee or donation is usually required, and you'll have to agree to have the pup spayed or neutered if

When Can I Get That Puppy?

Don't expect to buy a puppy on the day you want one. The best breeders plan litters years in advance and breed only a few each year, often with a long waiting list, so be prepared to wait a few weeks or months before taking home a new Boston.

the operation hasn't already been performed. When you make the decision to adopt a pup, choose him just as carefully as you would one from a breeder.

BEFORE YOUR BOSTON COMES HOME

It's almost time for your Boston Terrier to join the household. To make the transition easy, plan ahead. Your all-American hero will need a schedule you can stick to and plenty of doggy stuff, too. Save yourself a last-minute trip to the store by purchasing the basic supplies before picking him up from the breeder. The less hectic the first few days are, the better.

Puppy-Proofing the Home and Yard

It's amazing how much trouble one little puppy can find inside and outside your home if left unattended. Before your dog comes home, check over the house and yard for potential hazards. Don't forget to look underneath tables and inside corners. Here are some things you can do:

- To prevent him from falling and injuring himself, block off open stairways, decks, or balconies with baby or dog gates.
- Cover electrical outlets with baby locks and tack dangling cords to the wall or enclose them with cable wrap or a cord concealer.
- Install baby locks on kitchen cabinets to prevent your pup from swallowing toxic cleaners.
- Keep a tight-fitting lid on garbage cans, or store them in a locked cabinet out of your pup's reach.
- Store craft items up high where your pup can't reach and swallow pins or small pieces.
- Pick up children's toys promptly to keep your pup from chewing and swallowing small pieces.

- Check the yard for poisonous plants and remove them.
- Keep rose bushes and any plants with low, sharp branches in an enclosed area away from your puppy. Thorns can seriously injure a Boston Terrier's eyes.
- If your puppy has access to the garage, remove tools and toxic fertilizers and chemicals.
- Check fences and gates to make sure that they are totally secure. Dogs have a way of squeezing through gaps or digging underneath and escaping from the yard. Consult the website of the American Society for the Prevention of Cruelty to Animals (ASPCA) for a complete list of poisonous plants: www.aspca.org/pet-care/poison-control/plants.

Setting Up a Schedule

Dogs like a routine so that they know what to expect. Before your puppy comes home, set up a family meeting to plan his schedule. Discuss what time he will eat, go outside to potty, exercise, play, and sleep, and which family members will be responsible for those doggy chores. This way, everyone can enjoy your puppy while meeting his needs. Maintaining a schedule facilitates housetraining and will help your new Boston adapt to family life.

A crate is a den-like refuge for your Boston.

Be patient with your Boston puppy as he adjusts to his new life in your home.

Obtaining Supplies

Preparing for your Boston's arrival comes with a price tag, but don't worry. This breed isn't a fussy one and doesn't need a lot of fancy stuff to keep him happy. Many pet supplies last a lifetime, but the initial expense can be costly. If you have the time, it pays to compare prices at online stores, pet supply warehouses, and specialty shops.

Bed

Wait to purchase a dog bed for your pup until he's through the chewing stage. Leave your pup alone in his bed for a few minutes and he'll transform a plushy cushion into piles of stuffing. Instead, place an old blanket inside his crate. (Don't use towels because your dog will chew and swallow the stringy fibers, which can become obstructed in his stomach.)

Bowls

Your dog will need two bowls: one for food and another for water. Stainless steel bowls last forever and are easy to clean. Avoid ceramic and plastic, as these can crack and injure your dog's tongue and can cause chin acne. Food becomes trapped in the crevices and harbors bacteria.

Clothes

If you live in a cold climate, your Boston will appreciate a doggy coat or sweater to keep him warm during outings. Doggy raincoats come in handy if you walk your dog in the rain. Nothing fancy is required, although you'll find outfits galore for a Boston. Puppies wear a size small, depending on how large your pup is.

Collar and Leash

You'll find collars in different price ranges, but all your Boston needs is a simple flat or rolled lightweight buckle collar to help control and identify him. These styles are available in leather, nylon, web, and recycled materials.

Until he's an adult, the size of your Boston's neck will expand two or three times, so he'll need two or three different-sized collars. Don't buy one that's too big, hoping he'll grow into it. If it's too loose it could fall off or catch on an object and choke him. Purchase a collar that fits him at the time. The right size allows for two of your fingers to fit between the collar and your puppy's neck.

Choose a sturdy leather or nylon 6-foot-long (2-m) leash that will last a lifetime and teach your dog not to pull you while on a walk. Some Boston owners prefer using a harness if their dog pulls when walking. Instead of attaching to the dog's collar, a harness loops around the shoulders and body and attaches to the leash. Although it doesn't give you as much control as a collar and leash, a harness prevents the dog from gasping and coughing while he's pulling you down the street.

Skip retractable leads because they tangle easily and can slice through someone's leg. Plus you have no control over your dog when he's 10 to 16 feet (3 to 5 m) away from you and an aggressive dog approaches him.

Crate

Visit the pet supply store and you'll see crates in three styles: wire, which folds flat and provides plenty of air circulation; high-impact plastic, required for airline travel; and lightweight soft canvas that collapses for easy transport.

You need only one crate when your dog comes home. Whatever style you select, choose a size that's large enough for your Boston to stand up, turn around comfortably, and lie down in. Don't buy a giant crate, as your puppy will use the back of it as a bathroom. The bottom of the crate should be solid. Models with a wire floor raised over a solid pan can tear Boston toenails and splay their feet.

Food and Water

Most reputable breeders will give you one or two days' worth of the food your pup has been eating. Before using it up, purchase more of the same food. You can switch recipes once your puppy acclimates to his new routine.

Rather than use tap water, you'll need some bottled water for your pup for the first few days. Different water systems contain slightly different chemicals that can cause gastrointestinal upset. When you make the switch to your own water system, do so gradually so that his system has a chance to adjust.

Training Tidbit

Aside from providing entertainment and exercise, toys can be used to assist you in the training process. To train your puppy not to dig in the yard, build him a private digging space. Fence off the area and bury a few of his toys when he's not looking. Take him there and unearth one of his treasured objects. When he investigates and starts to dig, praise him. Repeat several times until he catches on.

Grooming Supplies

Low-maintenance Boston Terriers don't need much glamming up, but you'll still need to purchase a few grooming supplies to keep your dog in tip-top shape. These include a canine toothbrush and some canine toothpaste to brush his teeth, toenail clippers and/or a nail grinder to keep nails short, a rubber brush, and canine shampoo for regular brushing and bathing.

Identification

Doggy ID tags are available in pet supply stores and on the Internet. Purchase two with a sturdy O-ring in case one gets lost, and include your current address and phone number.

Bring your Boston home when you have time to spend with him.

Tattoos: A permanent way to identify your dog involves tattooing a number that will remain the same for your Boston's lifetime. Most tattoos are placed on an adult dog's stomach or inner thigh; their installation may require anesthesia because the dog may squirm. Sometimes these numbers fade over time, and whoever finds the dog may not realize that this is a form of identification.

Microchips: Microchip implants are reliable permanent identification available through veterinarians and animal shelters. About the size of a grain of rice, a chip is placed at the top of your dog's neck by your veterinarian. You must register your name, address, and phone number, along with your veterinarian's contact information, with the microchip registry and update this information every time you move or change your phone number.

Owners sometimes forget to register their dogs after having them microchipped. A study conducted by the Journal of the Veterinary Medical Association (July, 2009) found that of 1,943 dogs in shelters, 58.1 percent were microchipped, but the registries were unable to find any information on the owner or the person who implanted the microchip for 9.8 percent of the dogs, so be sure to follow through on this important step.

Canine GPS: Another way to help reunite you with your dog is to attach a canine global positioning system to his collar. If he becomes lost, you can track his location through your cell phone or computer.

Toys

Can a Boston ever have enough toys? Purchase a few different types, such as balls, chews, tugs, and plush and interactive toys, like the ones made by Nylabone, until you know which ones your dog prefers.

When selecting toys for your dog, size matters! Choose balls or small toys that are large enough that your dog can't swallow them. Avoid soft toys that your dog can easily tear apart because the pieces can become lodged in his throat, creating a choking hazard. Check playthings over carefully to make sure there are no small objects attached. Many toys have hard plastic loops or S-shaped hooks that retailers use to hang them on display racks. Be sure to remove these before giving the toys to your dog because he can swallow and choke on them.

BRINGING PUPPY HOME

After your pup turns nine weeks of age, he's ready to join your family. If possible, pick him up early in the morning so that you both have several hours to adjust to one another before bedtime. Choose a day when you can stay home, preferably at the beginning of a long weekend or your vacation. This will help your pup adjust to your routine.

Avoid bringing him home during holidays if you expect company and a lot of commotion. He needs some quiet time to figure out who everyone is.

For the first few days, limit visitors coming to see the new puppy. To avoid confusion, give him some time to bond with family members before meeting acquaintances.

What to Expect the First Few Days/Weeks

It may take your new Boston puppy a few days to settle into his new home. Don't expect him to gobble up all of his food at the first meal, but if he skips more than two meals or vomits more than twice, call your veterinarian because he may be ill.

Until your puppy figures out what housetraining is all about, plan to clean up a few bathroom accidents too. If you notice more than one or two loose, runny, or bloody stools, contact your veterinarian immediately because this may signal illness. Also notify your breeder if your puppy becomes ill.

Healthy puppies adapt to new situations quickly, especially after surviving the first few nights without whimpering. In his previous home, your pup was accustomed to cuddling up with his littermates at bedtime. Now he's surrounded by different smells and sounds, which can be a scary experience once the lights go out. To ease the transition, place your puppy's crate next to your bed. Put an article of your clothing inside the crate to give him a familiar smell and a big stuffed animal (without any dangerous pieces) he can snuggle up against. Tire your pup out before you put him to bed, and speak soft words of encouragement to him if he fusses.

If he's never slept in a crate before, let your puppy sleep on the floor next to your bed on a comfy blanket. Attach his leash to the bed frame so that he can't wander off. The next day, introduce the crate for a nap so that he has a chance to become accustomed to it before bedtime.

CHAPTER 3

CARE OF YOUR BOSTON TERRIER PUPPY

Keep your camera handy! The next few months with your new Boston Terrier puppy will be sure-shot memory-makers. But as you experience the joys of owning a four-footed friend, you'll also face the responsibilities of keeping him in tip-top shape. These include feeding him a healthy diet, maintaining his coat and skin in good condition, and making trips to the veterinarian for routine checkups, preventive care, and oh yes, preventing reproduction.

FEEDING YOUR PUPPY

Offering your Boston pup his first meal can be an enjoyable but messy adventure. When he dined with his littermates, he was accustomed to pushing and shoving for kibble crumbs spread out on a big round pan. Now he's graduated to eating alone from a bowl. Not every puppy understands what having his own deep dish is all about, so expect some sniffing, barking, and even refusing the food altogether. Or he may decide to dive in feet first.

Feeding a new puppy his first few meals sets the stage for a lifetime of good eating habits. Some Bostons can become picky eaters; others are always begging for any little tidbit they can wrangle out of you.

One way to prevent having a problem diner later on is to establish a consistent routine right from the beginning. Feed your puppy in a location free of distractions from the family hubbub and other pets in the household. Don't hover, but stay in the room while your puppy eats because no one likes to eat alone.

Pet your pup while he's eating to discourage him from becoming too possessive over his food. Once every two or three meals, pick up the bowl, wait a few seconds, and return it to him. Your pup will realize that you're in charge of his food and that guarding it by growling or biting your hand is unacceptable behavior. This submissive behavior comes in handy if a child approaches and reaches to pet your dog or take food out of the bowl.

What to Feed

In the early 1900s, Boston Terrier breeders fed their eight-week-old puppies 3 teaspoons of raw chopped beef and cooked vegetables one day, then cooked beef or lamb the next. By three months of age, the pups ate an eighth of a pound (57 g) of meat or fish and veggies a day.

Today, Boston owners have more meal choices than ever before. Dry food, or kibble, and canned,

The type of nutrition your puppy receives will affect his growth and development as well as his overall health and well-being as an adult.

or wet, formulas rank as the most popular, with semi-moist and frozen foods close behind. Seeking a healthier alternative to commercially processed foods, many people opt to cook their own recipes or serve up a raw diet.

Whatever type of nutrition you choose for your puppy, he needs a high-quality, well-balanced diet for his active lifestyle. A Boston pup's typical day involves plenty of wiggles, sprints around the house, ball chasing, and a nap or two. This schedule, coupled with a puppy's rapidly growing body, requires essential nutrients to keep him active, healthy, and strong.

Boston pups require about twice as many calories per kilogram of body weight and more protein and fat than their adult relatives. They need the right amounts of proteins, amino acids, carbohydrates, fiber, fats, vitamins, and minerals in each meal. All these nutrients combine to build muscle and bone.

The Association of American Feed Control Officials (AAFCO) establishes guidelines for all animal feed products and makes recommendations for how much protein, fat, and vitamins commercial food should contain. AAFCO recommends that puppies receive 28 percent protein, while adult dogs need only 18 percent. Protein is a critical part of a growing puppy's diet. If you feed a commercial diet, choose the puppy recipe.

Boston puppies also require omega-3 and omega-6 fatty acids for healthy brain and eye formation. The right balance of vitamins helps your puppy's body fight disease, absorb minerals, regulate metabolism, and grow normally. The puppy maintains and stores fat-soluble vitamins in the liver and fatty tissues; water-soluble vitamins, such as vitamins B and C, are flushed out every day and must be replaced.

For puppies, calcium and phosphorus are essential for proper development of strong bones and teeth. Most quality commercial dog foods contain all the vitamins and minerals that a puppy needs.

For the first few days, while your pup is acclimating to his new environment, keep him on the same brand of food the breeder fed. After that feel free to change brands gradually or start him on a homemade diet.

If you decide to give your new little one a dry food, choose small kibble pieces. Because the Boston is a brachycephalic (short-faced) breed, picking up food, chewing, and swallowing it can be a challenge, especially for a pup. Add the fact that the pup is teething and that his mouth may be sore and it's no wonder that he'll take a while to clean the bowl if the pieces are too large.

When you change to a new food, do it gradually over a week to ten days. This gives your puppy's system time to adjust and avoid an upset stomach, diarrhea, or vomiting. Mix in a quarter of the new recipe with three-quarters of the old recipe for three or four days. Then up the proportion to half new recipe, half old recipe for another three or four days. After that your pup should be eating all new food.

Puppies need a high-quality, well-balanced diet that is compatible with their active lifestyle.

Feeding the Right Amount

Knowing the precise amount to feed your new puppy isn't always easy, but begin by asking your breeder how much he or she gave your pup. For the first day or two, measure out the same quantity. If your pup finishes it quickly, you may want to add one-eighth of a cup more of dry food or another tablespoon of canned or homemade recipe to his bowl. New sights and sounds in a household build up an appetite!

Ask your breeder or veterinarian for the recommended amounts of food you should provide as your puppy grows.

If you feed quality commercial food, look at the proportion guidelines on the package, but these are only suggested measurements and may be too much for your Boston.

Ask your breeder or veterinarian for the recommended amounts of food as your puppy grows, or follow these guidelines:

- Up to 12 weeks, feed one-quarter to one-third of a cup, four times a day. Puppy recipe.
- From 13 weeks to 6 months, feed one-third to one-half of a cup, three times a day. Puppy recipe.
- From six months to one year, feed one-half to two-thirds of a cup, two to three times a day. Puppy recipe.
- One year and older, feed half a cup, twice a day. Change to the adult or maintenance recipe.

Just don't let your Boston puppy plump up. It's healthier to keep him lean rather than too fat. Look at his physique. You should be able to feel his ribs and see his waist. Dogs do have a waist, and your Boston's is located behind his ribs. If he's too hefty, you won't be able to feel them. If he's too skinny, the ribs stick out.

Feeding Schedule

Rather than leaving food out all day (called free feeding), serve your puppy his meals at set times. This encourages good eating habits and speeds up the housetraining process. When he's finished eating, you can take him outside to eliminate. Or, if he walks away from most of his food, you'll know he may be ill.

Free feeding contributes to canine obesity, which can lead to serious illness. When puppies are allowed to eat as much as they want, they usually do, and the pounds pile up. The other disadvantage to leaving a full bowl of food lying around is that it issues an open invitation to other dogs in the house to come help themselves. At the end of the day, you have no way of knowing how much your puppy has eaten.

When you feed your puppy, give him 15 or 20 minutes to finish the meal. After that time, pick up the leftovers and store them in the refrigerator or toss them in the garbage. This sends the message to your Boston not to dawdle over his food.

Depending upon their size, Boston puppies up to the age of six months need to be fed three or four times a day. If you work and your schedule isn't flexible and you can't be home to feed your puppy, enlist the help of a reliable friend or family member, or hire a professional pet sitter.

Sometime around six months you may notice that your puppy isn't ravenous at the mid-day meal. If so, try skipping it the next day and instead divide the food and add it to the remaining meals. From six months on, Bostons should be fed two meals a day—morning and evening.

When to Feed Your Puppy

When you pick your puppy up from the breeder, ask what time he last ate. He'll need his next meal three or four hours after that. At home,

Bottled Water

Your new puppy is going to feel slightly unsettled and may have a queasy stomach while he's adjusting to his new environment. During this time, or at least for the first few days, give him bottled or filtered tap water to drink in his water bowl and if mixed with his food. The concentrations of nitrates, iron, and magnesium in your household water system may be different from those at the breeder's, resulting in gastrointestinal upset. It's one reason why some Boston puppies suffer bouts of diarrhea after arriving in their new homes.

give him an hour or two to unwind before introducing the food bowl. Don't be surprised if he turns his nose up and walks away from the dish you lovingly prepared. Allow 15 to 20 minutes before picking up the bowl and hold off offering more food until the next meal three or four hours later.

On his second day in your new home, set a schedule of feeding your puppy when he wakes up in the morning, late morning, early afternoon, and at dinnertime.

GROOMING A PUPPY

A nine-week-old Boston puppy may be a handful, but along with his other needs he'll need regular sprucing up. It's not difficult once you get your routine down pat.

Start grooming your puppy the day after you bring him home. The idea is to begin establishing a consistent habit of doing so. If you choose a regular day and time during the week to attend to his maintenance, it will be easy to remember. Or jot down on

Multi-Dog Tip

When feeding your puppy with other dogs, give each one a designated spot in the room for their food bowl. If your puppy leaves his bowl to check out someone else's, patiently redirect him to his own bowl. Don't allow bigger dogs to eat the pup's food.

your calendar which day you've performed a grooming task so you know when it needs to be done again.

Why Grooming is Important
Establishing a regular grooming routine for bathing and brushing keeps your Boston's coat in good condition. Besides, you're more likely to spend time cuddling with a sweet-smelling dog who looks good. Don't forget to trim his nails regularly too. Short nails help him maintain balance and the ability to move freely.

Bonding
Besides improving your dog's appearance, regular grooming offers you a chance to spend some quality time with him. You'll build a strong bond and strengthen the trust you have between one another.

Health Check
Grooming your dog on a regular basis gives you the opportunity to check his body over for anything that may need medical attention: lumps, bumps, broken nails, fleas, ticks, or ear infections. During this time you can also examine his mouth and teeth for accumulated tartar, any broken teeth, or reddened or discolored gums.

Grooming 101
Teaching your puppy to like being fussed over may take a while. Start slow and be patient. The important thing is that he likes the grooming session and is a willing participant. It helps to use some small food treats to reward your dog after a bath or nail trimming.

For the first few sessions, don't do everything at once. Clip one or two nails or give a quick bath in the kitchen sink if it's big enough, rather than the bathtub, which might be too

Training Tidbit

Give your puppy a small food treat immediately after trimming each nail. After a few sessions, he'll realize that standing still for a nail trim has yummy rewards.

intimidating to a young puppy. This gives him time to acclimate to the process. Once your Boston becomes more accustomed to being groomed, you can perform all of the tasks at one time.

Grooming Supplies
Before beginning your grooming session, assemble all of the tools you'll need. Nothing is more frustrating that having to stop in the middle of a bath or nail trim to fetch something you've forgotten.

Keep all of your grooming supplies in a basket or small plastic organizer so all you have to do is pick up the container. A grooming table comes in handy because you don't have to bend down, but you can also use a countertop or outdoor picnic or kitchen table with a nonslip surface. Never leave your Boston on a table or countertop unattended because he could fall off. If you're comfortable sitting on the floor or on the couch, try that approach.

HEALTH CARE
Sometimes it takes teamwork to maintain your Boston in top condition. He depends on you to feed him the right diet and provide enough exercise, and he also needs a qualified veterinarian with a conscientious office staff to provide good health care.

Finding a Vet

The path to keeping your Boston active and lively begins with finding the right veterinarian. Dogs are living longer today thanks to advances in veterinary care, prevention, and monitoring early signs of illness. It makes sense to take the time to choose a qualified veterinarian who is sincerely interested in helping your dog to live a long and happy life.

Choosing a vet is one of the most important decisions you will ever make for your Boston. You'll want to be certain the person you select has the academic training and experience necessary to care for your pet and a true passion for animals and their well-being.

Unless you live in a small town where there's only one veterinarian or none at all, you'll have several veterinary offices from which to choose. These usually range from a small office with one veterinarian to a large clinic with several. Some vets have mobile clinics or specialize in alternative medicine, such as acupuncture or homeopathy, or clinical disciplines, such as dermatology or ophthalmology. With so many choices, the selection can be confusing.

Begin by asking for a referral from your puppy's breeder, dog-owning friends, or local shelter or kennel club because word of mouth is often the best resource. Or, if there's a college of veterinary medicine near you, contact it for a list of nearby veterinarians who may be affiliated with the school. Another way to find qualified veterinary clinics in your area is to check the American Animal Hospital Association's (AAHA) website at www. healthypet.com. It lists hospitals accredited by the AAHA that meet high veterinary care standards.

To help you narrow down your search, look at the websites of local veterinarians. Most post biographical information and photos of their offices, and they list their policies, treatment philosophies, services, hours of operation, routine fees, and locations.

After researching, call a few veterinary offices and arrange for an interview. Most hold open houses to give potential clients a chance to view the hospital or clinic and meet the staff.

What to Look For

Before visiting a veterinary office, ask whether you can bring your puppy along to meet the veterinarian and the rest of the staff. If he hasn't had his core vaccines yet, plan on carrying him; older immunized pups can tour on a leash.

Choosing a vet is one of the most important decisions you will ever make for your Boston.

Introduce your pup to the veterinarian and staff to see how they relate to one another. Hopefully, they will acknowledge his presence and seem genuinely glad to see him. Offering him a healthy treat also helps to let your dog know that visiting the vet can be a fun experience.

When touring the facilities, take a peek at the exam rooms, X-ray area, surgical facilities, and recovery rooms. All spaces, including the waiting area and the laboratory, should appear well lit, clean, and orderly. If the staff does not want to show you these areas, thank them politely and cross them off your list.

Most veterinarians are proud to display their credentials on their office walls, so take a few moments to look at those credentials to see where the diplomas are from and whether the vets have received any special training. The credentials should be from an accredited veterinary college, and the doctor should be a member of a professional veterinary association such as the American Veterinary Medical Association or a state or local veterinary association.

Questions to Ask

It's important to feel comfortable talking to the veterinarian and asking any questions without feeling silly. You're establishing a trusting relationship with your vet, so you should feel at ease with the way the doctor communicates with you, and the explanations he or she gives should be easy to understand. Also important, the staff

Schedule your puppy's first checkup within the first few days of bringing him home.

should seem friendly, compassionate, and eager to help you.

While you can inquire whether the veterinarian has experience treating Bostons, this is not mandatory. All purebreds and mixed breeds require the same excellent level of care, and a good veterinarian will have a network of specialists available for any necessary referrals.

Answers to the following questions may help you to make a final decision:

- Does the veterinarian keep up with the latest advances in veterinary care and offer continuing education for the professional staff?
- What does the veterinarian do if he or she has trouble diagnosing an animal's medical condition? Does the doctor refer you to a specialty clinic? Veterinarians are proud of the latest diagnostic equipment they may have added, so make sure you inquire about what may be new and how it may help your dog.
- Can you request an appointment with a specific veterinarian at each visit, or must you take whoever is available? It helps if you can establish a rapport with the same veterinarian.
- Do any of the veterinarians in the practice specialize in certain disciplines, such as orthopedics, oncology, ophthalmology, or dermatology? Bostons may need these services as they age.
- If you decide to purchase pet insurance, will the clinic accept it?
- If you have an emergency after hours, is the office open? If not, does the veterinarian recommend a nearby emergency clinic?
- What is the average wait time for making a nonemergency appointment?
- Does the veterinarian have a dog, and if so, what breed? Another dog owner may have a greater understanding and compassion for the human/canine bond.

- Are boarding and grooming services available? Are training classes offered?
- Find out how health records detailing immunizations, reactions to medications, illnesses, surgical procedures, and behavior traits are maintained. Many veterinarians are now using efficient computer programs to store and track this important information.

But despite recommendations, top academic qualifications, and state-of-the-art offices, there's always a possibility that you're uncomfortable with the veterinarian. That's all right. Resume your search until you find the right person and place for you and your Boston. A good relationship with your veterinarian is just as important as a referral or the latest technological resources. Never underestimate the value of a caring veterinarian who sincerely wants your Boston Terrier to remain healthy. Don't forget, too, that if you're ever unhappy with the level of care your Boston receives, another qualified veterinarian is only a few phone calls away.

First Checkup

After you've found a veterinarian with whom you're comfortable, schedule your puppy's first checkup. Breeders require new owners to take their pups to their own vets within 48 to 72 hours after bringing them home. If you've adopted an older puppy, don't wait until your puppy is sick before meeting the veterinarian for the first time.

Resist the urge to stress out before the first visit to the vet because your puppy will pick up on your emotions and feel nervous too! Maintain a calm and happy demeanor and it will rub off on your pup. This first experience should be a positive one so that he won't develop any painful associations with going to the veterinarian.

Before you leave the house, jot down some questions you want to ask. Once you arrive at the vet's office it's easy to become distracted and forget. Schedule enough time for the visit so that you don't have to feel rushed. Bring along any health records you received from your breeder, including the list of dewormings and vaccinations that have already been administered. Also bring a stool sample from that morning so it can be checked for worms and other parasites.

Once in the exam room, the vet tech will weigh your Boston and take his temperature and pulse. A normal puppy temperature is 100° to 102°F (38° to 39 °C), and a normal pulse is 120 to 160 beats per minute. Your veterinarian will greet your pup and ask about his health history. Use this opportunity to discuss anything that concerns you, particularly regarding feeding and behavior.

If you have any questions about a vaccination schedule, be sure to discuss this issue with the doctor as well. If you don't plan to show your Boston, another important issue to review is spaying and neutering. Don't forget to schedule an appointment for the procedure before you leave the office.

During the initial exam, the veterinarian will listen to your puppy's heart and lungs through a stethoscope, listening for any sounds of congestion, cough, abnormal breathing patterns, or early signs of heart disease. The body and other internal organs will be palpated to detect any signs of internal problems.

A good exam also includes checking your puppy's genital region and looking for any discharge. If you have a male puppy, the veterinarian will check to make sure that both testicles are properly descending. The vet will also examine your puppy's anal region for discharge or other signs of disease or parasites and his belly button for an umbilical hernia. This is a small rupture in the abdomen, usually

Emergency Care

If anything should go wrong on a weekend, holiday, or after your veterinarian's office has closed for the day, it is important to know the location of an emergency veterinary clinic closest to you. Your vet can probably recommend a veterinary hospital or 24-hour clinic, and you should keep this information handy in the event you cannot reach her for advice. Emergency clinics only handle urgent problems and generally do not perform routine checkups, vaccinations, or spaying and neutering. The ASPCA Animal Poison Control Center offers an emergency hotline at 1-888-426-4435. You can call any time, 365 days a year. A small fee will be charged to your credit card.

hereditary or acquired during the birth process when the umbilical cord separates from the placenta. Hernias are fairly common and can be surgically corrected when your dog is spayed or neutered.

The doctor will examine your puppy's ears with an otoscope, an instrument that probes the entire ear canal and eardrum, to ensure there are no parasites or infections present. Ears can often collect bacteria that emit a musky foul odor. Sometimes a foreign body, such as a blade of grass or a foxtail, can become imbedded and cause an infection.

The veterinarian will also look into your puppy's eyes to check whether they are clear and free from discharge. Too much staining on the skin underneath the eye may indicate a clogged tear duct. Your puppy's nose should be free from discharge, too.

Gently lifting your pup's lips, the veterinarian will open his mouth to make sure there are no swollen areas on his gums and that all his teeth look normal. Sometimes baby teeth are slow to fall out and the gums can become infected when adult teeth begin to come in. There shouldn't be any lumps, cuts, or scrapes inside the mouth, and the teeth should look clean and white.

A good checkup includes looking at your pup's skin for any eruptions or rashes or fleas, ticks, and other external parasites. The condition of the coat will be evaluated. A dull coat could signal an internal problem. Most likely your puppy will need flea, tick, and heartworm preventives along with a few vaccines, too, so expect the first visit to be on the pricey side. This overall checkup is very important to your puppy's long-term health.

When the veterinarian completes the exam and gives your puppy a clean bill of health, you'll breathe a sigh of relief. Ask when he needs to return for his next checkup. It's your job to keep up with his preventive care.

Vaccinations

During their first few weeks of life, puppies receive immunity from the colostrum in their mother's milk. After a few weeks, immunity begins to decline, although this occurs at different times for different puppies. To provide protection after puppies are weaned, a series of vaccines is administered.

While a healthy immune system gives adult dogs the best defense against disease, puppies—even strong ones—sometimes have not yet developed sufficient immunity. Vaccination protects them from certain deadly communicable diseases by boosting their immune system. Derived from viruses or bacteria that have been either killed or weakened (modified live), vaccines trigger the production of antibodies that prepare dogs to fight future infections, providing resistance that can last for months or even years. Some vaccines are given via injections using a syringe and a needle, while others are administered directly into the skin or into the nose.

Although veterinarians once recommended vaccinating dogs every year, there has been increasing debate about the risks associated with some immunizations. As a result, the protocol is different today. In 2006, the American Animal Hospital Association issued a new set of guidelines recommending

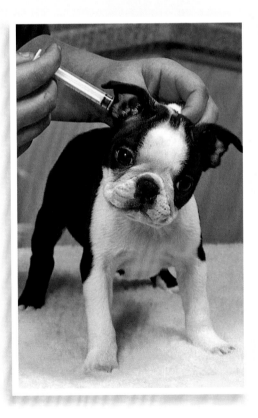

Vaccination is crucial to ensuring that your puppy remains healthy during the first few months of his life.

vaccination once every three years and booster shots every three years. You may want to discuss vaccination protocols recommended for your area with your veterinarian so you can make an informed decision about what may be best for your dog.

Core and Noncore Vaccines

Core vaccines (CAV-2 vaccine) are recommended for all dogs for vaccinations against distemper, canine adenovirus-2 (hepatitis and respiratory disease), and canine parvovirus-2. They should be given at least three weeks apart, at 9 to 10 weeks, 14 weeks, and 16 to 18 weeks, with a booster administered at one year. Following this series, the distemper, adenovirus, and parvovirus core vaccines should be given once every three years.

The rabies vaccine is also a core vaccine and required by law. It's required before your dog can get a license or be boarded at a kennel or transported in an airplane. The first rabies vaccine should be given between 16 and 26 weeks of age, although the booster protocol varies somewhat depending upon local laws.

Noncore vaccines are recommended for those dogs who are particularly susceptible to contracting leptospirosis, coronavirus, canine parainfluenza, kennel cough, and Lyme disease.

Once the initial core vaccines are given, the veterinarian can use a blood sample to measure the levels of protective antibodies already present in the body. This is called titer testing or serum vaccine antibody titer testing.

A high titer count reveals a high level of immunity to the disease, while a low titer count shows that a dog may still be susceptible. Many veterinarians recommend using a titer before routinely vaccinating a dog once a year. Titers are not available for bordetella, parainfluenza, or coronavirus.

Bordetella

Commonly known as kennel cough, bordetella (caused by *Bordetella bronchiseptica* organisms) is highly contagious and results from an inflammation of the dog's upper respiratory tract. Passed through the air, it can affect dogs of all ages and is often spread among dogs who spend time with one another in boarding kennels, veterinary clinics, grooming salons, and dog parks. Signs of the infection occur 2

Because many diseases are spread among dogs who spend time with one another in boarding kennels, grooming salons, and dog parks, it's best to keep your puppy at home until he is fully vaccinated.

to 14 days after exposure, and if there are no further complications, the symptoms will last about 10 days.

Comparable to whooping cough in people, kennel cough is characterized by a dry, hacking cough that sounds like honking and is followed by retching and gagging. Bostons may have a watery nasal discharge along with it. Despite the coughing, dogs will continue to eat and are alert and active. Severe symptoms produce lethargy, fever, loss of appetite, pneumonia, and even death in the worst cases. Bordetella infection can continue for as long as 6 to 14 weeks and may spread to other dogs during that time. In severe cases the veterinarian may prescribe antibiotics.

The best protection against bordetella is not exposing young puppies to other dogs who may pass it on. A nasal spray for both parainfluenza and bordetella can also be used in puppies as young as three weeks of age; it can offer protection as early as three to four days after vaccination.

A single injectable bordetella vaccine, as well as the one administered as a nasal spray, will not totally prevent infection. The injectable vaccine must be given in two doses, three to four weeks apart, and protection will not occur until one to two weeks after the second injection.

Coronavirus

A viral cause of diarrhea in puppies lasting several days, canine coronavirus (CCV) is passed through food contaminated by feces of an infected dog. Puppies can also contract it by licking a contaminated area. If younger than 12 weeks of age, puppies are particularly susceptible.

Coronavirus is highly contagious and mimics milder symptoms of parvovirus: vomiting,

Want to Know More?

The onset of some illnesses and conditions may occur during both puppyhood and adulthood. For more detailed health information, see Chapter 8: Boston Terrier Health and Wellness.

diarrhea, and depression. Only a laboratory test can differentiate between the two. There is no specific treatment for coronavirus, although keeping puppies from becoming dehydrated can help.

In areas where coronavirus is prevalent, dogs should be vaccinated against it beginning at or about six weeks of age.

Distemper

Similar to human measles, canine distemper virus can be deadly in dogs. It is transmitted through the air by the cough of infected dogs and through contaminated urine. Distemper virus destroys the skin, brain, eyes, and intestinal and respiratory tracts. Older dogs and puppies younger than six months of age are the most susceptible, although dogs of any age can contract it.

From initial exposure to the first signs of the disease 7 to 21 days later, symptoms may include a mild case of coughing, nasal and yellow eye discharge, diarrhea, vomiting, and fever. Severe symptoms include seizures, pneumonia, and a thickening of the nose and pads of the feet (the latter called "hardpad").

The distemper vaccines available prevent the disease with minimal side effects, but should be boostered.

Leptospirosis

Leptospirosis affects both animals and people throughout the world. There are many different

Some infectious diseases, such as Lyme disease and leptospirosis, are transmitted through contact with infected organisms in outdoor environments, so carry your Boston puppy if you take him on a public outing.

strains of the disease, but the canine vaccines that are available offer protection against only one or two of the more common strains.

Dogs can contract this disease through contact with infected urine from a dog or from a rat or other wild animal, or through bite wounds. Transmission also occurs through exposure to contaminated water sources (particularly stagnant or slow-moving water), food, or bedding.

Shivering, fever, and muscle tenderness are the first signs of infection, followed by vomiting and rapid dehydration. In severe cases, dogs develop hypothermia and become depressed before death. If a dog does manage to survive, he will have kidney damage. Veterinarians can diagnose lepto through a blood test.

The best prevention is keeping dogs away from contaminated water sources, wildlife reservoirs, and infected animals. Although a vaccine is available, it is one of the most controversial vaccines because it may cause an adverse reaction that can be fatal.

It is not recommended for puppies younger than eight weeks of age or for very small dogs.

Lyme Disease

Lyme disease is caused by an infectious organism carried by the deer tick. It was originally identified in Lyme, Connecticut, although cases have been diagnosed throughout the United States, particularly in the Northeast and upper Midwest.

For a dog to contract Lyme disease, an infected deer tick must attach itself and feed on him for about 48 hours. Symptoms include arthritis, which causes sudden lameness, swelling in the joints, swollen lymph nodes, lethargy, loss of appetite, and fever.

To prevent Lyme disease, dogs need protection from ticks through tick control products and should avoid areas of infestation when ticks are most active. Removing ticks as soon as possible may help control the disease.

Lyme disease is treated with antibiotics. If left untreated, it can cause kidney or heart damage. There is a vaccine for Lyme disease prevention, but many veterinarians do not recommend giving it to dogs who do not live in a tick-infested area. The vaccine provides only partial protection.

Parainfluenza

The canine parainfluenza virus is a major cause of infectious tracheobronchitis (kennel cough) syndrome. As with the symptoms caused by the distemper virus, parainfluenza symptoms range from a dry hacking cough to inflammation of the larynx, bronchial tubes, and trachea. The vaccine to prevent kennel cough includes *Bordetella bronchiseptica*, a bacterium, canine adenovirus-2, and canine parainfluenza virus.

Parvovirus

Highly contagious, canine parvovirus (parvo) is characterized by bloody diarrhea. Spread through contact with the feces of infected dogs, this virus also survives for five months and longer on objects such as food dishes, clothing, and floors. Insects and rodents can transmit the disease through fecal material and vomit as well.

For this reason, avoid taking your puppy out walking in public places, such as dog parks, parking lots, and pet stores where unvaccinated dogs may have defecated. This deadly virus can live in a large grassy area or even the tiniest

clod of dirt for at least six months after being deposited there by an infected dog. From 6 to 20 weeks of age, carry your Boston puppy if you take him on a public outing.

The appearance of the first signs of parvo varies from 7 to 14 days from the time of initial exposure. It is characterized by vomiting, diarrhea, dehydration, and bloody feces. Death may occur as early as two days after exposure. Adult dogs exposed to parvo show few symptoms, while puppies younger than six months of age are more susceptible. The most severe cases occur in puppies younger than 12 weeks.

Rabies

Rabies is contracted through the bite of an infected animal. The virus moves slowly from the point of the bite—from three to eight weeks—and spreads through the nerves of the bitten animal toward the brain. Once it reaches the brain, the dog will experience three stages ranging from anxiety and fury to paralysis, all within days of the virus having reached the brain.

There is no treatment for rabies, and vaccinating puppies between 16 and 24 weeks of age is the best prevention. Because the disease is fatal to humans as well as dogs, raccoons, coyotes, foxes, skunks, cats, and other mammals, the rabies vaccine is required by law in every state. Veterinarians may administer a one- or three-year rabies vaccine, depending on local laws and the incidence of rabies in the area.

Puppy-Specific Illnesses

Boston puppies are pretty hardy creatures with few breed-specific medical problems. This doesn't mean that an unexpected illness won't pop up. In a perfect world, your Boston would inherit only healthy, normal genes and live to a ripe old age of 14 or 15 years. But every breed is prone to developing at least a few genetic illnesses. Hopefully, breeders have tested for these prevalent issues and will not offer a puppy for sale without fully disclosing a health condition to the buyer.

Deafness

Boston Terriers, like several other breeds, may suffer from hereditary deafness. According to a Boston Terrier Club of America (BCTA) health survey in 2000, the incidence of deafness in Bostons was 3.8 percent.

With hereditary deafness, total and permanent hearing loss can occur in one ear (unilateral deafness) or in both ears (bilateral deafness) at about three to four weeks of age. Shortly before the ear canal opens at about three weeks of age, the blood vessels in the inner ear degenerate. The nerve cells in the inner ear then die, causing irreversible damage. The mode of inheritance for the defective genes is unknown, although both parents must contribute defective genes.

With diligent observation, a conscientious breeder can identify a bilaterally deaf puppy between three and four weeks of age. If the pup is asleep, he will not awaken or react to a loud sound. A unilaterally deaf pup is harder to detect.

Using special auditory equipment without sedation, a veterinarian or veterinary neurologist can make a definitive diagnosis of either bilateral or unilateral deafness through BAER (Brainstem Auditory Evoked Response) testing. This painless electrodiagnostic test consists of small electrodes placed under the scalp. These electrodes are so thin and sharp that the puppy hardly notices their insertion. Small earphones placed in the pup's ears emit a series of click sounds. The electrodes pick up the brain's response to the clicks.

Responsible breeders test for all breed-specific health issues before offering their puppies for sale.

There is no treatment for deafness, either in one or in both ears. Owners need to adapt their training methods by using sign language and other visual cues. Unilaterally deaf dogs can make great pets, but bilaterally deaf dogs may present unique training challenges. While some deaf dogs are good companions, others may develop anxious personalities because communication is restricted.

Juvenile Cataracts

Twenty different eye diseases can affect Boston Terriers, with juvenile cataracts being one of the most common problems. Cataracts can be inherited or can result from a nutritional disorder during puppyhood. In puppies, they may appear between 8 weeks and 12 months of age but can be detected as early as 8 to 12 weeks of age 90 percent of the time.

Genetic cataracts usually affect both eyes and progress rapidly. When a puppy has juvenile cataracts, it means that both parents are carriers. In a BTCA health survey, one out of five Bostons was found to be a possible candidate for early onset juvenile cataracts.

Any dog who develops cataracts between four and six years of age without an underlying medical problem, such as diabetes, is a carrier.

A cataract is a white spot over the lens of the eye that impairs vision. A veterinarian can recognize mature cataracts by dilating the eye and examining it with magnification and a strong light source, although a veterinary ophthalmologist can detect small cataracts with high-tech equipment. Reputable breeders will have their dogs' eyes tested before breeding them.

Observe your Boston's eyes and watch for a bluish, white, or milky substance on the eye, or redness, inflammation, or drainage around the eye. If your dog seems surprised when you approach him from the side, has a tendency to bump into things, or avoids jumping up or down, suspect cataracts. Immediately take your dog to the veterinarian. The vet will likely refer you to a veterinary ophthalmologist for further diagnosis and treatment.

Today, cataracts can be surgically corrected, although the procedure is expensive. Veterinary researchers are working hard to develop a DNA test to detect whether or not a dog is a carrier. Until that test is available, responsible breeders have their dogs examined by a veterinary ophthalmologist and certified clear for cataracts before breeding them.

SPAYING AND NEUTERING

The term "neutering" is a general term that describes either spaying or castration, although neutering and castrating have come to mean the same thing. The medical term for spaying a female is "ovariohysterectomy." This surgical

By the Numbers

Puppies can be spayed or neutered when they're as young as eight weeks of age, but many veterinarians recommend waiting until females are four to six months of age and males are six to nine months of age. Consult your veterinarian about the best time to have your Boston undergo this procedure.

sterilization involves removing both the uterus and the ovaries. The medical term for removing a male dog's testicles is "orchiectomy," also called castration.

There are many good reasons for spaying or castrating your Boston Terrier. Most importantly, these surgical procedures prevent the birth of unwanted puppies and help save your dog's life in the long run.

Pregnancy and giving birth can be life threatening for a Boston Terrier who must deliver pups by caesarean section, which can be costly as well. Spaying a female before her first heat cycle—usually between six and nine months of age—can also almost eliminate her risk of developing mammary cancer. Additionally, spayed females can't develop pyometra, an infection of the uterus that may be severe and possibly fatal.

Neutering your male Boston prevents the development of prostate problems as he ages and helps prevent testicular cancer, a common type of cancer in intact older dogs.

CHAPTER 4

TRAINING YOUR BOSTON TERRIER PUPPY

Intelligent and willing to please, your Boston Terrier waits and watches your every move before taking a step. When unsure which direction to follow, he will take the lead and discover clever ways to get what he wants. Sometimes these alternatives are less than ideal and can be downright annoying. But take heart! By implementing positive training methods, adding plenty of fun practice sessions, and maintaining your good sense of humor and patience, any dog can be trained to do very many things. Once you find a good trainer, teaching good behavior is only a few obedience skills away.

Start with the basics. Build your Boston's confidence by introducing him to new sights and sounds, using a crate when you can't watch him, and setting up the housetraining rules. From there you can proceed to teaching him the basic commands of *come*, *down*, and *sit*, and how to walk nicely. These elementary puppy skills come in handy, especially when guests come to visit, as no one really likes a pushy Boston.

INTRODUCTION TO TRAINING

Life with a well-behaved Boston Terrier has its rewards. You can trust him to respond reliably and quickly, plus you'll have a dog who's a joy to live with.

Why Training Is Important

Training is not cruel and unusual punishment. It actually enhances the relationship with your Boston Terrier and enriches the bond you establish with him throughout the years. Once he understands what you expect of him, you will get along much better. During the training process, you'll learn to decipher his language and he'll figure out what it is you're trying to tell him.

Training takes practice, and the more time and effort you put into the process, the more you will get out of it. If this is your first dog or even your first Boston Terrier, you may want to consider hiring a private trainer or think about signing up for a training class. Puppies usually start out in puppy kindergarten. After that you can join an obedience class for older puppies. Ask how many dogs are already signed up before committing to attending. Class size for puppies should be limited to eight to ten dog-and-handler teams per instructor. This ratio enables the instructor to give each team enough attention and time to respond to questions or special training circumstances.

During class your puppy will learn some basics, such as *sit*, *come*, *down*, and how to walk nicely on a leash. These elementary lessons with an instructor and other class participants will teach you the fundamentals of dog training while you benefit from others' trials and tribulations.

Teaching your Boston how to behave involves more than saying his name followed by giving him a command, followed by a little piece of food. Effective training involves interpreting canine body language, anticipating the dog's responses, timing the rewards, and varying the reward to keep him motivated to act appropriately.

The Importance of Positive Training

Your Boston will respond to your direction if you make it fun. Animal behaviorists believe that the old methods of punishments and harsh corrections may work once or twice, but in the long run they are ineffective. Your dog will not understand why you are angry with him, and you can't expect him to choose a different action the next time.

A yearlong study by the University of Pennsylvania, ending in 2009 and published in the journal *Applied Animal Behavior Science* (Elsevier), showed that aggressive dogs who were trained with aggressive, confrontational, or aversive training techniques, such as being stared at, growled at, rolled onto their backs, or hit, continued their aggressive ways. Nonaversive training methods, such as exercise or rewards, were very successful in reducing or eliminating aggressive responses.

Positive training lets your dog know that you are pleased with him, and he will repeat that behavior the next time. Rewards can consist of food, toys, or petting. Depending on what your dog does, you can use one, two, or all three types of rewards. You can also use playtime and games as positive reinforcement. The idea is to reward him every time he does something right. Once he's consistent, reward him with food, toys, or petting only some of the time, but verbally praise him every time. This way he'll work hard to please you, hoping that he'll receive a reward.

How to Get Started

Inside a Boston's gentlemanly exterior lies a rambunctious puppy just waiting for you to

Positive training is important for any dog—even a small one. It will help him fit into the family routine and enable him to feel secure because he will know what is expected of him.

Begin teaching your puppy good manners a few days after he's had a chance to settle into the household.

take the lead. To give him a healthy outlet for any shenanigans, begin teaching good manners a few days after he's had a chance to settle into the household.

Keep Training Sessions Short

Keep your training lessons short—about 10 to 15 minutes per session. You can repeat the session later on in the day, but each one should be brief. Plan to spend several training sessions because no puppy learns to do something perfectly in only one take.

Use Small Food Treats

It's a good idea to use some small food treats as rewards for training. You can use soft commercial food treats sized for puppies, pieces of string cheese, or cut-up apple pieces the size of a grape that are easy to swallow right away. Avoid hard, crunchy treats because they take a while to chew.

Give treats to your puppy immediately—within half a second after he completes the desired behavior. The faster you confirm the behavior you want, the easier it is for your puppy to understand what you're trying to teach him. When you give the reward, follow it up by saying "Good boy!" Avoid the trap of handing out treats during a training session just because your puppy looks cute. He will work harder to please you if he knows that he's getting a reward for having obeyed your command correctly than if he hasn't earned it. If he doesn't do something you like, don't yell or punish him. Simply withhold the reward.

Say a Cue Word Only Once

Say a cue word, like "sit" or "down," only once. Bostons are smart and can hear your command and follow it the first time. Repeating the cue word multiple times doesn't help your pup sharpen his listening skills; like a teenager, he'll tune you out.

Schedule Training Before Meals

Schedule your training session before your puppy's regular meal. This way he may pay closer attention to the instructions so that he can earn a tasty bite.

Choose a Training Time With No Distractions

Choose a time for training when no one will interrupt you and you don't feel rushed. Turn your cell phone off and forget about answering the doorbell if it rings. This will give you quality time to devote to the training process.

For the first few sessions, pick a room in the house that's large enough to move around in. When your Boston figures out what you want him to do, take your training lessons outside, preferably to a fenced-in area, or keep him on a leash when you are in an unfenced area. In an outside area, distractions will vie for your puppy's attention, so you'll need to become more interesting than the street noise, a fast-moving squirrel, or the scent of newly mowed grass.

Don't Train When Puppy's Not in the Mood

Don't train your puppy when he's hot, tired, or in the middle of vigorous playtime. You want him energetic and eager for a training session.

Don't Get Frustrated With Your Puppy

If you ever become frustrated with your puppy, don't get angry with him. Just quietly end the session and try again later in the day. Some Bostons have soft temperaments, and they become nervous and will stop paying attention to their trainers if they are yelled at. They can become scared of any training and decide that following directions is not for them. Stay calm

and relaxed so that your puppy will learn in a positive environment.

SOCIALIZATION

In or out of the house, a well-adjusted Boston Terrier puppy should be a delight to everyone he meets. He should eagerly approach strangers, want to explore objects he's never seen before, and love any social situation to which he's invited. For other puppies who were overly protected and missed receiving important developmental learning from their breeders early on, the world is a scary, frightening place. A

By the Numbers

Boston puppies are born loving the world, but sometime around five weeks of age they become more cautious of new people and situations. This is the ideal time for the breeder to begin socializing them. By the time they are 16 weeks of age, the fear response becomes so strong that it is difficult for them to remain receptive to different experiences. Despite the fact that puppies' immune systems are still developing during these early months, the American Veterinary Society of Animal Behavior (AVSAB) believes that puppies should receive socialization before they are fully vaccinated. The risk of infection is relatively small compared to the chance of death from a problem behavior.

Socialization is critical to your puppy's development, so introduce him to a variety of new people, places, and pets until he's about 18 months old.

Boston with a bad start will cower at the slightest noise, shrink from wanting to greet strangers, and detest going anywhere unfamiliar.

To give your new Boston Terrier puppy a solid beginning, socialize him. This involves spending time with him in various situations, meeting new people, encountering other dogs, and hearing interesting sounds. Introduce him to the world outside your home. With a little time and patience, your puppy will become a happy and well-adjusted member of the family.

What Is Socialization?

Your puppy comes into this world with a clean slate. It's your responsibility to help him adapt to family life and to assume his role as a model canine citizen in your community. Every experience he has will affect how he copes with future events—whether they are similar to or different from his previous encounters.

By giving him positive exposure to a variety of people, other dogs, and new sights and sounds when he's a puppy, he won't be traumatized by different experiences when he's older. At around five weeks of age, puppies enter a cautious stage where most new situations and people appear scary. This continues until sometime after 12 weeks of age, and by 16 weeks a fearful personality becomes dominant.

This means that during the first three months of life, socialization is critical to your puppy's social development. Regularly introducing him to a wide variety of associations with the world around him during this small window of opportunity will help him become a confident, well-adjusted dog. You're actually giving him the chance to develop his unique personality. The process should continue throughout his first year, as many puppies undergo a second fear stage between eight and nine months of age. Keep taking your puppy out of the house and introducing him to new experiences until he's 18 months old and even a few months longer if he needs more exposure.

Negative experiences during his first months can affect your dog for the rest of his life. Focus on giving your Boston quality experiences and introducing new experiences gradually without pushing him past the point of fear.

How to Socialize

The more new things you do with your puppy, the better, as long as you control the situations and don't overwhelm him. If he received minimal handling from the breeder early on, you'll need to socialize him on a very gradual basis, as he may be very fearful of anything out of the ordinary.

Take Your Puppy Places

You don't need to spend hours socializing your puppy each time you take him out. Multiple short trips are better than one or two large adventures. Get in the habit of taking your pup everywhere you go—countless five- or ten-minute trips several days a week are great confidence boosters. Need to pick up clothes from the dry cleaners? Take your puppy along. Making a carpool run? Pack along the Boston.

Have Strangers Give Your Puppy Treats

Carrying along some small food treats will help too. Ask strangers if they wouldn't mind giving your puppy a little cookie. Most folks love the opportunity to greet a Boston up close and personal, and your puppy will quickly learn that new people come bearing gifts and are not enemies.

Keep a Log

To help you remember how much time you spend socializing your Boston and what experiences you expose him to, keep a log of everything you do. You don't need to write a novel; a list of people, things, and sounds will suffice. Jot down your puppy's reactions to the encounters so that you have a record and can look back months later and see how he has progressed.

Ask Friends and Family to Visit

A few days after you bring your Boston into the household, start socializing him by asking friends and family to come visit and spend a few minutes petting and talking to him. Give them a few treats to give to your puppy. Include men, women, children, and people of all ages and sizes.

Let Your Puppy Be an Observer

Progress to taking your puppy out in front of your home or down the street and let him observe joggers, bicyclists, children on skateboards, babies in strollers, delivery personnel, garbage collectors, and people wearing a beard, heavy coat, helmet, pair of sunglasses, or carrying something large. If you can find someone using a cane, sitting in a wheelchair, walking on crutches, or carrying a backpack, you've hit a socialization payday! Your puppy will realize that these people are friendly and the situations harmless and that there's nothing to be afraid of.

Step the process up a notch by riding in the car, walking up and down steps, riding in an elevator in a building, strolling over a manhole cover, encountering a fire hydrant, or observing a plastic tarp flapping in the breeze.

Avoid Crowds

Avoid crowds, even after your puppy is old enough to walk on his own. He could be stepped on, or a child might suddenly run up to him, reach out, and frighten him. If, after a few months, your Boston seems happy, confident, and loving around the house, don't assume that you're done socializing him.

Carry Your Puppy Before He's Been Vaccinated

Before your puppy has received all of his vaccinations, make sure that you take him out of the house as often as possible, but carry him everywhere. Holding him in your arms, you can take him to public places such as the bank, cleaners, carwash, video store, garden center, office supply store, yard sale, stairway, or outdoor mall. Just don't put him down on the ground or let him sniff other animals because he may pick up germs.

After he's had his core vaccines, let him be a dog and stop carrying him. Clip his leash to his collar and hit the streets. Let him walk everywhere. If someone frightens your dog, do not coddle him and tell him it's okay, as this only reinforces his insecurity. Although it may be difficult, it's best to ignore his fear. Act as if nothing is wrong and your puppy will pick up on your strength.

Enroll in a Class

Enrolling your puppy in a formal obedience or agility class is an additional way to continue the socialization process while obtaining some specialized training as well.

CRATE TRAINING

A crate is not a prison. Nor should you consider it corporal punishment. Think of this small kennel as your puppy's private room and special place to relax. It's an absolute must when trying to housetrain your Boston and works wonders for all those times when you simply can't keep an eye on him and want him in a safe place. For puppies who love to chew, a crate helps save your furniture and treasured objects. This canine condo also proves indispensable when transporting your Boston in an airplane, serves as a safe means for car rides, and comes in handy when staying in hotels or visiting with friends. A

If you use a crate properly, your dog will consider it his den and may choose to go there on his own at times.

dog accustomed to sleeping in a crate will recuperate easier if he must spend time at the veterinarian's office.

However, a crate should not be used to contain your Boston 24 hours a day. It's mainly a place for your pup to sleep and stay if you can't watch him for an hour or two at a time. Although it's much more fun when you're around, puppies need to learn that it's okay to spend time away from you. But being separated from you is very stressful for some puppies, and anxiety sets in. Until a puppy relaxes and realizes that you'll return shortly, he may cry, howl, and bark for your attention.

Here's where remaining in an enclosure, such as a crate with the door left open and placed inside an exercise pen or puppy playpen, or a free-standing crate with the door closed, helps

teach the pup that alone time can be fun after all. You just might have to teach your puppy to regard his crate as his house within a home.

What Is Crate Training?

Crate training—teaching your dog to accept and like spending time alone in his crate—is one of the most important lessons you will ever teach him. Once they get the hang of it, most dogs like to sleep in a small, enclosed space because it provides security and protection. Convincing your puppy to accept his crate as a secure bed of his own will take some time and patience, but you'll soon discover that the effort proves worthwhile.

Although some people like to cuddle with their Bostons in bed, letting them sleep there all night is not a good idea, especially when

If your puppy is not ready for crate training, you can confine him safely in an exercise pen.

they're puppies. It doesn't take much to spoil a Boston and turn him into a brat. Your puppy needs to learn that you are the leader. When you allow him to snuggle next to you, he thinks that he is your equal and doesn't have to obey any commands you give him. He has no incentive to work to please you because he's already getting the biggest prize of all: sleeping next to you in the best bed in the house without having to do anything to earn the privilege.

When you take control of putting your puppy inside a crate and choosing when to let him out again, you send the message that you are in charge, not him. This paves the way for positive training in the future.

How to Crate Train

To train your puppy to accept his crate, introduce it gradually. The speed of this process depends on how your Boston was raised by the breeder. If your pup wasn't socialized properly and was kept confined or isolated in a crate or small pen throughout much of his puppyhood, hold off on crate training him until he seems more relaxed with strangers and new sights and sounds. Try using an exercise pen or baby playpen until he's ready for crate training.

For new puppies with some crate experience, or for those who have never slept in one before, begin introducing crate training early on the day you bring him home. Make it a comfortable place by putting a soft blanket, one of your old shirts with your scent, and a few of his toys in it. Your puppy may chew, so don't give him anything that can cause him to choke. Place the crate in the room where you spend the most time. At night, put the crate next to your bed so that your puppy won't feel abandoned in another room.

If you're using a wire crate, place a sheet over the top and sides to give it a cozier feel. Without the cover, too much open space may confuse a puppy who's just learning about remaining in a small area. Remove your puppy's collar, especially one with tags because they can get caught in the crate wires. If your puppy chews on the wire, he could get his jaw caught, so spray the wire with a chew deterrent.

Place a metal container filled with small food treats near the crate. For the first few days, keep the crate door open so that your puppy can wander in and around the crate to explore it. When he goes inside, praise him, shake the treat container, and give him a tidbit.

Come feeding time, create a positive association with the crate by placing the food bowl slightly inside the opening so that he doesn't have to go all the way into the crate, and leave the door open. At the next meal, place the food farther inside the crate. After a few days you can close the door. As soon as your puppy finishes his meal, open the door to let him out and remove the bowl.

A few times a day, call your puppy's name followed by the word "crate," and shake the treat container next to the crate. When he comes over to investigate the sound, give him a treat. If you have a hard-sided crate, throw a second treat inside the crate so that it hits the back wall. If you have a soft-sided or wire crate, toss it onto the floor of the crate, toward the back. Your puppy will run in after the treat. Praise him and close the crate door. Leave him inside for a few minutes and stay where he can see you. Let him out before he has a chance to whine or cry. If he does begin to make a fuss, wait until there's a quiet moment before you let him out. Otherwise he'll think that crying is the magic ticket out of the crate. Repeat, gradually increasing the time that he spends inside. Never leave a puppy crated for longer than three hours, except during the night when he's asleep.

HOUSETRAINING

On the day you bring your Boston puppy home, he won't have a clue where you want him to eliminate. At the same time, he's developing bladder control and remembers going wherever he wanted to when he lived with his littermates. Now suddenly he's expected to potty in a strange area with new smells and textures beneath his feet. It's no wonder, then, that he'll eliminate when and where the need arises.

Sure, no one likes to clean up a mess, especially after a Boston who uses the house as a restroom, but your puppy can learn what you expect of him. Start teaching him to eliminate outside instead of inside the day after you bring him home.

Pups are most receptive to these lessons when they're between seven and nine weeks of age, although you can housetrain a dog at any age. Bostons are intelligent dogs and housetrain quickly. With good instruction and follow-through from their owners, most Bostons figure out the housetraining routine by the time they're six to eight months of age. For optimum success, respond to his cues to eliminate consistently and set up a regular schedule.

What Is Housetraining?

Housetraining teaches your Boston when and where he should eliminate and to do it when you tell him to. In the beginning, you'll need to set the schedule and take him to the appropriate areas before he has to potty. Once he figures out the routine, he'll let you know when he needs to use the bathroom. Eventually, your puppy will control his bladder and wait until he reaches the right location.

It's your job to set your puppy up for housetraining success. Limit your dog's environment, use positive reinforcement, and crate your puppy when you can't watch him.

How to Housetrain

Training your Boston to poop and pee where you want him to can be surprisingly easy. The breed does not like to be in a messy situation and enjoys being clean. This fact helps speed the housetraining process along.

Don't give your puppy the run of the house until he's completely housetrained, and then you might want to wait until he's an adult. If you give him too much space, it's harder to keep an eye on him for potty training. Use baby gates or close doors to rooms you're not using to help confine him.

Follow these six steps and your Boston will master the bathroom basics in no time:

1. Begin by choosing a place in your backyard for your puppy to eliminate. You can train your Boston to use the same area every time, so select a spot that's away from flowers or plants that might suffer from your dog's daily visits. If you're not using your yard, take your Boston in front of your house or near the street, but plan to clean up after him each time.

Training Tidbit

Some trainers advocate giving a dog a small food treat to reward him for eliminating in the designated area outdoors. This may work with some breeds, but not most Boston Terriers. Intelligent creatures, they will run to the potty spot but hold their bladders until they receive their treat.

When housetraining your Boston, choose a spot in your yard where you want him to eliminate and take him to that same area every time.

2. Use the right tools: a crate, a collar and leash, and clean-up bags. Putting down newspapers or piddle pads on the floor is not necessary because your puppy can learn to go outside as soon as you bring him home.

   Puppies have an instinctive nature not to mess the space where they eat or sleep. Putting your puppy inside his crate when you can't watch him between potty trips teaches him to wait to relieve himself until he can visit the designated area.

   Attach the leash to your puppy's collar and lead him to the potty spot. Stand still and remain with him at that location without walking from place to place. This way he will exhaust the smells in that location and complete his business. Allowing him to walk from place to place only prolongs the trip outdoors.

3. Set a potty schedule. Your puppy needs to go to the designated area as soon as he wakes up in the morning, after a nap, after meals, and after playtime. During active play, your Boston puppy will need to go outside about every 30 minutes.

4. Observe your Boston's body language. Although every puppy is different, generally walking in circles with an intense look on his face or sniffing the ground is a clue that he is ready to poop or pee. Whisk your Boston outside to his potty spot when you see this activity. When he does go, praise him.

5. Accidents happen. Expect them, so be prepared and clean them up promptly. Ignore mistakes and don't even think of yelling or hitting your Boston with a rolled-up newspaper, which doesn't work anyway. He won't understand why you're angry and will begin sneaking around the house to eliminate where you can't see it. If you catch your puppy about to potty inside the house, distract him by calling his name or clapping your hands and take him outside to the potty area.

6. Stay calm and be patient. Housetraining takes time. Your Boston wants to please you but needs to develop the physical control to accomplish this.

BASIC OBEDIENCE COMMANDS

All Boston Terriers should know how to perform simple obedience commands. This will make your puppy more pleasant to be around and help him to recognize that you are his leader. Learning some basic obedience training commands gives him a mental workout, which is just as important as the role that physical exercise plays in warding off boredom and bad behavior. Following the rules will make your puppy feel valued and important. Besides, some commands, such as the *come* and the *down*, may save his life some day.

Begin teaching your puppy a few days after you bring him home so that he begins learning what you expect. Always say his name first, followed by the command, and keep your training sessions short—about 10 to 15 minutes—and make sure that they are fun for you and your puppy. Puppies are exuberant, so work off some of that energy before beginning any training sessions. Play a game of fetch or tug in the yard to take the edge off a little.

Dogs work well when a there's a treat involved. Include treats that your dog doesn't get at any other times. Use soft goodies so that he can eat them quickly and continue training without having to stop and chew. You can purchase commercial treats from the pet food supply store or cut up small pieces of hot dog, cheese, cooked chicken or ham, or bite-sized pieces of soft fruit.

Come/Recall

Although some Boston puppies will never leave your side, others are inquisitive and love to wander off in search of an interesting object or smell. These pups need some instruction to come when called.

Also known as the *recall*, the goal of training your dog to come to you if you call him is that he's less likely to choose something else to do. This involves establishing that returning to you is the best thing he can do. Always acknowledge your dog for doing what you've asked with praise, treats, a big hug, or enthusiastic pats on his chest. Always use an upbeat, happy voice to call him because this will entice him to respond to you.

If your pup misbehaves, never call him to come to you and reprimand or yell at him, no matter what awful thing he's done. Otherwise, he'll never trust that you won't do so again and will be less likely to respond when you call him the next time.

Want to Know More?

To learn intermediate obedience commands, see Chapter 9: Boston Terrier Training.

Why *Come* Is Necessary

Teaching your puppy the *come* command is one of the most important skills he can learn. Once your Boston reliably responds when you call him, you never have to worry if he escapes the yard or slips out the door and runs into the street. Even if this doesn't happen, collars and leashes can accidentally break, and relying on your dog to come can save his life.

Teaching the *Come*

The best way to teach your puppy the come command is to run the other way from him when you call his name. Dogs love a good game of chase, especially if their owners are involved. Hopefully, your Boston will never run out toward the street, but if he does, yell his name and run in the opposite direction. He'll be more likely to follow you. If you run after him, he'll only keep running into the street.

Basic obedience commands like the *sit* are the foundation for good manners and all future learning.

When you teach your dog the *recall*, use bite-sized pieces of food treats as incentives, especially tidbits he doesn't normally receive. Begin training inside the house in different rooms where there are few distractions. Once your Boston reliably responds indoors, take the training to the back yard, where there are mild distractions.

When outdoors, knot a long clothesline or a 15- to 40-foot-long (4.5- to 12-m) piece of rope onto his leash and clip it onto his collar. Use this to test his *recall* in front of your house or at the local park. Once he's mastered the *recall* in all of those locations and around multiple distractions, you may be able to trust him to come to you without the leash, but there's no guarantee.

To teach your puppy to come, say "Come" and his name. When he turns to look at you, praise him by saying "Good boy!" and give him a treat, a toy, or some love pats. Repeat several times.

Playing a *recall* game with your Boston puppy will help to reinforce the learning. Ask someone to hold your puppy in another room.

Multi-Dog Tip

Training a puppy with other dogs in the household can become mayhem before you know it. Everyone wants a food treat for good behavior and will jockey for position to win the reward, often crowding out your puppy. Before beginning a training session with your puppy, put the other dogs in another room. You can then give your puppy individual attention so that he doesn't have to compete with the other dogs.

Say your puppy's name, followed by the word "come" in a happy, upbeat tone of voice. When the assistant releases your pup, encourage him to come to you. Praise him when he does and give him a treat.

Down

When your puppy lies down on cue it shows that he has good manners. This etiquette also helps control his impulses in certain situations. While in this position, he can't jump on people, run out the door, beg food from the table, or chase after a squirrel. If you take him for a walk and meet a friend and decide to chat for a few minutes, your puppy can rest in a *down* position until you're ready to go again. Once he learns that lying down on command is a good way to relax, you'll discover many ways to utilize this behavior.

Although some Bostons are quick to learn the *down* command, other independent types view it as a submissive position and resist. They may require more training sessions and persistence, but eventually they will learn that lying down isn't so bad after all and may actually feel good about following your instructions.

Why *Down* Is Necessary

Teaching your dog to lie down on command has many other practical applications. During a visit to the veterinarian, he may have to lie down to undergo a procedure. If you become involved in therapy dog work with your Boston, he may be invited to lie down on a patient's bed.

Teaching the *Down*

To teach your Boston to lie down on cue, start with your pup in a *sit*. (See *Teaching the Sit* in the next section.) Say his name, followed by the word "down." Hold a treat between your fingers so that he can see and smell it. Hold it firmly and let him lick at it but not eat it. Put the treat

When your puppy lies down on cue, it shows he has good manners but it also helps control his behavoir in many different situations.

in front of his nose, and slowly move it straight down toward the ground between his front legs.

He will follow the treat with his head. Continue to hold it firmly, and when your hand is at the floor between your dog's paws, move it away from him as if to draw an L-shaped line along the floor.

Your puppy will follow the treat. When his elbows hit the floor, say "Good" and pop the treat into his mouth. If he goes only halfway down, reward him anyway. Take out another treat and repeat.

Sit

Prepping a Boston Terrier puppy to sit on a verbal cue is one of the easiest behaviors to teach a dog. It reinforces self-control because he must remain in this position until you give

him a release cue to move. For high-energy Bostons, knowing how to sit is the fast track to having a well-behaved dog.

Why *Sit* Is Necessary

The *sit* is the foundation of every type of training you will ever do with your Boston. It will become so familiar to your puppy, in fact, that he will often revert back to sitting on his own. This will happen if he wants something from you or seems confused when you're teaching him something new.

Asking your Boston to sit before being fed, prior to going outside, or when friends come to visit gives you an opportunity to praise your dog and reward him. It helps form a bond between dog and owner because it involves positive communication and interaction.

Having the right tools, such as a properly fitted collar and leash, can make leash training your dog easier and more effective.

Teaching the *Sit*

You can teach your puppy to sit in many ways, but using food to lure him into the correct position is the fastest and easiest. If your Boston does not respond on his own to sit and keeps backing up, do not push on his rear or bottom, as this exerts too much pressure on his legs and back. Ask someone to sit behind your puppy on the floor. Then hold a treat just above his nose and move it slightly back over his head while your assistant cradles his body in her legs so that he has no room to back up. He'll automatically go into a sit. Praise your Boston and give him an extra treat. Repeat several times until your assistant is no longer needed.

Walking Nicely on Leash

It's a fact: Some puppies naturally pull on the leash the first time you clip it onto their collars, while others don't. You can't much blame those pups who are excited about exploring the outdoors and can move faster than their owners. But with some practice, a lot of patience, and a determination never to allow your pup to pull, you can teach him to walk nicely beside you. If you allow him to tug even once, he'll continue to try pulling because sometimes it pays off.

Why Walking Nicely Is Necessary

If you give your puppy free rein to pull you in any direction, he will soon figure out that he can go wherever he chooses. Although your puppy is small, this doesn't seem like much of a problem because you can easily scoop him up in your arms if you have to, but as your Boston grows, this solution isn't so easy. Even a 25-pound (11.5-kg) Boston can knock you off balance and make you fall if he tries to yank you down the street.

Teaching Walking Nicely

A variety of methods will work to teach puppies to walk politely. No single method works with every dog, so you may need to try several different techniques.

Train your puppy to remain calm and to sit before you attach the leash to his collar. Wait until he follows your instruction before proceeding. If you give in and put the leash on anyway, he will learn that it's okay to remain out of control.

Once the leash is attached, stand still and let him perform his happy dance maneuvers, even if it takes five or ten minutes before he calms down. When he realizes that you're not going anywhere until he settles down, praise him and take your first step. Walk him around the house or garage for a few minutes before heading out the door. This will give him a chance to practice not pulling.

Every time your dog pulls or strains at the leash, simply stand still. You may have to repeat this reaction every few steps, but eventually your puppy will realize that when he pulls, he doesn't go anywhere. It's only when he doesn't exert pressure on the leash that he receives the reward of going for a walk.

PUPPY KINDERGARTEN

If you've never had a dog before, or even if you have but this is your first Boston Terrier, consider enrolling him in puppy kindergarten. This course is specifically designed for puppies between two to five months of age, and puppies attend with their owners. These classes help new owners pick up early training tips while their puppies benefit from socialization.

What Is Puppy Kindergarten?

Structured but low-key fun classes are led by a professional trainer and help provide positive reinforcement and puppy training. They're a great way for owners and their puppies to interact with other puppies and new people in a safe environment.

In a typical class, pups will play off leash, which teaches them how to be gentle and not too mouthy. They'll become accustomed to being handled by other people and receive exposure to odd props and sounds that will help build their self-confidence. You'll pick up some behavior basics, such as early attention training, waiting, and sitting, and have the opportunity to discuss problem behaviors such as biting and jumping.

Finding the Right Kindergarten for Your Puppy

To locate a puppy kindergarten class in your area, ask your veterinarian, breeder, or friends with puppies for referrals. Interview instructors over the phone before signing up for a session. Look for instruction that emphasizes positive reinforcement and uses toys, food treats, and play.

Skip strict classes that teach physical punishment, such as shaking or forcing your puppy onto his back and holding him there until he relaxes. These are no longer considered effective methods. Look instead for classes that use games. Bostons love a good contest with plenty of romping, but this doesn't mean that puppy kindergarten is a place to go wild. The instructor should lead the class and keep it peaceful and well organized.

Every bit of learning you expose your puppy to should be fun-filled and upbeat. That is the reason why you added a puppy to your household in the first place.

How to Find a Private Trainer

Years ago, if you wanted to train your dog your only alternative involved signing up with a strict trainer and a class at the local park or community center. Today, owners have their pick of private trainers, canine boarding schools, and a whole range of classes that teach everything from therapy work to agility competition to tricks and games to advanced manners to problem solving and to responding to a clicker or a signal. If none of these options appeals to you, turn on the television and celebrity dog trainers will give quick fixes for any canine problem.

Hiring a private trainer has become a popular alternative to enrolling in group classes. This person will come to your home and work with you and your puppy. Or if you feel more comfortable in a public location, you can arrange to meet there.

One advantage to working with a private trainer includes one-on-one instruction and the luxury of having the whole half-hour or hour-long session to focus on your puppy. If this is your first dog, you might need as much support as you can get, although hiring a private trainer is a very expensive alternative to taking your puppy to group classes. Once you've made the decision to go with a private trainer, choosing the right one can be confusing. Click around on the Internet and you'll see countless professionals, all promising to make your dog a well-behaved part of the household.

Start by asking your veterinarian, breeder, local shelter, kennel club, regional Boston Terrier club, or friends with dogs for referrals. Before hiring anyone, interview prospective candidates over the phone, check their credentials, and ask for

references. Just because someone has owned or trained dogs for many years doesn't mean that that person is the right trainer for you and your dog. Unless you're lucky, chances are you won't find a trainer who owns or has trained a Boston Terrier before, but that's okay. A good trainer should know how to train all breeds and will have experience working with small dogs.

Don't agree to sign up in advance for a large number of sessions or pay an exorbitant fee up front until you know whether you and your puppy like and can trust this person. Pay attention to how you feel about the trainer and how your puppy responds to the methods used. Also, stay away from anyone who encourages you to purchase expensive equipment that he or she sells or who offers a guarantee of training results. Dogs learn at different rates, and owners must spend time practicing with their dogs between sessions before the training takes effect.

When looking for a dog trainer, you'll find countless professionals with a variety of degrees and certifications listed after their names. Because there are many ways that someone can become a professional dog trainer, it's important to ask about this experience during your interview.

Trainers may apprentice with an experienced trainer before starting their own business, some have college degrees in animal behavior, and some have been educated through online vocational programs that may be combined with a mentoring program. Other individuals may have experience working in animal shelters or competing in dog sports. There is no required certification or licensing to become a professional dog trainer, and anyone who wishes to can call himself or herself a dog trainer.

To locate a private trainer, contact professional organizations that certify or recommend trainers, such as the Association of Pet Dog Trainers (APDT), the International Association of Canine Professionals (IACP), or the National Association of Dog Obedience Instructors (NADOI). Their websites include a long list of trainers, many with their own websites and qualifications.

PART II

ADULTHOOD

CHAPTER 5

FINDING YOUR BOSTON TERRIER ADULT

Who doesn't ooh and aah over a puppy? But the idea of saving the life of an adult Boston Terrier who desperately needs a home seems wonderful too. Considered an adult at one year of age, the full-grown dog you adopt still has a lot of puppy antics left in him. Well-cared-for Bostons can live 12 years or more, so you can anticipate a good span of lively love.

WHY ADOPTING AN ADULT IS A GOOD IDEA

A full-grown Boston makes an excellent companion for families and seniors. Purebred adult Bostons are available through breed rescue groups and local animal shelters.

While it's hard to imagine anyone giving up a Boston Terrier, it's not usually because the breed has a bad temperament. Adult dogs become available for many reasons, including their owners' divorce, loss of employment, and, subsequently, the home, or perhaps due to allergies or illness. Some breeders will place a Boston if they have too many dogs or are looking for specific features in a show dog.

Purchasing any dog may involve a risk. While you may not know an older dog's complete history, there's no guarantee with a puppy either.

Physical Certainty

There are many advantages to adding an adult dog to your family. An older dog from a reputable breed rescue can be much less of a gamble than a puppy. When you bring home an adult over the age of one year, you already know what he looks like. What you see is what you get. You won't have to guess how big he'll grow, wonder about the length of his body, or consider whether his ears will stand up or flop over. A good rescue coordinator evaluates the dogs brought into rescue and will know something about his personality, whether the dog has health problems, and whether he gets along with cats, other dogs, and birds.

May Be Housetrained

More than likely your adopted dog already knows about housetraining. Boston Terriers generally are clean dogs and think twice before making unwanted messes. Until your newly acquired adult dog acclimates to your routine, you can expect a few bathroom accidents in the house, but at least you won't

A great advantage to adopting an adult is that both his physical appearance and personality are already established.

have to teach him the housetraining basics. If you do, older dogs have the mental capacity to figure it out fairly quickly, and potty training should be easy.

May Be Obedience Trained

When it comes to training, the mature Boston may already know some fundamentals, such as walking politely on a leash, sleeping in a crate, or behaving in the house. If not, you can always teach a full-grown dog some new tricks. Older dogs are calmer than youngsters and have a longer attention span. They're more willing to focus on you and learn the tasks you teach them.

No More Constant Supervision

No longer interested in chewing, a grown-up dog doesn't require the constant monitoring that a puppy needs. This means that your shoes, furniture, and prized objects are safer from gnawing canine teeth. While sleeping in a crate is just as important for an older dog as it is for a puppy, you won't have to use the crate as a safe place for your dog to hang out if you can't watch him. Once he knows what you expect, he'll likely be well-behaved while loose in the house.

For busy families, not having to worry about watching the dog 24/7 leaves plenty of free time to simply enjoy him. If you're the active type, you can take your mature Boston out for longer walks or runs around the neighborhood. Over the age of 18 months, his bones are fully developed and you don't have to worry about injuring his already mature body.

Less Activity

For less active people who are content to curl up with a good book or enjoy short walks, having a retired canine who doesn't need to run a marathon everyday means the livin' is easy.

Meshing With the Pack

Mature Bostons come with life experience, and most have already learned what it takes to get along with people and other dogs. Although you'll need to socialize and introduce a new dog to the household carefully, your newly adopted Boston will be more likely to mesh with the pack faster than a puppy would.

Personality Is Better Developed

All puppies are cute, but Boston Terrier adult personalities don't come to the surface until they're about two years of age. Because an older Boston's disposition is already developed, a knowledgeable shelter or breed rescue coordinator can assess the dog for adoption suitability. When you apply to adopt, the organization makes every effort to match the right dog with the right owner.

ADOPTION OPTIONS

An owner who has decided to give up a Boston Terrier should call the breeder or the local shelter. Reputable breeders will take back a dog they sell if, for any reason, the owner can no longer keep him, regardless of the dog's age.

If the breeder won't take the dog back, the owner should drop him off at the local shelter. In some communities, a Boston Terrier breed rescue coordinator routinely checks the shelters to see whether any Boston Terriers are in need of homes. The shelter checker picks up the Boston and fosters him until a permanent new home becomes available. People who love Boston Terriers and volunteer to help them are always eager to help a homeless dog find a good forever home.

Reputable Breeders

To find an adult Boston to adopt, ask whether your veterinarian knows any homeless Boston Terriers, or contact the Boston Terrier Club of America (BTCA). Send e-mails to the breeder referral and rescue committee chairpersons letting them know that you are interested in adopting an adult Boston. You can also contact the BTCA affiliate clubs and e-mail or call their breeder referral or rescue coordinators.

Breeders maintain a network of other breeders, and once the word goes out that someone is looking for an adult Boston, people will try to help make a match. While

By the Numbers

According to Boston Terrier rescue organizations, the average age when most Boston Terriers are given up for adoption is five to six years. Although more dogs than ever before are in need of new homes, Bostons are often adopted fairly quickly.

When you adopt an older dog from a breeder, you'll likely receive information about his background, including his pedigree, a health history, and what training he's had.

not every breeder may have an adult dog ready to place, some may have a retired show dog or a one- or two-year-old show prospect they've been holding onto hoping that the right home will come along.

These dogs are available for several reasons. Perhaps the puppy developed a conformation fault or two, or the breeder has a better dog to show. Maybe the breeder has too many dogs and needs to find homes for those who can't contribute to the breeding program. Although other breeds may have problems with bad temperaments, this is not an issue with Boston Terriers. People don't usually give up Bostons because of personality problems.

When you adopt an older dog from a breeder, you'll usually receive information about the dog's background, including his pedigree, a health history, and what training he's had. More than likely he's already leash and crate trained and accustomed to traveling. Unless the breeder has small children, the dog may not have been exposed to kids and may not like them. If there are children in your home, you'll need to spend extra time training the Boston to feel comfortable around children. Although there's a fee to purchase

Multi-Dog Tip

Older Bostons have been around the block a few times and are accustomed to other dogs. More than likely they've spent some time being kenneled next to dogs in the shelter or breed rescue and are amenable to getting along with pets in their new homes. Introduce the adopted dog to your other family dogs on neutral territory outside the home before bringing them indoors.

an older dog from a breeder, it's usually less than what you might spend for a puppy.

Breed Rescues

BTCA members work with affiliated clubs and other purebred dog rescue groups throughout the United States. A Boston rescue begins with a call from a shelter, or volunteers visit shelters looking for Bostons. Packing a collar, leash, and adoption forms, volunteers meet the dog and legally transfer the Boston to their care. Shelters maintain their own procedures, and rescue workers keep an open dialogue with them. Shelters check the identification of the volunteer to verify that she will make every effort to find a new home for the dog.

With breed rescue groups, there is no deadline for the dog. After pickup, they will keep him until the right match with a new owner comes along. The Boston's new lease on life begins with a physical assessment. Looking for fleas, ticks, infections, sores, and wounds, the volunteer schedules a visit to the veterinarian for spaying or neutering, if needed, and a complete physical examination.

Temperament testing is another part of the breed rescue process. A volunteer exposes the dog to kids, other dogs, and cats to determine his reactions. If a Boston dislikes children or cats, he'll need to have a home without kids or cats.

When adopting a rescued Boston, you should expect to pay a fee. Usually the charge isn't nearly as much as what you'd spend for a puppy, but you should consider it. Although each breed rescue group

> ### *Want to Know More?*
>
> If you've decided that a puppy might better fit your lifestyle, see Chapter 2: Finding and Prepping for Your Boston Terrier Puppy for tips on how to find the right Boston puppy for you.

sets different fee schedules, none makes a profit. The affiliated volunteers must charge a fee to recoup their own expenses for food, veterinary care, and routine dog supplies such as collars, leashes, toys, and bedding. If medications are necessary for eye or ear problems, these fees will be passed along in the adoption fee. If your new Boston isn't already spayed or neutered

Expect a rigorous screening process before you can take home a Boston Terrier because volunteers want to feel confident that the dog will remain with you for the rest of his life and won't need another home.

By adopting an adult dog, you're not only giving him a vital second chance at having a good home, but you may be saving his life.

by the time you're ready to take him home, you may need to pay some of that expense as well.

When contemplating an adoption, expect to answer some questions and to fill out an application. There's a rigorous screening process before you can take home a Boston Terrier because volunteers want to feel confident that this dog will remain with you for the rest of his life and won't need another home. You might need to supply references

from a veterinarian who can attest to the fact that you've provided good veterinary care for a previous dog, and you may need to have had previous experience with a dog or have spent time researching the breed. The rescue coordinator will want to know whether you have a securely fenced-in yard and a stable environment and may visit your home to check things out.

A family with a new baby might not meet the qualifications for a Boston, as coordinators worry that the dog may not receive much attention. Or if you already have too many dogs, your chances of adoption are minimal. Ultimately, whether or not you'll take home a Boston depends on the rescue coordinator's sense about you as a responsible dog owner.

To complete an adoption, most rescues require adopters to agree to care for the dog properly and to return him if they can no longer keep him. You should receive some basic Boston Terrier care information about behavior, health, training, feeding, and grooming.

The volunteer will provide a record of any veterinary treatment the dog has received during his stay, along with a list of any medications he has been given. When you take your dog to the veterinarian for a checkup, bring this record along with you.

Shelters

When seeking to adopt, visit your local animal shelter. If you find a Boston Terrier, you've struck canine gold, but don't count on it. If a Boston does go to a shelter, he won't stay there very long, as breed rescue

Adoption Consultants

Once you make the decision to add an adult Boston to your household comes the task of tracking down the dog of your dreams. Finding a quality adult Boston requires the same diligent detective work as locating a healthy, happy puppy from a reputable breeder. Breed rescue and shelter coordinators will be only too happy to help you choose the Boston Terrier who best matches your lifestyle.

Training Tidbit

A day after you bring your adopted Boston home, begin socializing him just as you would a puppy. Take him walking in the neighborhood, and introduce him to people and other dogs you meet on the street. This will help him become accustomed to the sights and smells of his new community and will speed up the adjustment to his new digs.

coordinators work hard to pick up homeless dogs. And because Bostons are a popular breed, people looking for a good dog grab them up quickly. If they're not adopted quickly it's because there's a deadline. The shelters seldom have enough room for all of the dogs who need homes and must move them quickly.

One reason why Bostons wind up in a shelter rather than going back to the breeder is because some owners don't want their breeders to know that they can no longer care for their dogs. In these cases, you may find a dog with a show history or from well-bred parents but his paperwork, including his health history, may not accompany him.

If you're choosing between two Bostons and no one at the shelter can assist you, consider the dog's interest in you. Dogs at the back of the pen who are shy require more work than you think. You'll need to spend a lot of time socializing them before they will enjoy the company of others.

CHAPTER 6

BOSTON TERRIER GROOMING NEEDS

Giving your Boston Terrier a little hands-on pampering goes a long way toward enhancing his natural beauty. Like feeding him a nutritious diet, giving him enough exercise, and providing positive training, regular grooming is an important part of taking care of your dog and keeping him healthy.

Boston Terrier aficionados love the breed's distinguished look and natural charisma, but the bonus comes with its short, tangle-free coat. Although Bostons don't require the same amount of glamming up that long-coated breeds need, their skin and coat should be regularly bathed and brushed. When a Boston's coat is well cared for, it's smooth and glossy to the touch, making your little guy a joy to invite into your lap. Cuddling up with him on the couch is a lot more fun when he's soft and washed than when he's rough and stinky. You like to feel clean and fresh, so it stands to reason that your dog loves the same feeling too. In addition to coat care, keeping your dog's ears and eyes clean, trimming his nails, and brushing his teeth also are all important parts of the grooming process and should be done regularly as well.

To keep your Boston healthy and sweet smelling, choose a set time to attend to his sprucing up. The good thing about a Boston is that he's easy to groom, and the whole process doesn't take much time. But if you feel that you may need the assistance and skills of a professional groomer, by all means select one whom you feel comfortable hiring. With a little research and referrals from reliable sources, it's easy to find a qualified person you can trust.

BRUSHING

While some breeds have a double coat that helps insulate them from the cold and wet weather, the Boston Terrier is a single-coated breed. Bostons may feel chilly from time to time when the temperature dips, but the good news is that they require less brushing than long-coated dogs.

A short coat is easy to maintain; it won't tangle and you don't have to worry about removing knots in it, but it does require daily brushing. Another advantage is that Bostons aren't big shedders, so you won't see clumps of hair scattered about your floors. Nevertheless, they still shed somewhat, and their little black and white hairs will stick to your clothes, furniture, and carpets.

Why Brushing Is Important

Brushing your dog isn't just for beauty's sake. It serves a healthy purpose by removing the dead hair before it falls out on its own. Brushing also stimulates the natural oils in your dog's skin and gives the coat a healthy, shiny appearance. It also benefits you because you collect the hair in the brush rather than on your clothes and throughout the household.

When you go over your dog with a brush, comb, or grooming glove, you can also check his body for the presence of any unusual bumps, growths, or wounds. If you do see something that doesn't look right, contact your veterinarian immediately. This gives you the opportunity to detect a problem in the early stages and obtain treatment before a serious situation develops.

Going over your dog's coat also helps you spot the presence of fleas or ticks. On black Bostons, they may be difficult to find, especially around the base of the tail, so push the hair aside and look closely at the skin. Fleas and ticks blend easily into brindle coats, too.

Shedding Facts

Shedding is a natural part of a dog's hair growth cycle. Hair grows, dies, falls out or sheds, and grows again. Most dogs grow new hair within 130 days, depending on their breed type, overall health, diet, and the weather. In colder climates, Bostons develop a thicker coat to help keep them warmer during the winter and then shed it in the spring when they no longer need the extra protection.

Training Tidbit

Begin training your Boston to enjoy the grooming experience the day after you bring him home. Pet his entire body and handle his feet for just a few minutes every day. This teaches him that it's alright to let you handle his body and he'll learn to relax enough to enjoy spa treatments, both at home and at the grooming salon.

Once your Boston becomes accustomed to the procedure, he'll look forward to the pampering and attention you lavish on him—which sure beats having to wrestle him every time he needs to be groomed.

How to Brush a Boston

It only takes a few minutes to brush a Boston Terrier. You can use a rubber brush, a rubber grooming glove, or even your fingertips, but regardless of the tool you use, do it once a day for the best results.

For the first few brushing sessions, your Boston may be a little fussy and wonder what a brush is all about. If so, let him sniff it and just spend a few minutes gently brushing his coat. It may take him a few sessions to relax enough to enjoy the entire process.

For easy grooming, follow these steps:

1. Place your Boston on a grooming table; if you don't own one, you can use a kitchen or bathroom counter. This makes it easier for you to reach your dog and harder for him to wriggle away.

2. Using a brush or grooming glove, start brushing your dog's coat the same direction the hair grows, i.e., from the head toward the tail.
3. Next brush down his sides and legs, then down his neck and chest. Don't forget the top of his head.
4. If the brush fills with hair, remove the hair and continue brushing.
5. After most of the dead hair has been loosened, use a damp towel to wipe the coat down.

Once your Boston is comfortable with brushing, ask a friend or family member to lightly brush him with you seated at his side or directly in front of him. This lets your dog know that anyone can perform this task in the event that you can't brush him or you decide to let a groomer perform the task.

BATHING

A healthy coat is a clean coat, and it takes only a few minutes to freshen up your dog. Once he becomes accustomed to the spa treatment, he'll enjoy the special time you spend together.

Why Bathing is Important

Petting a clean and odor-free Boston is a whole lot more pleasant than cuddling with a dog who desperately needs a close encounter with some soap and water. Before you think that bathing dries out a dog's coat, guess again. Somehow a myth began circulating years ago

To keep your Boston Terrier looking and feeling his best, brush him daily.

Before bringing your dog to his bath, have all your supplies set up and ready to go.

that too much bathing dries out canine coats, but this is false.

Regular hygiene for people, as well as dogs, keeps the skin free of debris and odor. Boston Terriers who exhibit in the show ring are bathed before they show—often every week or every other week—and they have luscious, healthy coats that glisten and gleam.

How to Bathe a Boston

Boston Terriers are great sink soakers because they're small enough to fit inside most large kitchen sinks. They can also be bathed in the bathroom tub, or outdoors in a plastic tub with a sprayer attached to the hose if it's a warm day.

To make the process as stress-free as possible, assemble everything you need before you begin the bath: nonskid mat to provide traction in the sink or tub, a sprayer attachment for the faucet nozzle for getting your dog wet and rinsing off the soap (or you can use a plastic pitcher or small bucket), shampoo, conditioner, towels, cotton balls, and some small food treats. This way you won't have to stop in the middle of the bath to go get something you need, leaving your dog unattended and at risk for getting injured.

Follow these easy steps:

1. For your Boston's first bath session, just put enough warm water in the sink or tub to cover his feet.

2. Let him remain standing, but hold him firmly the entire time so he doesn't try to jump out.

3. Swish a little water over his feet, but don't bother with the soap just yet. Tell him to stay.

4. After a few minutes, say "Okay" and gently lift him out of the sink and place him onto the towel before drying off his feet. Tell him what a good dog he is and give him a tiny food treat.

5. For the next session, spend a few more minutes. Fill the tub or sink with a little more water and splash it over his whole body, or use a sprayer to wet him completely, but avoid getting water in his eyes or ears.

6. First, use a washcloth to wash his face.

7. Next, apply a small circle of shampoo at the back of his neck.

8. Using a rubber brush, rub the shampoo into the coat from the back of the neck down the back toward the tail. Don't forget to wash underneath his body. Don't get shampoo in his eyes or ears.

9. When you are done shampooing, rinse the soap out of his coat completely.

10. A conditioning rinse is optional.

11. When you are done rinsing, towel dry your dog or use a dog hair dryer on a low or no-heat setting.

12. Start drying the coat from the neck down the body. The drying process may take twice as long as bathing.

13. Dry your dog completely to prevent him from becoming chilled.

EAR CARE

A healthy ear should be free of dirt and excess wax, and without sores or inflammation. While Boston Terriers don't have floppy ears like some other breeds that are prone to infections, their small erect ears do collect debris and, occasionally, ear mites. Earwax can be a problem, too. While small bits of earwax are normal, a heavy buildup can become a source of major irritation.

If you notice your dog shaking his head or scratching his ears a lot, this may be a sign that his ears are bothering him. If they are extremely warm or sensitive, or if he whimpers when you touch them, there may be a problem. If he's rubbing his ears along the carpet or against your legs, peek into them. Checking your dog's ears every few days for signs of infection and cleaning them if necessary should be part of your regular grooming routine.

Why Ear Care Is Important

Even if your Boston isn't fussing with his ears, it's a good idea to develop the habit of regularly inspecting them for early signs of redness, which would indicate an ear infection. Although it may sound odd, smell the ears too because a mild infection will cause a musky, foul odor.

By cleaning the ears often, you will keep them healthy and may be able to prevent a full-blown ear infection. Left untreated, ear infections can develop into chronic conditions that are painful and may cause hearing loss.

Also, when an infection causes excessive scratching or head shaking, a blood vessel may rupture and the blood will accumulate between the skin and the cartilage of the ear or the flap. A hematoma, a blot clot that causes swelling of the ear, can give it a cauliflower appearance. Hematomas may dissolve, but in some cases your veterinarian may need to drain the blood from the area through surgical repair. To avoid this process and annoying ear infections, it's much easier to prevent problems in the first place by keeping your Boston's ears clean.

How to Clean Your Dog's Ears

Gather all necessary materials before you begin cleaning your dog's ears.

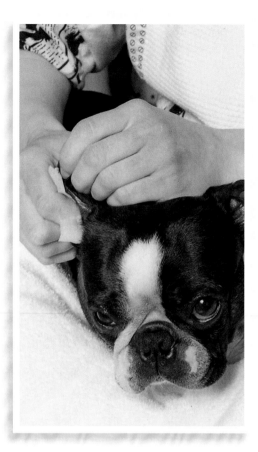

Inspect and clean your dog's ears and eyes as part of his regular grooming routine.

5. Gently wipe out all the folds and crevices inside of the ear. You may need to add more ear-cleaning solution and use several cotton balls or strips of cotton until they come out clean.
6. Repeat this process for the other ear using fresh cotton balls or strips.
7. Never use cotton swabs; they can damage the inner ear.
8. Never use baby wipes to clean the ear, as they contain drying agents that are harmful to a dog.

Your Boston may resist ear cleaning and will shake his head afterwards. Give him a small food treat to entice him to let you handle his ears again next time.

EYE CARE

The Boston Terrier is all about expression, and his eyes tell his story. But because they protrude and are more vulnerable to becoming irritated and injured, checking his eyes for any signs of redness or irritation should be a normal part of your grooming routine.

Always inspect your dog's eyes after he's been playing outdoors, and think twice about taking him on outings to wooded areas or low brushy spots where they will surely attract pollen or thorns that can cause irritation or damage.

If you notice that your Boston is pawing at his eyes or blinking a lot, or that his eyes are watering, you'll need to take him to your veterinarian.

1. Every time you groom your dog, wipe out his ears with a dry cotton ball or one slightly moistened with mineral oil.
2. If you detect a problem, pour a little ear-cleaning solution into one of your dog's ears. If your dog's ears are already clean, you don't need to use an ear-cleaning solution.
3. Massage the ear at the base back and forth a few times.
4. Wrap your finger around a cotton ball or strip of cotton and gently rub the inside of the ear. Don't poke too far into the ear, though, because you may cause injury.

Want to Know More?

For more detailed information on conditions and disorders of the eye to which your Boston may be prone, see CH8: Boston Terrier Health and Wellness.

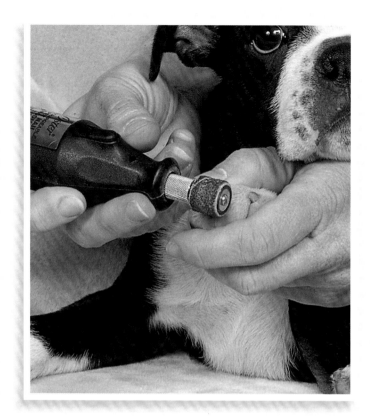

Nail care keeps your dog's feet healthy.

Why Eye Care Is Important

Some eye problems or injuries can result in a serious condition or loss of vision. Don't hesitate to contact your veterinarian if you suspect something is wrong. For example, discharge coming from your dog's eyes may signal an infection. Obtaining treatment as soon as possible may prevent a more serious situation from occurring.

How to Clean Your Boston's Eyes

Cleaning your Boston's eyes is an easy grooming task that takes just seconds. Follow these steps:

1. Soak a cotton ball or gauze pad in warm water.

2. Start at the inside corner of the eye and gently wipe out toward the outside.

3. Repeat if you notice any discharge from the eyes.

While most Bostons don't have excessive tear staining, some do. To prevent tear stains, wipe underneath the eye with a cotton ball moistened with warm water and dry it thoroughly. A small dab of petroleum jelly rubbed into the skin beneath the eye may help repel the dampness.

NAIL TRIMMING

Manicures and pedicures aren't limited to humans. Your dog will appreciate some attention to his feet too, which besides feeling good will help keep them healthy. Make trimming your dog's nails part of your weekly grooming routine. It'll be easier to keep track of when they need cutting.

If you hear nails clicking on your floors, it means that you've waited too long to give your dog a pedicure and his nails are too long. Contrary to what many people believe, not every dog wears his nails down automatically running or walking on concrete, so it's your job to see that his feet are properly cared for, which includes regular toenail trimming. Some dogs' toenails grow faster than others no matter where they play. Nail growth depends on many factors, including body chemistry, nutrition, and the shape of the nails.

With each successive doggy pedicure, both you and your dog will gain confidence and the process will go more smoothly. Put aside your fear of cutting a nail too short and making it bleed. Sooner or later that may happen, but even experienced groomers occasionally clip a little too close. You can always have your vet or a professional groomer give you some pointers or show you how to trim nails properly before doing it for the first time.

Why Nail Trimming Is Important

Your Boston's nails should never curve over and touch the ground. When this happens, it throws off him balance because he cannot stand evenly on the pads of his feet and he loses traction, which impairs walking. For an elderly or overweight dog who has difficulty walking, having long nails only adds to this problem. In the worst cases, nails that grow too long past the pads of the feet can cut into the pad itself. A dog with bad feet will have a hard time going anywhere, so there's every reason to keep the nails nice and short.

Untrimmed nails can cause other problems as well. When nails are too long, their pointed tips can catch on objects and clothing and can snag or break, often causing bleeding and pain. Your veterinarian may have to surgically remove a badly broken nail, especially if it becomes infected.

How to Trim Your Boston's Nails

Some Bostons may find grooming tools scary, so let your dog see and sniff everything before you begin. Keep nail trimming sessions short, too. Most dogs don't like standing on a table for too long and become stressed by this strange procedure until they get used to it.

Before you even begin trimming your Boston's nails, massage his feet every day so he becomes accustomed to your handling them. Then, for your first nail trimming session, simply trim one or two nails. At subsequent sessions you can trim additional nails as your dog grows comfortable with the process.

Boston Terrier toenails are black, which makes it difficult to see where the vein inside the nail, called the quick, is located, but don't let this prevent you from getting the job done. Cut your dog's nails outdoors in bright light or use a flashlight so you can see the quick (pinkish portion) in the center of the nail.

There are several types of nail trimmers you can choose from, including an electric pet grinder. Many Boston owners use a nail trimmer first to remove most of the length of the nail, then a rotary nail grinder to get even closer to the quick. The grinder makes a whirring noise, so let your dog see and hear it before you use it.

Follow these steps:

1. Put your dog on a grooming table with a grooming arm and noose to hold his head steady.
2. Give him a little food treat to relax him.
3. Gently lift your dog's paw and press your index finger and thumb on a toe. This extends the nail and holds it in place.

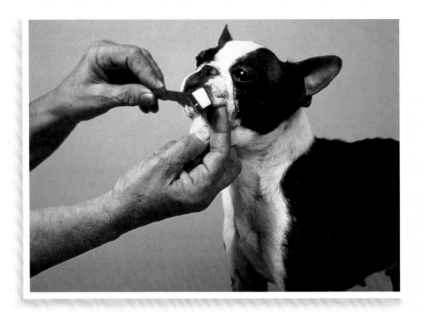

To brush your dog's teeth, use both a toothbrush and toothpaste especially formulated for dogs.

4. Locate the quick and clip off the portion beyond it toward the tip.
5. If you clip too closely and the nail bleeds, apply a little styptic powder to the nail, which will stop the bleeding. This may sting a little, so if you choose not to use it, the bleeding will eventually stop on its own.
6. Repeat with the other toes.
7. If your dog still has his dewclaws, or thumbnails, clip those too.
8. Give your dog a treat and tell him what a good boy he is.
9. If your dog has brittle nails that crumble easily when they are trimmed, try supplementing his diet with omega-3 fatty acids using fish oil capsules to restore nail strength.

The best treatment for Boston Terrier nails is to trim them once a week and frequently check to make sure they are intact. With practice, your nail-rimming skills will improve and your Boston's feet will benefit from your diligence.

DENTAL CARE

Like people, dogs need their teeth brushed regularly. With a tendency for tooth overcrowding and spaces for bits of food to become trapped, a Boston's mouth is prone to developing periodontal disease. This leads to decayed gums, infection, tooth loss, and other health problems.

The problem begins when a dog eats. A hard brown coating of calcium salts from saliva, known as tartar or calculus, forms on the teeth. Beneath that surface, a thin layer of sticky bacteria, or plaque, begins to build up, causing periodontal disease.

Why Dental Care Is Important

Plaque accumulates on a dog's teeth every day, but regular brushing keeps it under control and helps prevent periodontal disease.

While brushing takes care of most of the plaque, it doesn't remove the crusty tartar that forms in crevices and hard-to-reach places. Because of overcrowded teeth and their propensity to build up plaque and tartar, Boston Terriers need a good professional cleaning, known as prophylaxis (or prophy) twice a year. During the cleaning, which is usually performed under anesthesia, the veterinarian will check for fractured or abscessed teeth and remove any tartar buildup.

Without regular dental hygiene, bacteria from the plaque and tartar can enter the bloodstream and cause infections that damage your dog's heart, liver, and kidneys.

How to Brush Your Boston's Teeth

To brush your dog's teeth, use a toothbrush and toothpaste especially formulated for dogs. You can also use a finger toothbrush that fits over your finger, or wrap a piece of gauze around your finger. Doggy toothpaste is nonfoaming and digestible, so you don't have to worry about

Along with regular brushing, dental chews and bones help to remove tartar and plaque buildup.

rinsing it out of your dog's mouth. Available in poultry, fish, and beef flavors, the toothpaste has a taste that is actually loved by most dogs. Don't use human toothpaste because it can upset your dog's stomach.

To get your Boston used to having his teeth brushed, you'll have to proceed slowly. Don't expect to brush all his teeth the very first time, as it will take a while before he feels comfortable having a toothbrush in his mouth. Spend a few minutes once a day on your dog's dental hygiene after he's eaten.

Follow these steps:

1. Place some toothpaste on your finger and let your dog sniff it or lick it off.
2. Repeat the application of toothpaste on your finger, gently lift your dog's lip, and rub one of his teeth for a brief second or two with the toothpaste.
3. Next, try spreading the paste on the toothbrush and let your dog lick it off.
4. Repeat the application of paste on the toothbrush and gently lift his lip and try brushing a tooth or two in a circular motion.
5. Once your dog relaxes enough to allow you to brush more than one or two teeth, brush a few more teeth, including the ones in the back because these are most susceptible to periodontal disease.

Add a few more teeth every day until you've brushed all 42 teeth. Keep the process fun, and praise your dog for accepting the brushing.

By the Numbers

Like people, dogs have two sets of teeth in their lifetime. The first set erupts through the gums when a puppy is about three to four weeks of age. These baby teeth will fall out at about four months of age, making way for the adult teeth. By the time the dog is about four months of age, all 42 adult teeth should erupt, including the molars. You can begin brushing your dog's teeth at this age.

TAIL CARE

Your Boston's tail requires some attention. Beneath deep-set corkscrew or inverted tails, a pocket of debris can form and cause infection if this area isn't wiped and dried.

Regularly wipe the tail area with some warm water and a doggy shampoo. Be sure to rinse and dry it thoroughly.

HOW TO FIND A PROFESSIONAL GROOMER

If the whole process of sprucing up your dog seems overwhelming, you can opt to entrust your dog's regular maintenance to a professional groomer. That's fine. Just find an experienced, reliable professional who has a good reputation, cares about your dog, and understands what a Boston Terrier needs.

Although you'll save money by not having to purchase all of the grooming essentials, keep in mind you will have to transport your dog to the grooming parlor or pay extra for a professional to come to your home. You'll also have the grooming expense.

Before taking your dog to the neighborhood grooming parlor, check out all nearby facilities. Knowing what to look for will alleviate any worries you might have about your dog's safety

and well-being. Ask your veterinarian or friends with dogs for referrals. Word of mouth often carries the best references.

While many pet supply stores offer grooming services, these services are not necessarily superior to those provided by an independent professional. Anyone can call themselves a dog groomer, so visit grooming shops and see for yourself. Ask about the groomer's experience and whether the individual has worked with Bostons before. Many reputable groomers belong to the National Dog Groomers Association, although other qualified professionals have graduated from grooming schools or apprenticed under other good groomers.

If you go mid-morning when most shops are the busiest, you'll have a good idea about what to expect. Look for a shop that is clean and has a pleasant smell. Other than the odor of wet dog, you shouldn't smell, anything especially urine or feces. Watch how the groomers treat the dogs. They should be handled gently but firmly, as not every dog enjoys being there. Observe whether dogs are left unattended on grooming tables; left alone with a grooming noose around his neck, a dog could fall or jump off the table and choke. Look at the drying cages. Dogs should never be left unsupervised in one of these because an unattended hot air dryer can burn them. Hand blow dryers are a better option because the temperature can be monitored.

Once you choose a groomer, discuss the services that will be performed on your dog before you leave him. Give specific instructions about what you want so there won't be any surprises when you pick him up.

If your dog has never traveled without you or has never been groomed before, expect him to feel anxious. With experience, your dog will learn to adjust to the situation.

CHAPTER 7

BOSTON TERRIER NUTRITIONAL NEEDS

If your Boston catches a whiff of your steak sizzling on the grill, it's no wonder he'll perform a happy dance and lick his chops. Dogs love food—the tastier the better. And why shouldn't they? They're omnivores and will eat anything if you let them.

Your job is to make sure that your Boston receives a healthy meal, not just what he wants to eat. When you can combine wholesome ingredients and appetizing food, he has the best of both edible worlds. It's not hard to feed your dog a good diet as long as you pay attention to the basics of good nutrition—carbohydrates, fats, proteins, minerals, vitamins, and water.

To provide proper nutrition, you can choose to give your dog a dry or canned food you purchase, cook his meals yourself, or serve up a raw diet. Don't forget that treats should be healthy, too. They can be nutritious or full of empty calories, so watch out that your Boston doesn't gain too much weight from eating excessively or consuming unhealthy foods.

WHY GOOD NUTRITION IS ESSENTIAL

All dogs—and especially Bostons—benefit from eating a complete and balanced diet of carbohydrates, fats, proteins, vitamins, and minerals. Other than preventing your dog from going hungry, good nutrition helps in many ways. It aids in fighting off certain diseases, maintains a healthy coat and skin, and promotes longevity. At the very least, the food your dog eats provides the energy he needs to function. Good nutrition also provides the structural components, vitamins, and minerals that are necessary for building and maintaining strong muscles and bones.

Building Blocks of Nutrition

Everything your dog eats contains varying amounts of nutrients—the substances that your Boston Terrier needs to live and grow. Six basic types of necessary nutrients include carbohydrates, fats, proteins, minerals, vitamins, and water. Carbohydrates, fats, and proteins provide energy, while the combination of minerals, vitamins, and water all contribute to the maintenance of overall health.

Carbohydrates

Carbohydrates are found in foods that are rich in sugar or starch, such as cereals, bread, rice, wheat, and pasta. Excellent sources of nutrients, they provide energy and are easily digested. Unused carbohydrates are stored in the body as converted fat and as glycogen in the muscles and liver.

There are two types of carbohydrates: simple carbohydrates, which are quickly digested and absorbed by the body, and complex carbohydrates, which provide energy for a longer period of time.

It's important to feed your dog the most nutritious types of carbohydrates you possibly can. Many commercial dog foods contain between 30 and 70 percent carbohydrates. Canned dog foods can contain carbohydrates, but they often consist of sugar in empty-calorie sources in the

A well-balanced, nutritious diet will help your dog look and feel his best.

form of sucrose, propylene glycol, and corn syrup. Higher quality foods contain complex carbohydrates from whole grains, which are much more nutritious.

Try to avoid foods that contain carbohydrates with little nutritional value. You can search for them on a dog food label. The following are some examples:

- rice flour: in the form of a fine powder, it is the end process of milling rice
- beet sugar: dried residue from the sugar beet
- corn gluten meal: dried residue from corn after the removal of starch and bran
- brewer's rice: rice sections discarded from the manufacturing of beer, containing pulverized dried hops

Proteins

Proteins are among the most important nutrients in a dog's diet. Dietary protein comes from animal or plant sources and contains ten specific amino acids that dogs cannot produce on their own. They are necessary for all aspects of growth and development and are vital to the immune system. They are responsible for producing hormones, building enzymes, regulating metabolism, repairing damaged tissue, and strengthening hair and skin.

Dog food manufacturers use beef, chicken, turkey, lamb, and duck as sources of protein. Other sources include fish, fish meal, liver, eggs, milk, and milk products. Some grains and beans, such as rice, wheat, corn, barley, and soy, also contain protein.

When deciding how much protein to feed your Boston, also consider the type of protein it is. If you feed a commercial recipe, you know exactly what kind of protein it contains by reading the label. Not all proteins are created equal: Some are easier for your dog to digest and to absorb, while others are harder or impossible for the body to break down, even though they are technically called proteins. From best to worst, the easiest proteins to digest are: eggs, fish meal, milk, lamb, beef, and chicken.

Fats

Fats and oils contribute essential nutrients that enhance the flavor of food, enticing Bostons to enjoy their meals. For those dogs who are picky eaters and need help maintaining their weight, the right amount and type of fat in the diet can make all the difference in the world.

Compared to carbohydrates and proteins, fat is a much more concentrated form of dietary energy, providing more than twice the amount of calories. Fats have many functions. They make the texture of food more palatable and aid in the absorption of vitamins, especially vitamins A, D, E, and K.

Oils are a form of fat derived from plants and animals called essential fatty acids (EFAs). The body needs EFAs to maintain healthy skin and hair and to assist with kidney function and reproduction.

Some commercial dog foods may contain more fat than what the body really needs, which causes obesity, while some weight-reducing or homemade diets can be deficient in necessary fats. To prevent deficiencies, essential fatty acids should constitute at least 2 percent of a dog's daily caloric intake, although the recommended amount of total fat percentage in food for an adult Boston is 9 to 15 percent.

Minerals

Compared to other nutrients, which are large and complex, minerals are simple molecules that perform important functions in the

Whether you choose to serve your Boston Terrier a homemade diet or buy a commercial dog food, it should contain the healthiest ingredients he loves to eat.

body. They're responsible for building bone and cartilage, transporting oxygen in the blood, producing hormones, and regulating the functioning of nerves and muscles.

Minerals are divided into two categories: macrominerals and microminerals. Macrominerals are inorganic nutrients needed by the body in relatively high daily amounts. They include sulfur, calcium, phosphorus, magnesium, and the electrolytes sodium, potassium, and chloride. Microminerals are inorganic nutrients needed in minute daily amounts, such as zinc, copper, manganese, iodine, and selenium.

Quality commercial dog food contains adequate amounts of minerals. Homemade diets, on the other hand, may provide too much or too little of certain minerals, which can seriously affect the overall balance of nutrients your dog requires and become harmful over time. For example, excess copper can cause liver damage in dogs that cannot excrete it normally, too much phosphorus can be harmful in dogs with kidney disease, and an extra supply of calcium can cause skeletal damage, including osteochondrosis in puppies less than six months of age. Always consult with your vet before feeding your dog a homemade diet to ensure that complete and balanced nutrition is provided.

Vitamins

Vitamins fortify the immune system, regulate metabolism, and help the body function and grow. They also are responsible for numerous chemical reactions that occur in the body, aiding in digestion, reproduction, blood clotting, and the normal development of muscle, bone, skin, and hair.

Vitamins are divided into two groups: water soluble and fat soluble. Although the body does not store water-soluble vitamins, fat-soluble vitamins are stored in fatty tissue and in the liver. Fat-soluble vitamins include vitamins A, D, and E. Water-soluble vitamins include thiamin, riboflavin, niacin, pantothenic acid, pyridoxine, folic acid, biotin, vitamin B12, Vitamin C, and choline.

Quality commercial recipes contain an adequate amount of vitamins, so there's no need to supplement a prepared recipe. If you choose to add a daily supplement, check with your vet first. Excessive amounts of most vitamins won't cause a problem, but excessive amounts of vitamins A and D can be harmful; too much vitamin A can be toxic to the liver, and excess vitamin D can lead to kidney damage.

Water

Forget energy drinks or designer beverages; your dog just needs plain old water to remain in tip-top shape. Water is the most important nutrient of all, and it's necessary for everything the body needs to do. It transports necessary nutrients throughout the body and carries waste materials from the system via urine. It also assists digestion and regulates body temperature.

Sixty percent of a dog's body is water, and losing only 10 percent of it seriously jeopardizes his health. Exposed to hot weather for only a few hours, a dog can quickly become dehydrated if deprived of water. Normally, your Boston should drink two and a half times more water than the daily amount of food he consumes. Hot weather increases the need for water by two or three times this.

Considering this nutrient's role in your Boston's health, the quality of the water should be high. Household tap water is safe, but yours may be high in nitrates, iron, or magnesium, which can pose a health risk. Filtered water is a healthier option.

To foster good water drinking habits in your dog, pick up his bowl every morning and thoroughly wash it before refilling it—if you wouldn't want to drink out of your dog's bowl, he won't want to either. Also, dirty water bowls harbor harmful organisms. If you use a ceramic or a plastic water bowl, check it regularly for scratches that can trap bacteria. Replace it if necessary. Stainless steel bowls are the best options for resisting scratches and the easiest to keep clean, plus they last forever.

To encourage your dog to drink enough water, make sure it's tasty. Keep it cool in the warm months and serve it room temperature in the winter.

To know exactly how much water your dog drinks throughout the day, measure the amount you put in the bowl in the morning and measure it again in the evening.

By the Numbers

Most Boston breeders recommend switching your dog from a puppy recipe to an adult maintenance diet by the time he's one year of age.

Dry foods provide the most popular and diverse meal base for dogs.

WHAT TO FEED

Whether you choose to serve your Boston Terrier a homemade diet or buy a commercial dog food, it should contain the healthiest ingredients that he loves to eat.

For Bostons, food tidbits should be small. Short-faced breeds with an underbite and dental crowding have difficulty picking up food and chewing and swallowing it. If the pieces are too large, your eager eater may try to gobble it all in one bite and can choke. Add to that the Boston's tendency to have food allergies and coat dryness from time to time and it becomes necessary to give careful thought to the foods you select.

Today, there's a host of recipes and ways to feed your dog a healthy diet: commercial dry and canned food, semi-moist food, and homemade or raw diets. Your veterinarian can also supply a prescription diet and suggest supplements to booster your dog's nutritional requirements. Nutritious treats may also be occasionally included as part of your dog's diet. While treats and bones can't supply all of your Boston's needs, they can help reward his good behavior.

To know whether a food agrees or disagrees with your Boston, look at his coat and skin. It should have a natural shine to it without dandruff or itching. His stools—one to two a day—should be firm and not bulky, running, or frequent. Your dog should not have frequent bouts of diarrhea, vomiting, or ear infections, or constantly want to lick body parts, scratch continuously at his skin, or chew at his feet obsessively.

The wrong food for your Boston can cause dietary allergies, which are the body's inflammatory reaction to certain proteins in the food. Any protein, including those in meat, chicken, or grains, can trigger a problem. Avoiding high levels of proteins in the diet can help manage seizures.

Commercial Food

Today, the aisles of pet food stores are piled high with dog food in bags, cans, and boxes, as well as frozen and semi-moist food varieties in the sections reserved for frozen and refrigerated foods. With so many choices available, it's difficult to know what kind of food suits your Boston best. Different dogs do better on different types of food, and each type has advantages and disadvantages.

To choose a good recipe for your dog, read the label and the list of ingredients. Look for foods containing high-quality proteins, such as beef, chicken, turkey, fish, or lamb as the first three ingredients. Avoid meat by-products, meat meal, and meat from unidentified sources. These are inferior parts of the animal that people would never eat. Select carbohydrates with whole grains, such as brown rice or oatmeal, as these are the most nutritious. Avoid formulas containing mostly wheat, corn, soy, gluten, water, and cereal by-products. Because many Bostons don't metabolize a high percentage of grains in dry diets completely, flatulence may be a problem. Boston breeders say that corn and soy are big gas producers.

Inferior dog foods often contain nine ingredients that you should avoid:

- Butylated hydroxyanisole (BHA) and butylated hydroxytoluene (BHT): These preservatives prevent spoilage and extend shelf life, but some studies say they are carcinogenic. Look instead for vitamin C and vitamin E (mixed tocopherols) used as preservatives.
- Ethoxyquin: This preservative is linked to impaired liver and kidney function.
- Propylene glycol: This liquid, used to prevent food from drying out, may cause central nervous system impairment and changes in kidney function.
- Propyl gallate: This antioxidant prevents fats and oils from spoiling but may cause skin irritation.
- Coloring agents: Red dye 40 and yellow dye 5 brighten food but show a link to cancer.
- Phosphoric acid: This is a clear liquid serving as a flavoring agent and emulsifier (an ingredient that binds oil and water together). While it prevents discoloration, it may irritate the skin and mucous membranes.
- Sorbitol: This synthetic sugar substitute used to flavor food may cause diarrhea and intestinal upset.

Training Tidbit

To retrain your finicky dog to eat his food, offer him meals at regular times, and pick up the dish and throw away uneaten food after 20 minutes. Don't give him any additional food or snacks until the next meal. Some dogs will hold out three or four days before they begin eating all of their food. That's alright. When your dog is hungry enough, he'll eat what he's given.

- DI-alpha tocopheryl acetate: This synthetic form of vitamin E is not easily absorbed.
- Menadione sodium bisulfate vitamin K3: This synthetic form of vitamin K may irritate mucous membranes.

Dry Food

Dry food, or kibble, is convenient, but not all dry foods are created equal. While kibble tends to be low in fat, which helps keep your dog's weight in check, it can contain ingredients that consist of more bulk than actual nutrition.

Not every Boston loves kibble. To entice their picky eaters to eat all of their dry food, some Boston breeders will add in a few spoonfuls of chicken-flavored canned food. Some like to serve a basic dry food diet but add a little fresh steamed or finely chopped or grated vegetables and fruits every day, such as green beans, carrots, apples, pears, berries, broccoli, squash, or spinach.

Dehydrated Food

This relatively new type of food has all the water removed from it and preserves the vitamins, minerals, and other nutrients. Mixed with warm water, it has a long shelf life and may be refrigerated if your dog doesn't eat it all at once.

Semi-Moist Food

Mostly water, semi-moist food contains a high amount of salt, sugar, and artificial flavors and colorings. In the pet supply stores, these foods are generally found in the frozen and refrigerated food sections; instructions for their preservation before use and in serving to your dog should be followed.

Frozen Food

Frozen commercial foods are more expensive because they contain a higher ratio of meat to grain. They also contain fewer preservatives and additives and can be safely stored for six months. Once opened, they last for two days.

Canned Food

Many Bostons like the taste of canned food because of its strong aroma and flavor. Sometimes Boston owners will even use canned food to supplement the dry food they give their dogs.

Many canned foods contain a higher percentage of water than protein, but look for a canned food containing a whole protein, such as meat, poultry, or fish as the first ingredient. More expensive than dry food, many canned food recipes are high in fat. Look for a canned recipe containing whole vegetables, not grain by-products. Always refrigerate leftover portions.

Noncommercial Food

Opponents of commercial dog food claim that drying, freezing, heating, or canning food causes spoilage and rancidity. By making your own meals you can give your Boston exactly what he needs.

Home-Cooked Diets

To prepare a balanced home-cooked diet, include 30 to 60 percent protein. This should consist of fresh-cooked lean chicken, turkey, duck, beef, lamb, venison, pork, or fish. Other options include eggs, beans, lentils, tofu, and peanut butter. Thirty to

Want to Know More?

For more information on special diets for seniors, see Chapter 13: Care of Your Boston Terrier Senior.

Limit the number of treats you offer your dog, and make sure they consist only of healthy ingredients.

60 percent of the meal should consist of carbohydrates in the form of cooked grains, such as rice, millet, and barley. Other options are potatoes, rolled oats, winter squash, and whole-grain bread.

Vegetables and fruits are important also and should compose 10 to 30 percent of the meal. Feed raw veggies if they can be finely chopped or lightly steamed. Calcium and phosphorus supplements should be added, but check the amounts with your veterinarian. Fats in the form of a teaspoon of salmon oil, flax, borage, and canola or olive oil is also necessary. Don't forget a natural canine multivitamin/mineral supplement, but check with your veterinarian for the correct dosage.

Raw Diets

Some dog owners believe that raw diets are better for their dogs. The recipes are more natural, and you can avoid artificial preservatives and by-products and use only quality ingredients. But preparing a fresh raw diet for your dog at every meal presents a challenge because it requires advance planning and organization.

For your dog to derive the most nutrition from a raw diet, the recipe should be nutritionally complete and contain the right proportion of ingredients, including vitamins and minerals. It's also important to handle the food correctly to prevent bacterial contamination. Wash your hands and cooking utensils thoroughly after handling raw meat.

Dehydrated raw diets have recently become available for dogs. These are dry ingredients that require reconstitution with water. For people who want to feed their dogs a raw diet but may not have the time to shop for food, this offers a convenient alternative.

Special/Prescription Diets

Today, there are specialized diets for every canine medical condition. While many manufacturers are providing these diets, your veterinarian can also suggest healthy ways to feed your dog.

Just about every veterinarian stocks special dog food recipes to target specific metabolic processes. These include therapeutic diets for kidney, heart, and skin problems. Sold only through veterinary offices, these formulas are often very expensive and contain either nutrients in reduced amounts or nutrients in amounts that are elevated above typical levels for healthy dogs.

Beneficial for only short periods of time, these diets are not designed to be used long term. If your veterinarian prescribes a therapeutic dog food, ask why this diet is beneficial, and if you cook your own dog food, ask what ingredients you should or should not include to derive the same benefits.

Multi-Dog Tip

To make sure that each dog eats his own food and doesn't steal from another bowl, supervise mealtimes. Stand between your dogs and redirect them to their own bowls if one dog tries to sneak a mouthful. Within a few feedings, they'll stay in their own area.

Supplements

Always consult with your vet before adding supplementation to your dog's diet. If you feel the need to supplement your dog's food, consider coenzyme Q10 (CoQ10). This antioxidant is required for energy production by cells and helpful for dogs with heart disease, allergies, and periodontal disease.

Chondroitin sulfate and glucosamine are beneficial supplements for dogs with arthritis. This combination supplement increases the synovial fluids to restore cushioning between the joints.

Treats and Bones

Who doesn't love giving their dog an extra treat and a special bone to chomp on. Just make sure any treat you provide is healthy and safe, such as the ones made by Nylabone.

Treats

For Bostons with a tendency toward obesity, treats should be fed in moderation. Some contain a high amount of sugar, salt, and extra calories that your dog just doesn't need. Before purchasing treats, read the label on the package. The ingredients should be just as healthful as your dog's regular food.

Sure, your dog loves them, but avoid rawhide and cow hooves. Hooves are often dangerous because they can easily splinter, and your dog can swallow sharp pieces and break teeth. Rawhide pieces can become caught in your dog's throat or block his digestive system.

You can substitute store-bought treats with fresh, nutritious cut-up pieces of fruits and vegetables. These are full of fiber and provide a healthy alternative.

Bones

Raw bones make a great occasional snack, but avoid making them a major part of your dog's

Adult dogs over the age of one year should eat two meals a day.

diet. Be careful about feeding chicken, turkey, fish, or pork bones; they can easily splinter and cause intestinal injury. Raw chicken legs and wings have the perfect calcium/phosphorus ratio and are small enough for a Boston to handle, but give them cautiously.

Some dogs can manage a meaty raw bone that's large enough not to break. Feed your dog only raw bones, as cooked bones can splinter into sharp fragments. A better choice is to have the bones pulverized by a butcher and cooked. Raw bones may carry bacterial infection.

WHEN TO FEED AN ADULT DOG

Adult Boston Terriers thrive when they eat regular meals at specific times every day. With regular meal times, they're less likely to overeat and housetraining will be easier.

How Often

Adult dogs over the age of one year should eat two meals a day. Eating only one meal a day can actually cause a dog to gain weight because his metabolism slows down during the hours he doesn't eat, and then the food he consumes is processed too quickly after it is ingested.

When to Feed

The two meals a day you feed your Boston should be divided into a morning and evening meal. Keep the time span between the two fairly even so your dog doesn't have to go too long between meals.

OBESITY

While some Bostons are picky eaters, others love to eat and can't seem to get enough out of their food bowl. Oversized portions can pack on the extra pounds in no time. Several studies estimate that one third of all pet dogs in the United States are overweight. How does this happen?

It comes down to calories in versus calories out. When a dog eats more calories than he burns through normal metabolism and exercise—whether in the form of carbohydrates, fats, or proteins—the excess calories turn into fat.

Another reason for obesity may be found on the commercial dog food bag or can label. The feeding recommendations printed on these products generally overestimate the number of calories a dog really needs. As a consequence, many owners overfeed their dogs by following the feeding directions manufacturers provide. Bostons who eat too much of a home-cooked diet or a raw recipe can also end up eating too many calories and gaining weight.

Treats add up too. Many commercial goodies contain sugar and extra calories. Using their soft, pleading eyes, Bostons

Monitoring the amount of exercise your Boston receives daily helps him to stay fit and keeps his weight in check.

How Can You Tell Whether Your Boston Is Overweight?

A Boston Terrier is considered obese if he weighs more than 15 percent over the breed's average 15- to 20-pound normal healthy weight. You can tell whether your dog is at a good weight by looking at his body condition. Stand over him and look down at his body. He should have a definite waist, and you should be able to feel his ribs without seeing them sticking out.

know how to wrangle extra tidbits from their owners. Because many owners don't perceive the breed as needing much exercise, extra calories don't have a chance to burn off, so it's easy for Bostons to become obese.

Extra weight isn't just unattractive, it's unhealthy. It places excess pressure on a dog's joints and heart. For obese Bostons with luxating patellas or an elongated soft palate, the extra weight causes additional symptoms and pain. Obesity can cause many canine diseases and conditions, including diabetes, respiratory distress, osteoarthritis, liver disease, and heart disease. It also aggravates epilepsy.

Reversing Obesity

If you want to prevent your dog from suffering the unhealthy consequences of being overweight, you will have to provide regular exercise along with a proper diet.

First, gradually cut down on the amount of regular food and treats you feed. If your dog seems really hungry, add a few pieces of steamed or grated fresh vegetables to his regular meal. These will fill him up without adding too many extra calories. Avoid corn, beans, and broccoli because they cause digestive upsets, including gas.

While there are diet or "light" dog foods available, these are designed as maintenance diets for dogs with special needs rather than weight loss. Feeding meals at set times rather than leaving the food bowl down all day helps control how much your dog eats.

When it comes to serving portions, avoid eyeballing the amount. Always measure how much food you feed your dog so you know exactly how much he is getting. This comes in handy when you have to adjust the portion size.

Increasing the amount of exercise your Boston receives also helps him lose weight and improves his cardiovascular system. Walking him a few more minutes each day will speed up his metabolism and burn off those extra calories. If he hasn't gone strolling in a while, start slowly with a ten-minute outing. Add a minute each day until you've worked up to 20 to 30 minutes. You can divide this time up into several short sessions if needed. From there you can add little challenges like hills.

In hot weather, the best time to exercise your Boston is first thing in the morning before the ground heats up. Bring along water, and make the exercise routine a fun time for your dog. Skip the hard routines of ball chasing and marathon running; these activities should be reserved for conditioned dogs who are already in good shape.

CHAPTER 8

BOSTON TERRIER HEALTH AND WELLNESS

Your Boston Terrier relies on you to provide him with a healthy and happy life for as long as possible. Prevention is the first line of defense against illness. Make sure that your dog visits the veterinarian regularly, receives protection against parasites, and that you can administer first aid treatment if he ever needs it.

Bostons are a sturdy breed with only a few genetic illnesses, but despite the best of care there's always the chance of developing cancer, allergies, and ear and eye infections. Besides conventional medicine, don't overlook alternative treatments, as they often work wonders. All forms of health care are part of the commitment you took on when you added a Boston to the family. When he looks up at you with his soulful deep brown eyes, you know he's grateful.

ANNUAL VET EXAM

Taking your Boston to a qualified, compassionate veterinarian once a year is an essential part of caring for him. Assuming he isn't sick or needs emergency care, an annual wellness visit gives the doctor an opportunity to spot a problem in the early stages and possibly avert a more serious issue later on.

Once you're at the office, a veterinary assistant usually begins the routine physical exam by weighing your dog, taking his temperature, and checking his pulse. When the veterinarian enters the exam room, he or she will greet your Boston and ask you questions about his health history, including any behavior problems that you're concerned about.

A good exam includes looking at the overall condition of your dog's coat for any eruptions or rashes and for fleas, ticks, or other external parasites. The doctor will check the nose and mouth, look at your dog's teeth and gums, examine the eyes and ears for any signs of infection, and feel the neck for anything unusual in the lymph nodes or thyroid area.

Using a stethoscope, the veterinarian will listen to the heart and lungs for normal functioning, then feel the kidneys, liver, and intestines for any abnormalities. In

Want to Know More?

If you're wondering how to find the perfect vet for your dog, see Chapter 3: Care of Your Boston Terrier Puppy.

A dog with internal parasites will show signs of lethargy, weight loss, or irregular bowel movements.

addition, he or she will feel the genitals for any discharge. After checking the spine, the vet will also palpate the muscles, abdomen, and internal organs for the presence of any problems. Once a year, the veterinarian will draw blood for a heartworm test and to establish a baseline to compare to later samples if there's a medical problem. If your dog is ill, the doctor may order a fecal exam, urinalysis, or X-rays for a specific problem.

The exam time gives you a chance to discuss an overall health care plan for your Boston, including when to spay your female or neuter your male if that hasn't already been done. During this initial visit, discuss when your dog needs vaccines or titer testing and what you are feeding your dog.

PARASITES

No one likes the idea of nasty pests threatening a Boston Terrier's health and comfort. Parasites include the external variety that lives on the outside of your dog's body and the internal variety that dwells inside the body. Both types can wreak havoc on your dog's life. Depending upon your dog for their survival, they weaken his immune system and cause illnesses ranging from mild itching to death. With routine veterinary care, parasitic infestations are completely preventable or managed with medication.

Internal Parasites

Hiding inside your Boston, internal parasites can cause a lot of damage before you even realize your dog has them. They're responsible for a range of symptoms, including diarrhea, weight loss, anemia, dry hair, and vomiting. Early diagnosis is important to obtain treatment as quickly as possible. The five most common internal parasites in dogs are heartworms, hookworms, roundworms, tapeworms, and whipworms.

Heartworms

Far from having a heart, heartworms can kill your Boston Terrier. These long, slender worms are transmitted in the larval stage to a dog from a mosquito bite. Entering the bloodstream, the larvae travel to the heart and develop into adult worms that can grow more than a foot (30 cm) long. These adults begin a life cycle of producing larvae that circulate through the blood and reproduce in the body. One dog may have as many as 250 heartworms.

Signs: Heartworms cause inflammation of the surrounding arteries and damage the heart and lungs. In advanced cases, they produce congestive heart failure, weight loss, and death.

Treatment/Prevention: Only a blood test can determine the presence of heartworms before any symptoms appear. Treatment is available for heartworms, but it's expensive, dangerous, and may not always be effective, especially if the infestation is strong.

It's far safer to prevent heartworms. To guard your dog against this deadly condition, preventive medication is available. Puppies as young as three months of age can receive heartworm preventives. A prescription tablet taken once a month or a topical treatment is safe, convenient, and effective.

Hookworms

Hookworms are small, thin worms about 1/8 inch (0.3 cm) long that stick to the wall of the small intestine and suck blood. Dogs come into contact with hookworms by ingesting the larvae in contaminated food, water, and soil,

or through the skin. Puppies become infected through their mother's milk or through their mother's placenta. Hookworm larvae become adults in the intestine and reproduce quickly. One adult female hookworm can produce up to 20,000 eggs a day.

Signs: The signs of hookworm infestations include diarrhea, weight loss, anemia, and progressive weakness. Your veterinarian can detect the presence of these parasites by examining your dog's stool sample for hookworm eggs through a microscope.

Treatment/Prevention: To prevent your dog from getting hookworms, pick up feces daily in your yard and when walking in the neighborhood or park, and pick up after your dog so he does not contaminate the soil. Above all, don't let your Boston step in or eat any other dog's fecal material. Medications are available to kill hookworms.

Roundworms

The most common of all internal parasites, roundworms are 3 to 5 inches (7 to 10 cm) long and live in a dog's intestines. Resembling long strands of spaghetti, their eggs are passed from mothers to their puppies in the womb or during nursing. The worm eggs hide in muscle tissue and form cysts that lie dormant for years. Eggs may also live in soil in the environment— sometime for years—before they can infect a new host. A dog can also ingest roundworm larvae after consuming a small rodent that is carrying developing worms.

Signs: Puppies with roundworms will have soft, watery stools at about five weeks of age, followed by spaghetti-like worms in the stool a day or two later. Vomiting or lethargy may follow. Other symptoms may include excessive gas, weight loss, or an extended stomach resembling a potbellied appearance.

Treatment/Prevention: Your veterinarian

can confirm the diagnosis of roundworms by examining a stool sample and by performing a fecal flotation exam. Deworming medication can be given to infected puppies, but this affects only the worms in the intestinal tract and not the larvae. It rids the body of the worms during a bowel movement. The medication anesthetizes the worms so that they release their grip on the intestine and pass with the stool. Once passed, they cannot survive in the environment and they die.

Second and third doses are necessary to expel the eggs that hatch a few weeks later. Treatments are not available to kill the eggs; however, once the dog is cured, common preventives in flea control and/or heartworm medications can be used.

Conscientious breeders will give new puppy owners the dates that deworming medications were administered. Many breeders will give their dams this medication before they are bred.

Tapeworms

Tapeworms are flat worms that may reach 8 inches (20 cm) in length and are made up of many small segments about l/8 inch (0.3 cm) long. This parasite attaches itself to the small intestinal wall by hooklike mouthparts.

Bring a Sample

When taking your Boston for a veterinary exam, bring along a fresh stool sample. As part of his checkup, your veterinarian will check it for worms or their eggs. Parasitic infestations can weaken a dog's immune system and cause illnesses ranging from mild itching to death, but with routine veterinary care they are completely preventable or managed with medication.

The segments are mobile, break off, and crawl out of the anus and the surface of fresh feces. Dried segments can be seen stuck to the hair around a dog's anal region. They look like grains of rice and contain tapeworm eggs.

When dogs swallow a flea that contains tapeworm larvae, they become infected. The tapeworms hatch in the dog's intestine and anchor themselves to the intestinal lining. If dogs eat rodents carrying these parasites, they may ingest tapeworms.

Signs: While tapeworms are not particularly harmful to dogs, when present in large numbers they can cause liver damage, debilitation, and weight loss. The dog may scoot his rear along the ground or carpet because the segments are irritating to the skin.

Treatment/Prevention: A routine fecal examination may not reveal the presence of tapeworms, although the white, mobile segments can be detected when crawling on the dog or in the stool.

Oral and injected medications to kill tapeworms are available and do not cause side effects. Controlling fleas on the dog, inside the home, and outdoors will prevent tapeworm infection. A flea-infested environment may reinfect a dog in two weeks.

Whipworms

A very thin front portion and a thick end resembling a whip handle give adult whipworms their name. Unlike roundworms, hookworms, and tapeworms, which live in a dog's small intestine, whipworms dwell in the large intestine, specifically the cecum, which is where the small intestine and large intestine meet.

Dogs become infected with whipworms by ingesting food, water, or dirt contaminated with whipworm eggs. Once the eggs are swallowed, they remain in the body for one to

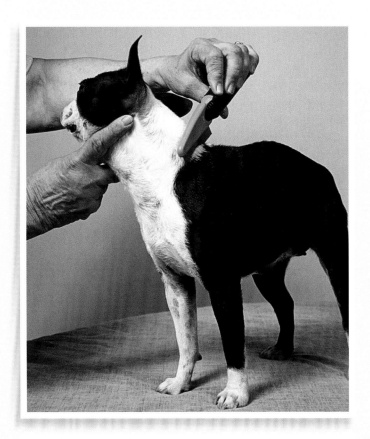

If your Boston begins to scratch himself frequently, he may have fleas. Using a flea comb can help you spot fleas in his dark coat.

three months until they hatch and mature into adults. Burrowing into the intestinal wall, they thrive on the blood supply and lay eggs.

Signs: Large numbers of whipworms will produce inflammation of the intestinal wall leading to diarrhea and weight loss, while small amounts of worms produce few signs of illness.

Treatment/Prevention: Your veterinarian can diagnose whipworms through a routine fecal examination. Deworming medication can help control whipworms. Because whipworms can live in infected soil for years, even withstanding freezing temperatures, you should pick up feces in the yard on a daily basis. Replace infected soil with new soil, gravel, or pavement. To prevent contamination, apply a bleach solution to kennel runs.

External Parasites

External parasites, such as fleas, ticks, and mites, can make your dog's life miserable. Besides, who wants to cuddle or pet a Boston with fleas or ticks? Fortunately, there are easy preventives you can use to control these pests.

Fleas

Sometimes you have to look hard to find tiny black or reddish brown fleas on the Boston Terrier's black or brindle coat. These six-legged wingless insects are slightly smaller than a sesame seed and possess the incredible ability to jump and burrow in and out of a dog's skin. They can easily jump from ground level to leap onto a dog in the blink of an eye.

Fleas feed on blood, and female fleas consume about 15 times their body weight. The digested blood is excreted and dries as "flea dirt," which helps to identify an infestation.

Fleas have a short, fast life cycle lasting from two weeks to eight months. They need a warm, humid temperature—70° to 85°F (21° to 29°C), with 70 percent humidity— in order to survive, and these pests thrive in warm, moist winters and springs.

It only takes two days for females to begin laying eggs after mating. They can produce up to 50 eggs per day. After the eggs are laid, they fall off the dog and burrow into soil outdoors or in various places inside the house, especially in bedding and carpeting. Up to six days later, they begin hatching into larvae that feed on flea dirt. The larvae transform into pupae and develop into adult fleas that begin looking for a host on which to live. Once a flea begins feeding, it will die within 24 hours if removed from its food source.

Signs: If you didn't spot the nearly invisible fleas on your dog, you'll be made aware of their presence by his intense biting, scratching, chewing, and restlessness. Far more severe than a mere annoyance, fleas cause severe discomfort and pose a serious threat to your dog's health, including anemia in puppies and debilitation in adult dogs. Fleas transmit tapeworm infection and produce flea allergy dermatitis (FAD), the most common veterinary dermatological condition.

To help spot fleas on your Boston, use a flea comb. If you see or feel dark grit in his coat, remove some and put it on a white paper towel. Add a drop of water; if the grit dissolves and turns red, it's flea feces.

For some dogs, the occasional fleabite may not present much of a problem, especially if you treat the situation quickly, but for dogs with weakened immune systems, fleas can cause major damage. A poor diet, stress, and unsanitary conditions will worsen the slightest flea reaction.

Some dogs are highly sensitive to flea bites. Fleas inject saliva containing irritating antigens and histamine substances that produce intense itching sensations. The constant scratching tears at the coat and produces hair loss and red, inflamed skin and hot spots. It's no wonder that dogs with flea allergy dermatitis become obsessed with tearing at their skin and cause immense damage to it.

Treatment/Prevention: Contrary to what some people think, dogs do not have to have fleas, and you do not have to live with them. Getting rid of fleas used to involve complicated treatments applied to your dog, his bedding, your house, and your yard, as well as keeping up with daily vacuuming and flea combing. Today your veterinarian can prescribe preventives that are safer, easier, and more effective to use.

Natural remedies, such as fatty acid supplements in the form of omega-3 and omega-6 help to reduce the amount and

Multi-Dog Tip

In multi-dog households, it is a good idea to separate pets if you suspect any of them have a contagious condition such as parasites, or an infectious disease such as kennel cough, distemper, and so forth.

effects of histamine, although the best line of flea defense is to permanently eradicate their existence on your dog, in your home, and outdoors. Also, by feeding your dog a natural diet, you can boost his immune system and resistance to all parasites.

Grooming your dog weekly, especially in warm weather, will alert you to the presence of fleas. Powders, sprays, and bathing products containing pyrethrin, which is made from chrysanthemums, a natural flea repellent, are helpful.

Washing your dog's bedding once a week in hot water and using a cedar-filled dog bed, which repels fleas, will help prevent infestations too. Steam clean your carpeting and clean upholstered furniture and drapes before flea season. At least once a week, sweep between cracks, crevices, along baseboards, and under rug edges, furniture, and beds to catch any flea eggs, larvae, and adult fleas. Sprinkle borate flea control powder around floor edges.

To rid your outdoor environment of fleas, apply natural diatomaceous earth around your garden. Nonparasitic nematode worms that naturally live in soil can consume flea larvae and other garden pests. Harmless to people and pets, those nematodes eat many types of pests that live in soil and are readily available in garden centers or through organic garden catalogues. In warm weather, prevent fleas from moving in on your dog by not taking him to exercise in large grassy areas that may be infested. Because tall grass and leaves are favorite nesting areas for fleas, keeping your lawn mowed short so that sunlight has a chance to kill larvae makes good flea prevention sense.

Mites

Boston Terriers are particularly vulnerable to demodectic mange. The mite *Demodex canis* is responsible for this disease.

A study by the Boston Terrier Club of America health survey revealed that almost 10 percent of Bostons have had localized demodectic mange and 5 percent have had the generalized form. The difference between localized demodectic mange and the generalized form is the severity of the skin infection. Fewer than five spots of mange is considered "localized"; more than 5 spots is considered "generalized."

Signs: While mange spots usually occur on the face, they can occur anywhere, including the feet. Mange-causing mites are microscopic, so you can't see them with the naked eye, but mange shows up as dry, scaly, bald patches on the skin. With secondary infection, the skin can become red and inflamed. Most puppies have mites. Nursing pups inherit them from their mothers during their first days of life.

Treatment/Prevention: Diagnosing mange can be difficult because symptoms look like other skin conditions. Stressed and undernourished puppies and young dogs with weakened immune systems are particularly vulnerable to mite infestation. Strengthening the immune system helps prevent mange from returning.

It was once believed that the mange caused by demodex mites could be transmitted through contact, but this is a myth. The disease is caused by a genetic defect in the immune system. Usually the condition resolves itself in time. However, severe infections can be treated with repeated medicated bathing dips and topical ointments and creams.

Ringworm

Ringworm is not caused by worms at all. It is a fungal skin infection caused by fungi that live on the surface of the skin and in the skin follicles. The fungi survive by feeding on dead skin tissue and hair.

Always check your dog for fleas and ticks after he has spent time outdoors.

Signs: Ringworm usually causes a round, hairless lesion and scaly skin. Patches of hair loss occur on the face, ears, tail, and paws. It may or may not be itchy, and the skin may or may not be reddened and inflamed. The characteristic "rings" that people develop from ringworm don't always look circular on dogs, however, and can look irregular as lesions grow. Puppies and young dogs are susceptible if their immune system hasn't fully developed, but healthy adult dogs usually have a resistance to ringworm.

Treatment/Prevention: Your veterinarian cannot diagnose ringworm simply by looking at the skin. Because 50 percent of the fungi will glow under ultraviolet light, the vet may use an ultraviolet lamp (black light) to detect it. A hair or skin sample from the lesion placed under

a microscope can also be used to detect the presence of ringworm.

Ringworm symptoms will usually resolve independently within two to four months without treatment. An antifungal drug that inhibits fungal reproduction is available to reduce contagion or to ease discomfort if your dog is suffering. It does have some side effects, so discuss whether or not to use it with your veterinarian. A lime sulfur dip can also be administered twice a week, but special care must be taken when using it because it can stain clothing and has a strong smell of rotten eggs.

Ringworm transmission occurs after direct contact with another infected animal or person, and it can be passed back and forth from dogs to other pets and people, and then back again by touch. The fungal spores can live a long time in the home environment. When a dog comes into contact with infected carpeting, bedding, furniture, and grooming equipment, he can pick up the spores. Infected soil can also cause ringworm because the fungi can live for months. Following a dog's exposure to ringworm, lesions may appear 10 to 12 days later.

To decontaminate the environment and kill ringworm spores on surfaces, apply a 1:10 solution of bleach and water (one part bleach to 10 parts water). This kills 80 percent of the spores. Daily vacuuming helps rid the household of spores. Remember to dispose of vacuum bags after each use. Steam cleaning of carpets and furniture will also help. Use the bleach solution to wash down crates and kennel areas, and wash your dog's bedding in very hot water.

Ticks

Ticks are far easier to spot than fleas and mites, although you hope to never find them on your Boston. Resembling flattened spiders, these hard-bodied eight-legged creatures cling to the body. After attaching themselves to your dog, they begin feeding on his blood.

Ticks are dangerous parasites because they cause anemia, heart damage, rashes, fevers, and painful joints. They're also responsible for spreading Lyme disease, Rocky Mountain spotted fever, Texas fever, tick paralysis, tularemia, babesiosis, and canine ehrlichiosis.

Cold, frosty fall weather does not kill ticks, and the spring and summer months are generally tick season, especially in wooded or grassy areas. Rodents, deer, and other animals are primary tick carriers. The parasites jump from these animals onto bushy plants and grass and latch onto a dog's chest, neck, or head, although it's not uncommon to find them clinging to ears, the tail area, or between the toes.

Signs: Ticks commonly embed themselves in the places just listed but can be found elsewhere on the body. The places where they attach can become red and irritated.

Treatment/Prevention: To prevent ticks from plaguing your Boston, treat the environment and your dog at the same time. Maintain his health through a good diet and frequent grooming so you can spot ticks early on. Remove a tick as soon as you see it. Do so carefully because just pulling it off can leave body parts still attached to your dog. Using tweezers, grasp the tick firmly near the head and pull it gently off your dog's skin. Drop the tick into the toilet or into a jar filled with alcohol to kill it.

Keeping your dog out of grassy and wooded areas during exercise will reduce exposure to ticks. Remove leaves and clear brush and tall grasses in your yard and kennel areas to reduce the tick population outside your home. There are products available to treat the yard, but many of them may be toxic. Choose environmentally safe

By the Numbers

The word cataract comes from the Greek word for waterfall. It was thought that opaque material flowed into the lens of the eye like a waterfall, causing blurred vision. Cataracts in Bostons can appear between 8 weeks and 12 months of age, in adults between 4 and 6 years, or in seniors.

With a characteristically flat face and short muzzle, some Boston Terriers are born with abnormally small openings to the nose, which can impair breathing. Surgery can correct this condition.

tick sprays and apply them in your yard every 30 days during peak tick months.

Many of the new oral and topical products that prevent and sterilize adult fleas will also work on ticks. In heavily tick-infested areas, consider a tick collar in addition to a topical once-a-month product for the best protection. Discuss options with your vet if you are unsure which products are best for your dog.

BOSTON TERRIER HEALTH ISSUES

Although fairly healthy, like other breeds Boston Terriers are not completely free from hereditary health issues and genetic diseases that may crop up. Despite feeding your dog a healthy diet, providing enough exercise, and obtaining regular veterinary care for him, you can't help the genes your Boston may inherit from his parents.

Brachycephalic Airway Obstruction Syndrome (BAOS) or Brachycephalic Syndrome

With a characteristically flat face and short muzzle, some Boston Terriers are born with abnormally small openings to the nose or nasal cavity and relatively long soft palates. This makes it difficult to inhale and impairs breathing. Without enough oxygen, dogs breathe through their mouths, producing wheezing, snorting sounds and foamy nostrils.

Signs: It will be hard to miss the signs if your Boston avoids exercise, becomes short of breath after mild exertion, has abnormal or noisy breathing when he becomes excited, or snores loudly while he is asleep. He will likely refuse to go out walking in hot weather because he will not be able to control his body heat through panting; he also will have blue gums from lack of oxygen. This condition can be debilitating and life-threatening if your dog exercises in hot weather.

Treatment: Surgery can enlarge the nostril openings in some Bostons and shorten the long and swollen soft palate. It should be performed before the age of one year.

Eye Problems

Set wide apart, Boston eyes are big and beautiful, making them prone to external injuries. They are also susceptible to cataracts and congenital defects. Some eye problems occur in puppies, while others are of adult or senior onset. The more you know about these conditions, the better the chances of obtaining a healthy dog from a breeder. If you notice anything unusual in your dog's eyes, take him to the veterinarian immediately.

Cherry Eye

According to a 2001 health survey conducted by the BTCA, cherry eye occurs in about 6 percent of Bostons under two years of age.

Signs: Caused by a congenital defect, the condition occurs when the gland situated below the inner corner of the eye protrudes and flips up to emerge from the eye.

Treatment: Although a round pink mass bulging out of the corner of the eye can look scary, cherry eye can be treated with topical anti-inflammatory medication. Surgical intervention may be necessary to return the eye to its normal appearance, however. The gland should not be removed because doing so may cause *keratoconjunctivitis sicca*, or "dry eye."

Distichiasis

Bostons may suffer from distichiasis, a growth of extra eyelashes from the glands of the upper or lower eyelid. These eyelashes, called distichia, rub on the cornea, causing irritation that produces excessive tearing and inflammation. Corneal abrasion may also occur, eventually causing damage to the cornea.

Signs: Signs include a darkening of the cornea, corneal ulceration, or white areas on the cornea. A Boston may also squint or have tearing, or you may see redness from blood vessel accumulation.

Treatment: A veterinary ophthalmologist should examine the eyes; he or she will be able to identify eyelashes from the gland

Many different eye diseases can affect Boston Terriers, but most can be treated or corrected.

openings on the edge of the eyelids. If the offending eyelashes are fine and small enough, a dog may not require treatment. In mild cases, or if the dog isn't a good candidate for surgery, ophthalmic lubricant ointments may be applied to protect the cornea and to coat the lashes if there is tearing. In more serious cases, surgery can be performed to remove the lashes and kill the offending hair follicles. Repeated surgeries may be necessary, as new hairs may erupt at new locations.

Entropion

Entropion is a rolling in of the eyelid. If inherited, it usually develops within a few months of birth, but it can be acquired later in life.

Entropion usually affects the lower eyelids and causes the hair on the surface of the eyelid to rub on the eyeball. Not only is this painful, but it also causes corneal ulcers that interfere with vision.

Signs: An affected dog will squint and tear excessively, although some dogs will show no signs of discomfort. If you suspect that your Boston has entropion, look for tearing, a thick discharge from the eyes, squinting, and difficulty in seeing the eye itself. A dog may also try to rub his eyes along the furniture or bedding.

Treatment: A veterinary ophthalmologist can diagnose entropion by performing a thorough ocular examination. Using fluorescein dye, the vet can detect any corneal ulcers that may have developed due to constant rubbing of the eyelashes. Dye sticks to the damaged sections of the cornea and will show up bright green under examination.

If this condition is left untreated, the cornea will try to protect itself from the rubbing eyelashes by developing scar tissue. While there

is no medical therapy to correct entropion, the condition can be corrected surgically.

Keratoconjunctivitis Sicca (KCS)

Another name for "dry eye," *Keratoconjunctivitis sicca* occurs in 1 in 50 Boston Terriers. This condition is caused by inadequate tear production caused by injuries to the tear glands, such as infections or traumas. Prolonged cases can cause the nerves of these glands to become damaged. Also, without good lubrication the eyes lose their ability to wipe away offending substances that accumulate on the surface of the eyes and are unable to protect them from bacteria.

A knock on the head near one of the tear-producing glands can also lead to KCS. Sometimes KCS can be caused when the gland of the third eyelid is surgically removed by mistake.

Signs: In its early stages, KCS may look like simple conjunctivitis, but the eye later develops a gooey yellow discharge.

Treatment: Diagnosis is obvious in advanced cases. A veterinary ophthalmologist must evaluate the condition and determine a course of treatment. A delicate surgery may eliminate the problem, while various topical therapies, including artificial tear solutions and ointments, may help. If the condition is left untreated, the dog will suffer from repeated painful and chronic eye infections, scarring on the cornea, corneal ulceration, and eventual blindness.

Patellar Luxation

The patella, or kneecap, is the movable flat bone at the front of the knee. It slides up and down in a groove in the long upper bone of the hind leg, called the femur, which allows the dog to bend or straighten his leg. When the groove doesn't develop deeply enough, the patella shifts out of place and luxates, or pops out of place. This affects the hind legs and causes limping in three-legged style.

Patellar luxation affects many small and toy breeds, including Bostons, with females 1.5 times more likely to be affected than males. According to a survey conducted by the BTCA, respondents reported a 9.6 percent incidence of luxating patellas.

Signs: The onset of symptoms can begin any time, even from the first day a puppy begins walking, although most owners notice the problem when the puppy is four to six months through one year of age. Dogs with patellar luxation will have intermittent bouts of lameness, which may appear as skipping or hopping after trotting or right after standing, turning, or jumping. Some dogs may hold up their legs completely.

There are four stages (or grades of severity) of luxation. In grade 1, there is little discomfort and only occasional lameness. In grade 2, luxations occur more frequently and the lameness lasts longer. Knee joints with damaged cartilage are inflamed, painful, and lose motion. Sometimes Bostons with grade 1 or even grade 2 luxations may not show any signs of the problem and will run and jump without any interference. In grades 3 and 4, dogs will show signs of lameness and disability, but it may not always be severe.

Puppies should not be required to jump or climb extensively because too much pressure on developing joints can lead to injuries and slipped patellas. Wait until at least 18 months before doing any serious running.

Puppies should not be permitted to jump or climb extensively because too much pressure on developing joints can lead to injuries and slipped patellas, which may cause lifelong disabilities.

Because overweight dogs have more of a problem when the patella slips, it helps to keep your dog at an average healthy weight.

Treatment: To diagnose patellar luxation, a veterinarian can palpate the knee joint and use X-rays to determine the severity of the condition and see whether there are any other problems. Many dogs with grade 1 luxation don't usually require treatment, and some manage well with only occasional pain-relieving anti-inflammatory medications. Grades 2, 3, and 4 require surgical correction.

Knowing how to recognize potential health problems and how to handle them is important to your dog's overall well-being.

Pet ramps also help a dog move around the house without adding any pain or further damage to the patella.

GENERIC HEALTH ISSUES

Despite the best of care and excellent breeding, any dog can develop a health problem. The important thing is to identify it and to obtain treatment as quickly as possible.

Allergies

Bostons aren't immune to allergies. They can develop them just as people do when the immune system acts to protect the body against offending foreign substances, or allergens. Common allergens are pollens, molds, specific foods, and flea saliva. Allergy-producing substances enter the body through breathing, eating, bites, and skin contact.

After a foreign substance enters the bloodstream, the body produces antibodies in white blood cells to attack it, which results in an allergic response.

Signs: While people react to allergens by wheezing or having runny eyes or other abnormalities, dogs develop skin irritation and itching. Spring and summer are the worst times for allergies in dogs, but some are allergic all year round. The location of the irritation and itching depends on the source.

Inhaled allergens most commonly cause irritations on the face, feet, and underarm areas, although other areas of the body may be affected. The most common inhaled allergens are mold; mildew; grass, tree, and wood pollens; and dust mites.

Food allergies cause skin irritation around the head, ears, and neck, and it's not unusual for dogs to chew their feet in an attempt to soothe it. Puppies less than six months of age and dogs older than six years of age are the most likely to develop food allergies. The most common food allergens are wheat, corn, soy, beef, chicken, and dairy products.

Flea allergies produce constant licking and scratching, leading to skin rashes and secondary infections. They pop up wherever fleas are mostly found, usually the rear, tail, and groin areas.

Treatment/Prevention: To diagnose an allergic reaction, your veterinarian may use a blood test or a skin test to screen for antibodies for common allergens. You can help determine the cause of an allergy by keeping a log citing when the problems started and what changes occurred. Also write down the ingredients in your dog's diet and keep notes on his environmental exposure.

Medications such as antihistamines and corticosteroids may help, but only on a short-term basis; steroids have serious side effects if used in excess. Natural anti-inflammatory drugs and fatty acid supplements can also help reduce allergic reactions.

Cancer

As in people, cancer is caused by an uncontrolled multiplication of damaged cells. These cells can invade organs and tissues in any part of the body. Cancers can be slow-growing over a period of years or aggressive (sarcoma or carcinoma). Malignant tumors rapidly destroy healthy tissue and spread to other parts of the body.

Signs: Signs of cancer include weight loss with or without loss of appetite, difficulty breathing, persistent lameness, bleeding from an open sore or a sore that doesn't heal, and chronic diarrhea or difficulty in eliminating.

Treatment: Diagnosis requires clinical tests such as blood tests and X-rays. Cancer is the leading cause of death in dogs, but 50 percent of all forms of canine cancers are completely curable. With early detection, some types of cancer can be treated with surgery, chemotherapy, radiation therapy, or all three. Many advances in canine treatments are available today.

Ear Infections

Ear infections plague all dogs. Deep ear canals trap moisture and ear wax, which creates a warm and humid environment perfect for bacteria and yeast to thrive.

Signs: Signs of ear infection are head shaking and persistent rubbing or scratching at the ears. The inside of the infected ear becomes inflamed and red (with a Boston's black ears the hair will take on a reddish cast) and will often have a bad odor.

In severe cases, dogs will lose their balance because the infection spreads to the middle ear. Chronic ear infections that cause head shaking could lead to the formation of a hematoma, or blood blister, under the skin.

Treatment: To diagnose an infection, your veterinarian will examine the ears with an otoscope. The vet may also extract some earwax and examine it under a microscope to check for the presence of ear mites or yeast.

To keep your dog's ears healthy, clean them

frequently. Use a cotton strip with medicated cleaner and gently clean the outer portion of the ear; never enter the ear canal. Adding fatty acids to the diet helps control ear inflammation caused by allergies. To treat ear infections, your veterinarian may prescribe medication and repeated ear cleaning.

Eye Infections

Dogs can develop an eye infection from a viral, bacterial, or other microbial agent, or from an airborne allergen. Not always serious, an eye infection may cause great discomfort to your dog if not treated. Some eye infections do not endanger a dog's general health, while others require immediate veterinary attention to prevent further complications.

Signs: Signs of general eye infections can include a bloodshot or inflamed appearance, discharge, pawing or scratching at the eyes, and squinting.

Treatment: A veterinarian can perform an ophthalmoscopic examination to test a dog's vision, depth perception, and identification of objects. A veterinary ophthalmologist may perform more sophisticated testing procedures, such as a flourescein stain test to determine whether there are any tears or lesions in the cornea of the eye.

Treatment will depend on the cause of the infection, but medicated eye drops, oral medications, or eye scrubs that are pH-balanced may be recommended.

Skin Problems

Itchy skin can plague a Boston Terrier as early as six months of age. The BTCA health committee's report reveals that almost one-fifth of Bostons in the survey suffered from allergic dermatitis or other allergy problems. Parasites, bacterial infections, and fungal infections are other sources of skin problems.

Signs: Atopic dermatitis (AD) is one of the most common skin problems suffered by Bostons. Those with AD are hypersensitive to environmental allergens, such as grass and weed pollens, and may also be sensitive to dust mites, molds, and other allergens. Exposure to allergenic substances creates an immune response that results in itchy or reddened skin or runny eyes. The feet, ears, and face are most affected.

Treatment: Fatty acid supplements, frequent bathing with hypoallergenic shampoos, avoiding

Chiropractic care can benefit dogs who suffer from musculoskeletal problems resulting from injury or old age.

known allergens, and effective flea control all help to reduce itching. Although a veterinarian may prescribe a corticosteroid to reduce itching, this should be used as a last resort.

ALTERNATIVE THERAPIES

Your dog relies on you to keep him healthy. By taking advantage of all forms of veterinary medicine—traditional, also known as conventional or Western, and alternative methods, or a combination of both, called integrative—you can obtain the best care.

Conventional Western medicine focuses on treating the disease itself, while alternative or natural therapies focus on overall wellness and healing of both body and mind. Integrative medicine uses all therapies to prevent and treat disease.

Alternative therapies are all about treating the entire dog and not just symptoms of the disease. This means feeding a healthy diet, providing enough exercise, and evaluating everything about your dog's lifestyle and environment to correct any disorders and to establish balance and well-being.

An advantage to using alternative treatments and natural remedies is that they have fewer side effects than conventional therapies. Sometimes there may be no conventional treatments available for a particular condition, and alternative therapies may succeed or provide healing relief. Today more veterinarians than ever before are incorporating all types of healing options that were once considered alternative.

Acupuncture

Developed in China more than 4,500 years ago, acupuncture is one of the oldest forms of medicine practiced on both people and animals. Once thought of as hocus-pocus therapy, the American Veterinary Medical Association now regards it as an integral part of veterinary medicine.

Based on the Chinese concept of a central life force called Qi (or Chi), acupuncture works on a biochemical level. The theory is that in a balanced, healthy body, Qi, which is stored in major organs, flows smoothly along pathways called meridians. But if Qi is obstructed, reduced, or in excess, the body becomes imbalanced, or diseased. To restore balance, disposable hair-thin sterile needles are inserted slightly below the skin along affected meridian points to stimulate the release of endorphins and other pain-relieving anti-inflammatory hormones into the bloodstream. This adjusts Qi and restores balance in the body, resulting in the return of health and well-being.

Initially considered helpful in treating dogs with arthritis, spondylosis, and hip dysplasia, acupuncture is now also used to treat diseases of the major organs, such as the heart, liver, and kidneys, and problems in the nervous and circulatory systems. As an adjunct therapy to treat cancer, acupuncture helps reduce nausea and improves a sense of well-being. Whether used as a primary or additional therapy in conjunction with conventional treatment, acupuncture can even be a powerful alternative when the risk from surgery or anesthesia is high.

Chiropractic

For a dog experiencing moderate to severe muscle and joint pain resulting from injury or old age, chiropractic therapy often helps. It realigns the vertebrae in the spinal column by using manual manipulation to relieve discomfort. It is also thought to produce other healthy responses in the body.

During a typical session, a veterinarian or veterinary chiropractor (practitioners should be licensed by the American Veterinary Chiropractic Association) uses the hands to manipulate the spine. If a vertebra is displaced, the chiropractor will relieve the displacement with a small hand-held alignment tool that produces a quick pulse to tap the vertebra back into place. The amount of pressure is low.

Although it's a natural approach to many health and performance problems in dogs, chiropractic care does not replace traditional veterinary medicine or surgery; it's a drug-free alternative therapy. Not a quick fix, it may require numerous sessions to improve comfort and performance levels.

Herbal Remedies

Another form of ancient medicine practiced on people and animals, herbal remedies contain excellent sources of minerals that can have medicinal effects on dogs. Herbs have many functions and are helpful for a variety of common conditions. Alleviating pain and relieving symptoms, these special plants boost the immune system, help balance the body's organ systems, and offer nerve-calming benefits.

Veterinarians who specialize in using herbal remedies will recommend nutritional support in addition to conventional treatment for severe problems. This gives dogs the advantage of having a range of therapies. To locate a veterinary herbalist, contact the Veterinary Botanical Medicine Association (www.vbma.org).

Herbs can be used in cooking food for your dog or given as a medication, but they're not a quick fix. They take longer to work than traditional medicines, so don't expect to see any improvement in your dog's condition for at least 60 to 90 days after beginning treatment. Never use them in place of a veterinary consultation, especially in life-threatening or serious conditions. Herbs support and improve general physical well-being and are not intended to be used alone.

You can supplement your dog's nutrition by offering certain herbs as a tasty treat. Occasionally add a pinch of dried or twice as much of these fresh herbs to his food: alfalfa, parsley, thyme, dandelion, red clover, raspberry or blackberry leaves, basil, comfrey, linden flowers, or fenugreek. He'll lick the bowl dry!

Homeopathy

Conventional medicine believes that symptoms are part of the illness, while homeopathy sees the symptoms as the body's natural reaction

Now more commonly used with pets, herbal remedies are helpful in alleviating pain, reducing stress, and boosting the immune system.

to fighting the illness. Treating and ridding the body of the illness therefore involves stimulating symptoms rather than suppressing them.

An ancient folk remedy turned to a science, homeopathy works on a simple principle of "like cures like." This means that the very substance that produces signs of illness in a healthy dog can be used in small amounts to cure a sick dog. A trained homeopathic veterinarian matches the symptoms of the dog to the remedy.

Remedies are administered in the form of pellets or liquids, and 70 percent of the preparations have an herbal origin. They are very delicate, and there is a specific way to prepare them. They're diluted in stages to produce different strengths of the substance, and different strengths produce specific benefits without being toxic. They isolate any energy blockages that cause the illness and restore balance in the body. This relieves the symptoms and cures the problem. Dogs usually like the sweet taste of homeopathic remedies.

There are no side effects to homeopathic remedies, and using them is relatively inexpensive. Today, more veterinarians are incorporating homeopathy into their practices than ever before.

Physical Therapy

Twenty-four hours after a dog has suffered a serious injury or has undergone surgery, swelling occurs, joints stiffen, and muscle loss begins. Here's where physical therapy comes in. Gone are the days of performing surgery or putting on a cast and discharging a patient without some form of physical rehabilitation 48 hours later.

Aside from the psychological benefits of providing follow-up care, physical therapy decreases pain, increases strength, and improves mobility and circulation. Physical therapy helps a range of orthopedic disorders including osteoarthritis, hip and elbow dysplasia, luxating patellas, and anterior cruciate ligament injuries. This type of rehabilitation can also benefit Boston Terriers with weight management issues.

Veterinarians specializing in physical therapy offer the latest in physical medicine and rehabilitation. Canine physical therapy includes:

- Hydrotherapy: Warm water helps increase flexibility and mobility of the muscles.
- Therapeutic Ultrasound: Uses high-frequency sound waves to treat soft tissue injuries.
- Low-Level Laser Therapy: Increases the quality and strength of tissue repair, decreases inflammation, and provides pain relief.
- Heat and Cold Therapy: Helps decrease pain and inflammation. Cold therapy is used in the first 72 hours after surgery or trauma and heat therapy later in the healing process to increase blood flow and increase muscle flexibility.
- Massage: A focused deliberate touch using a variety of strokes. Utilizes soft tissue manipulation to achieve different goals such as relaxation, stimulation, and increasing circulation.
- Pulsed Signal Therapy: A painless electrical field surrounding healthy joints is used to help regenerate cartilage to treat arthritis and other injuries.

Canine Vital Signs

- A dog's normal temperature is between 100° and 102.5°F (38° and 39°C).
- A small dog's normal heart rate is 90 to140 beats per minute.
- A dog normally takes 15 to 30 breaths per minute.

EMERGENCY CARE AND FIRST AID

One minute your Boston acts normally; the next instant something is terribly wrong. For example, a bite or a broken bone is painful and frightening for your dog, and he won't understand what has happened to him. If you panic, your dog will too. Assess the situation as calmly as possible. Is this an emergency requiring an urgent trip to the doctor's office, or can you give your dog first aid treatment at home? Remain clear-headed, call your veterinarian, and explain your dog's symptoms. You'll receive instructions about what's best for your dog.

If you need to transport your dog to the veterinarian's office, gently tuck him into a large towel or a blanket and carry him that way. Try not to jostle him if you suspect any broken bones.

To prevent your dog from panicking or struggling against you, you may need to restrain or muzzle him. Take a strip of gauze, a necktie, or any other piece of long fabric and loop it around your dog's muzzle, cross it under the chin, and tie it up behind the ears.

Emergency first-aid procedures can increase your dog's chances of a full recovery—and may even save his life.

Bites and Stings

Warm weather brings out harmful pests that may be bothersome to your dog. Lacking thick coats and long hair, Bostons and other breeds with short coats are easy targets for insect bites, spider bites, bee and wasp stings, and snake bites.

If your dog is stung by a bee, carefully remove the stinger with tweezers. Mix some baking soda and water and apply the paste to the affected area. If there is swelling, apply an ice pack to relieve the pain.

Give your dog an antihistamine as soon as possible. Call your veterinarian about the correct dosage. If your dog has trouble breathing or develops hives, rush him to the veterinarian immediately. He's likely having an allergic reaction and requires emergency treatment.

Only three types of spiders pose a threat to canine health—the black widow and other widow spider species, the brown recluse, and the hobo spider. Symptoms of spider bite venom pop up 30 minutes to 6 hours after a bite. These include extreme pain around the bite, muscle spasms, and possible breathing difficulty. Depending on the biting pider, a white ring may develop around the reddened bite site within four to eight hours.

If your Boston is bitten by a widow spider, your veterinarian will administer pain medications and muscle relaxants to ease your dog's symptoms while the spider venom runs its course, but recovery will take several days. Antivenin is given to senior dogs and puppies, who are more at risk.

Ice packs slow symptoms of brown spider and hobo spider bites, and the veterinarian can give corticosteroids to help stop tissue damage if caught early. The vet may prescribe antibiotics as well.

If your dog is bitten by a snake, immediately transport him to the veterinarian. Signs of a snake bite include lethargy, vomiting, diarrhea, salivation, swelling at the bite location, and shock.

Bleeding

For small cuts that barely penetrate the skin and don't leave gaping wounds, remove any dirt or debris that may be sticking to the area and clean it with water or some hydrogen peroxide. Don't try to cover the cut with a bandage because a small wound will heal if left open and kept clean.

More serious bleeding with spraying blood signals a cut artery. Apply gentle pressure to the blood flow with a clean cloth, bandage, or your hand if you have nothing else. Don't worry about cleaning out the wound until the bleeding has stopped. If the bleeding starts again, transport your dog to the veterinarian as soon as possible.

Lacking a thick coat and long hair, Bostons are easy targets for insect bites and stings. For his safety, always supervise your dog while he's outdoors.

Broken Bones or Other Injuries

If your dog yelps in pain and can't put any weight on his leg, a bone may be broken or fractured. Keep your dog as still and calm as possible until you can stabilize the broken bone. Make a splint to support the leg, and use strips of cloth to tie the ends of the splint to the limb. Carefully transport your dog to the veterinarian immediately.

For broken bones that break through the skin, cover the area with a wet cloth. Don't try to cover the protruding bone with a splint, as you may injure it further.

If your dog is hit by a car and you're not sure whether or not the spine is damaged, gently place him onto a rigid object like a table or a board before moving him. Transport him to the veterinarian immediately.

Frostbite

Wet and exposed to the outdoors too long, parts of a dog's body with little or no coat protection, such as the ears, tail, scrotum, foot pads, or toes, are likely to become frostbitten. These areas will swell and develop a blue-black or white color. In one to three weeks these tissues will dry up and turn black, eventually falling away from the body.

If you suspect that your dog has frostbite, soak the body part in warm (103° to 105°F/ 39° to 41°C) water for 15 to 20 minutes, or until the skin returns to a healthy pink or red color. Don't massage circulation back into the frostbitten area, as this increases the damage.

You may have to restrain your dog from biting or scratching at the frostbitten skin because it becomes painful when circulation returns to the area. Dead tissue needs to be removed, so it will be necessary to take your dog to the veterinarian for examination and treatment.

Heatstroke

Hot weather and Boston Terriers don't mix because Bostons are subject to heatstroke. Heat stroke occurs when the dog's body produces or absorbs more heat than it can dissipate. Dogs can cool themselves off only by sweating through their paws or panting, which isn't very efficient. Bostons have an especially difficult time staying cool because their short noses have little room for air to circulate.

Your dog depends on you to keep him comfortable. Never leave him in a car with the windows closed in warm weather, even if it's parked in the shade. The interior temperature rises quickly and can kill your dog. Refrain from taking your Boston outdoors in hot and humid conditions. Exercise him early in the morning or late in the afternoon when the weather has cooled off.

To recognize signs of heatstroke, look at the color of your dog's gums. Healthy gums should be a deep pink. If you press them with your finger, they should return to pink within two seconds. If they are pale or white, your dog could be in shock. Bright red gums may signal overheating. Other heatstroke symptoms include thick, sticky saliva, depression, weakness, dizziness, vomiting, diarrhea, shock, and coma.

Normal canine body temperature is between 100° and 102.5°F (38° and 39°C). Moderate heatstroke occurs when your dog's body temperature rises to between 103° and 106°F (39° and 41°C). Deadly heatstroke occurs when his body temperature climbs above 106°F (41°C). If you suspect that your Boston is suffering from heatstroke, lower his body temperature by cooling him down immediately. Apply towels soaked in cold water to his abdomen and beneath his armpits. Place a wet cold towel on the ground and let him stand on it. If necessary,

Flat-faced breeds are prone to heatstroke, so don't take your Boston outdoors in hot and humid weather.

immerse his body in cool (not cold) water. When your dog cools down, transport him to the veterinarian.

Poisoning

Leave it to a curious Boston Terrier to find toxic foods, plants, household cleaners, and garden and automobile products when you're not looking.

You wouldn't think that foods and other products you keep around the house could cause a problem for your Boston, but several items can poison your dog. How toxic a substance is depends on how much of it your dog has ingested, his overall health, and any underlying allergies or sensitivities he may have.

For example, while one raisin or one M&M may not produce any harmful effects, a small

piece of xylitol from a few pieces of sugar-free gum can be deadly. If a dog is severely allergic to peanuts and he smells a peanut, he could have a fatal reaction. While a healthy dog may safely absorb a small amount of cat food or nuts, one who has recently recuperated from a bout of pancreatitis could fall ill again. Theobromine, a chemical in chocolate, is toxic to dogs. For a 20-pound Boston Terrier, ingesting 1 pound (0.5 kg) of milk chocolate can be lethal. To be on the safe side, children should be taught never to share chocolate or any other human food with their dog.

If a dog eats a toxic food and nothing happens, this doesn't mean the food is safe. Perhaps not enough was eaten, but many effects of toxic foods are gradual and will show up later on.

Foods that are toxic to dogs include:

- alcoholic beverages
- avocados (leaves, seeds, skin, stem)
- cat food
- chocolate
- coffee
- cola drinks
- eggs (raw eggs and raw egg whites)
- fish (uncooked)
- garlic
- grapes
- hops (used in home beer brewing)
- iron supplements (human)
- macadamia nuts
- marijuana
- moldy foods
- mushrooms
- onions
- onion powder
- potatoes (especially toxic are green potatoes, leaves, stems, skins, sprouted potatoes)
- raisins
- rhubarb
- salt
- tea
- tomatoes (especially toxic are green tomatoes, leaves, stems)
- tobacco
- trash
- walnuts
- wild mushrooms
- xylitol (contained in chewing gum and candies)
- yeast and dough containing yeast

You should know basic first aid and have a first aid kit available in the event your Boston should ever have an emergency.

Disaster Preparedness

No one expects a disaster, but planning ahead for your pet's safety in the event one occurs may save his life. Set aside some time to make a plan and assemble an emergency kit especially for your dog. Keep a leash near the front and back doors so you can take him out of the house securely. Stock up on at least five days' worth of nonperishable dog food and water, and store them in a covered container that's ready and easy to transport. Include a dog bowl, medications, a canine first-aid kit, and clean-up bags. A towel, paper towels, trash bags, grooming items, and a spray container of diluted household bleach will all come in handy too. If possible, having a few toys and a pet blanket or crate on hand will help reduce your dog's stress.

Pack a current photo and description of your dog to help others identify him in case you and your dog become separated and to prove that he belongs to you. Your dog's feeding schedule, medical conditions, behavior problems, and the name and number of your veterinarian should be included in case you have to board your dog or place him in foster care.

It's also a good idea to make arrangements with a trusted neighbor or friend to take care of your dog in case a disaster strikes when you're not home. Give them a key to your home or let them know where they can find a key on your property.

When you must evacuate your home, even if you think it may be for only a few hours, take your dog with you. If you are given the order to evacuate, follow it. Don't wait until the last minute; if you do, you may jeopardize both your own and your dog's safety.

Many household and garden plants are poisonous to dogs. Besides azaleas, cyclamen, oleander, sago palm, and tulips, more than 100 plants and shrubs are toxic if ingested. If you're unsure whether your Boston has eaten a poisonous plant, contact your veterinarian immediately or the ASPCA National Animal Poison Control Center at 1-888-4ANIHELP (888-426-4435) or 1-900-443-0000. Expect to pay a small fee for a phone consultation.

The following are also dangerous to your dog if he swallows or comes in contact with them:

- antifreeze
- batteries
- blue-green pond algae
- citronella candles
- cocoa mulch
- compost piles
- bleach
- drain cleaner
- fertilizers
- flea products
- fly baits containing methomyl
- kerosene
- pesticides
- slug and snail baits containing metaldehyde
- swimming pool chemicals
- toxic lawn and garden products

Always store common toxic substances out of your dog's reach and know the signs of toxicity or poisoning. These include pawing at the ears, eyes, or mouth and watery eyes and/or runny nose. The dog may have increased thirst, salivation and frequent swallowing, and breathing may be difficult or labored. Diarrhea, cramps, blood in the feces, or any uncoordinated movements, shivering, seizures, or shock all signal time to rush your dog to the veterinarian.

CHAPTER 9

BOSTON TERRIER TRAINING

Every year the Boston Terrier Club of America (BTCA) holds an obedience trial at its National Specialty, which is held at a location that rotates annually around the country. This is the most prestigious obedience competition for Boston Terriers, although many regional clubs hold obedience trials for Bostons too. When obedience became a popular activity for Bostons and their owners at the end of the 1980s, the club sponsored its first obedience trial in 1989. The breed's first Obedience Trial Champion (OTCH) was Brother Mack Duff, owned by Ellen Dresselhuis. Another top-winning obedience in Boston Terrier history was Connemara's Kitty O'Shea, UD, owned by Sara Casey. This dog was the only Boston to earn a Utility designation—another top obedience title. Visit a trial today and you'll likely see several Bostons competing in intermediate obedience. Boston Terriers excel in obedience competition because of their enthusiasm, desire to please, and overall intelligence. Like many other breeds, they do best with gentle but firm leadership, and they thrive when praise and tasty tidbits are freely given.

While obedience competition may not be your thing, it does build a bond between you and your dog and creates a lasting partnership. There's something about training seriously enough to compete that sharpens your practice sessions. Regardless of how seriously you approach your training, obedience increases your dog's self-confidence and challenges him to learn and succeed.

Your Boston Terrier can learn anything you teach him. That he may put his own spin on it is another story. Tell a Boston to heel and he may interpret that as speed walk. Ask him to stay and he may think that you're talking to someone else. Sure, the *down-stay* command might work for a few seconds, but so does scooting on his elbows and belly crawling across the floor. Bostons are clever and curious, and although they're eager to please you, they sometimes try to reinvent the wheel. They want to obey the command, but they want to do it their way. Training your Boston to follow intermediate obedience commands isn't too difficult, but it requires time, patience, lots of positive reinforcement, and a positive attitude. Keeping a sense of humor doesn't hurt either.

BEFORE YOU TRAIN

Your adult Boston already knows basic obedience commands from puppyhood, but

For a simple but effective way to train your Boston, use tasty treats, a toy, or praise to reward him when he responds correctly to a command.

now it's time to expand his repertoire and take his training to the next level. As an adult, he's definitely ready now for some new challenges. But just because you're upping the behavior bar doesn't mean that you should rush the lessons and sacrifice positive training methods. There's always time to teach your dog new tricks, so remember to take it slow and remain calm and patient during training.

Obedience doesn't mean yanking, pulling, yelling, or hitting your dog. Ever. A leash should never be used as an instrument of punishment either. Teaching your dog some advanced behaviors involves showing him what you want him to do while using the right command words.

The activities should be fun for your dog and a satisfying experience for both of you. You're working with your dog and you need to trust

each other to succeed. Recognize that every Boston has different training requirements. One may need a little practice every day to remember his routines, while another may require only occasional refresher lessons. To achieve the most success from your obedience training, it helps to know what makes your Boston tick, whether it be praise, treats, or some playtime.

Let your Boston think that learning something new is all his idea. Pair that with an endless supply of tasty treats when he complies with your requests, and he'll catch on quickly. Remember to motivate him to pay attention to you by keeping your training sessions short. Several 15- to 20-minute training sessions are far more effective than one hour-long lesson. Having fun with your dog while you're training him will help him learn faster than using stern, harsh methods.

INTERMEDIATE OBEDIENCE COMMANDS

For a simple but effective way to train your Boston, try using the lure-and-reward method. To do this, lure your dog into the desired position with a small piece of food, then give him the treat. He'll soon realize that when he's in the right place, he receives the reward. When goodies are involved, Bostons respond well to this technique. If you're worried that your dog won't behave and will obsess about the food, take some extra time and be patient. Above all, keep trying; your dog will respond.

Clicker training is another popular training method that works well for many Bostons. Lure your dog into a precise position with a click sound from a plastic clicker—an inexpensive device you can buy at most pet supply stores. Then hand him a treat or reward him with praise. Clicker training also works with desired movements or behaviors. The click lets the dog know that he did what you wanted him to do and that a treat is coming. Bostons learn quickly with clicker training because it uses positive reinforcement to precisely mark the desired behavior. Clickers can be tricky to master, but once you figure out the exact timing it's a useful tool. If you don't want to use a clicker, you can use a marker word—like "Yes!"—to achieve the same effect.

Heel

It's a joy to step out with your dog and take him for a walk on a leash, especially when he strolls nicely beside you without pulling or lunging. If he stays on the left side of your body with his neck level with your leg or in the heel position, that's a bonus. Heeling comes in handy if you must exercise your dog on a crowded sidewalk and you don't want him bumping into other people. When your Boston remains at your side, you don't have to worry about falling over him because he's continually crossing in front or behind you.

When walking with your Boston, it's nice if he stays next to you, but if he's a little ahead or lags a little behind, it's not critical as long as he doesn't pull on the leash. But if you decide to enter him in obedience competition, he must heel precisely by your left side. And if you sign him up for more advanced obedience work, such as freestyle competition, heeling in the right place at the right time is a must. Even going jogging or bicycling with your dog requires him to remain in the heel position.

How do you train your Boston to walk on a leash nicely at your side? Ask three trainers and you'll hear three different responses. But whatever method you select, don't pull or jerk on the leash if your dog rushes past you. This can injure your Boston's neck and frustrate him.

All methods require you to hold the leash in your right hand and keep your Boston on your left side. Place your right hand holding the leash in the middle of your waist. You can use your left hand to grab the leash to prevent your dog from crossing in front of you and knocking you over. Otherwise,

Training Tidbit

Don't use a retractable leash to train your dog to heel. The elasticity in the leash gives your dog too much room to forge ahead of you. Instead, use a harness or collar and a 6-foot (2-m) leash because this gives you more control over your dog's movement.

Want to Know More?

For a refresher course on how to teach basic obedience commands, see Chapter 4: Training Your Boston Terrier Puppy.

your left hand should rest at your side while you're walking and the leash should hang loosely in front of you.

Before teaching your dog to heel, he should respond to the *come* command every time you use it. This preparation will help focus his attention on you during the *heel* command training. Keeping some food treats handy while you're training and using them to reward your dog when he places himself in the heel position will help motivate him.

Once your dog learns to heel via any method, never move if your Boston pulls you, no matter what the circumstance. This will send a clear message to him that pulling on the leash won't be tolerated.

How to Teach It: Method 1

1. Say "Heel" in a quiet, firm voice, and start walking with your dog.
2. If he starts to pull on the leash, even a little bit, and you feel even the slightest bit of tension on the leash, come to a complete stop. Don't make eye contact with him; ignore him completely.
3. Say "Heel" again in the same quiet, firm voice and begin walking.
4. Again, if he starts to pull, stop abruptly and don't look at him.

This method requires your patience, but Boston Terriers are smart dogs, and after a few starts and stops he'll realize that every time he rushes ahead, he will not be allowed to continue walking.

How to Teach It: Method 2

1. Give your dog the *heel* command and start walking with him at a brisk pace.
2. When he pulls ahead of you, abruptly turn the other way, walk a few more steps, and then stop. Don't jerk the leash; just use it to prevent him from going in the other direction. Don't say anything to your dog either. This will encourage him to watch your body for directional cues.
3. Repeat this exercise several times, making frequent turns in different directions, even zigzagging, before stopping for about five minutes. After a few turns, your dog will move closer to your left leg and look up at you.
4. When he's standing in the *heel* position, scratch his chin and say "Good boy" and give him a treat. It won't take long before he's naturally heeling.

Test out how much he's learned by walking in a straight line. If he forges ahead again, simply turn in the opposite direction, walk a few steps, and stop. You may have to repeat this pattern several times during your walk, but eventually he'll catch on.

How to Teach It: Method 3

You can lure your Boston into the *heel* position by just using treats and a long stick.

1. Place a yummy food treat at the end of the stick. This treat shouldn't be something your dog already receives at home; use something like a small piece of a hot dog or cheese.
2. Holding the leash in your right hand, place the stick with the treat in your left hand.
3. Move the stick until your dog is in the *heel* position, then say "Good boy" and let him lick the treat off.
4. Reload the stick. Say "Heel" and walk a few steps.

5. Move the stick to the *heel* position. When your dog positions himself in that spot, let him lick the treat off.

6. Repeat several times.

After your Boston is heeling reliably, make staying in the *heel* position a game by running and turning and giving him the stick when he is able to maintain the position.

Stay

The *stay* is probably one of the most practical and important commands your Boston Terrier will ever learn. It could even save his life. If the door suddenly opens and your dog dashes out of the house after another dog, he could run into traffic and get hit by a car. Or if he's not hit, he can easily become lost trying to return home. By telling him to stay, you can open the door without worrying about losing him.

Besides the safety factor, teaching your dog to stay proves useful if you need to maintain control over his behavior. If your Boston wants to jump up and greet guests who enter your home or people he meets outdoors, keeping him in one spot restrains his exuberance. Perhaps you just need your dog to stay on the patio while the children play in the pool or to stay and not gobble up a chicken bone that falls on the floor.

Whatever the reason, the idea of the *stay* command is to teach your Boston to remain in one spot in a *down* or *sit* position until you

The *stay* command teaches your dog to remain in place until you release him.

tell him that it's okay to move. Don't feel guilty about training your dog to stay because it's basically asking him to do nothing. Sure, it's a lot of work to teach him to remain still, but it's well worth the investment of time and energy.

Whether you give your Boston the *down-stay* or the *sit-stay* command, there are a few basic principles to follow. When you tell your dog to stay, it means that he must hold this position until you tell him he can move. You may use treats to reward for staying, although some dogs are too distracted by treats. Hand out the goodie to maintain the *stay*, not after it. Give the treat while your dog is still in the correct position. The treat is for holding the *stay*, not for breaking it.

How to Teach It

To teach the stay, follow these steps:

1. Begin with your dog in a sitting position. With your right hand, make a stop sign gesture a few inches (cm) in front of your dog's face and say the word "Stay."
2. While he remains in the same position, give him a small food treat. The trick is to reward him before he moves.
3. Take one or two steps backwards.
4. If your Boston hasn't moved and remains in the same position, give him another small food treat.
5. If your dog does get up, put him back in the same position by gently guiding his collar.
6. Repeat the beginning instructions, but this time decrease the time you expect him to stay.
7. After the briefest time he remains, release your Boston from the *stay* before he gets up and say "Okay."
8. Move toward him and give him a big pat on the chest. You can also give him a treat too if you want.

9. Practice several times and gradually increase both the distance you move back and the time you wait between giving him the command and releasing him. To release him, give a verbal cue that it is alright to move, such as "Yes, good boy!" and follow up with some energetic petting.

Down-Stay

For an energetic Boston Terrier, lying down quietly when you ask him to and staying there shows that he has good manners. The posture is also helpful for his safety in multiple situations. If you're exercising with your dog outdoors and he starts limping, you can give the *down-stay* command and examine his foot to assess the injury. Or, if he needs to remain in a shady spot and cool off for a few minutes, a *down-stay* will convince him to chill out.

Telling your dog to lie down and stay put can also help him calm down and relax after vigorous playtime. O,r if he becomes too excited, resting in this position will soothe him into a relaxing state. Remaining in a *down-stay* has other benefits. If you're walking with your dog and meet a friend or a small child who wants to pet him but feels intimidated with your Boston's bouncy attitude, the *down-stay* is reassuring to the child. This position also proves invaluable if you want to chill out on

Multi-Dog Tip

Take the time to work with each of your dogs individually. It can be confusing to work with one dog and give him a reward for doing a desired behavior when the other dog is performing an unwanted behavior.

the sofa and read or watch television but your dog wants to play. Once he knows how to comply with a *down-stay*, you will always find ways to use it.

This includes competing in obedience. To qualify for a Companion Dog title (CD), your Boston Terrier must remain in the long *down* or *down-stay* for three minutes while the owner walks a distance away. In Open (CDX) or intermediate obedience, the dog must remain in the *down-stay* while the owner walks away and remains out of sight for five minutes. The exercise demonstrates that your dog has confidence that you will return to him. To train dogs at this level, owners build up the time out of their dogs' line of vision for short periods. They gradually extend the distance to as much as 100 feet (30.5 m).

How to Teach It

When you begin training this command, know that some Bostons don't like lying down on a cold, hard floor or on the cement outdoors. If you sense some resistance, try teaching the *down-stay* on a rug or the grass. Use the *down-stay* when you want your dog to remain in this position and wait for you for more than a minute or two. It's more comfortable than sitting and staying. Before training the *down-stay*, your dog should also understand the concepts of staying and sitting.

Follow these steps:

1. Tell your dog to sit.
2. Show him a treat in your hand.
3. Say your dog's name, followed by the word "Down."
4. Slowly draw the treat forward and downward toward the floor.
5. As soon as your dog lowers his body and his elbows touch the ground in an effort to get the treat, say "Good boy!" and give it to him.

6. If he keeps trying to pop up, place your hands gently over his shoulders to help guide him downward.
7. Repeat a few times, waiting a few seconds longer each time before giving the treat. Release your dog with an "Okay, good boy!" to let him know it's permissible to move.
8. Repeat without the treat in your hand that you have been using to lure him downward.

Aside from showing that your energetic Boston has good manners, the *down–stay* is also helpful in ensuring his safety in a variety of situations and can calm him down and relax him after vigorous playtime.

9. Gradually change your hand movements until you are using only an abbreviated hand signal, and give your dog a treat when he complies with the *down-stay*.

10. Say "Down" before giving the hand signal.

11. Repeat several times, moving a few steps away from him each time.

12. Practice the *down-stay* in other locations. By practicing in public areas, your dog will naturally be distracted and not pay close attention to you. That's okay—he needs to follow directions in every circumstance.

13. Repeat the *down-stay* and require your dog to remain in the *down* position, regardless of the surroundings.

Sit-Stay

When you teach your Boston to sit, he should assume that you mean for him to stay there until you say that it's okay to move. If he hasn't figured this out yet, you may need to go back to the basics and reteach him how to sit. This command proves invaluable in social situations as well as at home. If you're waiting to see the veterinarian, putting your dog into a *sit-stay* will keep him relaxed and well behaved.

Teaching your dog to sit and stay prepares the foundation for other intermediate and advanced obedience exercises, but you don't need to spend a lot of time practicing. In fact, three ten-minute practice sessions throughout the day are far more effective than one or two hours of training. Your dog is more likely to retain these short lessons rather than the longer ones and won't become bored.

If you want to earn an obedience title on your Boston Terrier, knowing how to remain in a sitting position is a mandatory exercise. To qualify for a Companion Dog title (CD), your Boston Terrier must remain in the *sit-stay* or long *sit* for one minute while the owner walks a distance away. In Open (CDX) or intermediate obedience, the dog must remain in a *sit-stay* while the owner walks away and remains out of sight for three minutes.

How to Teach It

To teach your Boston to sit and stay, follow these steps:

1. Begin the *sit-stay* by heeling your dog for a minute or two. This will remind your dog that you are in charge and that it's time to listen and pay attention.

2. While he is on your left side beside you, heel your dog to a specific spot and tell him to sit.

3. Note the exact location. If your dog gets up, you will want to return him to this precise spot. Once he sits in a certain spot, it is marked with his scent, so he will know that he is returning to the exact location.

4. While your dog is sitting, tell him "Stay." Use a hand signal by holding your left palm up like a stop sign in front of his face about 2 inches (5 cm) from his nose.

5. Hold the leash about 1.5 feet (.5 m) away from the clip and hold it vertically above his head. Keep the leash tight without jerking your dog. This will hold your dog in position.

6. Lead off with your right foot and pivot around in front of him. Use your right foot rather than your left so that your dog doesn't think that you're going to begin

If you want to participate in dog shows, your Boston must know how to remain in a standing or sitting position.

heeling again.

7. Remain in front of your dog for a few seconds and maintain eye contact with him.
8. Return to the original position beside him in the same way you originally moved.
9. Release him with an "Okay!"
10. Give him a small food treat.

If your dog moved at any time during the exercise, begin again. Practice several times, but keep your practice sessions short and sweet.

Stand

If you're participating with your Boston Terrier in competitive obedience for his Companion Dog title (CD), one of the exercises your dog must pass is the *stand* for examination. This is also useful when you want to groom him or when he needs to go to the veterinarian for an examination. Or if you're walking with your Boston on the street and someone stops and wants to pet him, you can use this command to discourage jumping up on the stranger. The *stand* also comes handy when you want to photograph your dog or wipe his muddy feet. Your Boston doesn't have to remain as still as a statue, but it is expected that he doesn't try to run off or try to sit down.

Although it's a lot easier to teach the *stand* command to a dog with a laid-back personality rather than to a Boston who's a perpetual motion machine, any dog can learn to stand still for a few minutes.

How to Teach It

1. Start with your dog in the *stand* position. If he's sitting, place your arm under his stomach with the palm of your hand toward the top of his chest and gently lift him.
2. With your other hand on his collar, walk forward one step and say "Stand."
3. If your dog begins to sit, take another step forward.
4. Repeat this routine for about five minutes a day.

When he's standing, use the time to groom or pet him. After you return from an outing, practice the *stand* command. Once he knows how to stand on command, take two steps away from him while facing him and tell him to stay. Praise him when he doesn't move. A few seconds later tell him "Okay! Good dog" and give him a treat, which lets him know that he can move.

CHAPTER 10

BOSTON TERRIER PROBLEM BEHAVIORS

Looking at your Boston cuddled peacefully in his dog bed, it's impossible to imagine your little darling doing anything wrong, but sometimes bad behavior just happens. A stranger sneaks up and scares your boy and he nips at her hand, or the mail carrier knocks at the door and your normally quiet Boston barks up a storm. Perhaps a friend comes to visit and your dog won't stop jumping up on her. Then when she tries to pet your dog, he shows signs of aggression by baring his teeth and growling. Or if you leave him alone all day, he digs up the new vegetable garden, chews up the couch pillows, or whines and cries from the separation. In your dog's mind, these are all natural solutions to threatening situations, and he doesn't realize that they're problem behaviors for you.

In fact, problem behaviors are the most common complaint of dog owners and the leading reason why dogs are taken to shelters or euthanized. While no dog does everything perfectly, you don't have to accept problems you can't control.

Here's where positive, consistent, and fair training comes into play. Teach your dog to obey basic commands, including accepting a bath and having his toenails trimmed, and teach him to give up toys and food when asked. You may have to alter your environment by making sure that your fence and gate are secure so that your dog can't escape or make time to give him more exercise to tire him out and prevent boredom so that he doesn't go looking for trouble.

AGGRESSION

Aggression is the number-one reason why most people give their dogs up for adoption or hire a professional behaviorist or dog trainer. For some breeds, this problem behavior is a constant source of worry to owners, veterinarians, humane societies, and law enforcement officials. Fortunately, as a breed, Boston Terriers aren't known for exhibiting aggression, but every so often a Boston with an overly intense personality pops up.

Aggression can encompass a range of behaviors that take many forms for a variety of reasons. A dog's aggression toward a person can include growling, showing teeth, snarling, or charging at someone. Any type of biting, whether it tears the skin or does or does not leave a mark, such as nipping, mouthing, or snapping, is an aggressive act.

Most dogs will give warning signals before biting, but owners who are bitten often fail to notice them. When a dog exhibits aggressive behavior, it's important to evaluate the situations that led up to it. Examine where and when it happened and what else may have been happening at the same time. Did something happen to your dog to prompt this response? There are many reasons why a dog might behave inappropriately. Once you learn as much as you can about the incident, you can begin to understand what motivated your dog to act aggressively.

In many cases, an aggressive dog is defending his territory, protecting his possessions, or guarding his food. When dogs are afraid of something, they exhibit a flight response by trying to get away. If escaping isn't an option, a dog will fight and try to defend himself. This is called the fight or flight response. A fearful dog is far more likely to become aggressive, especially if cornered or trapped.

Finding a Canine Behaviorist

There are other ways to correct errant behavior, including taking your dog to special obedience classes or hiring a professional trainer. But if nothing works and you're still at your wits' end, you may decide to retain the services of a canine behaviorist. This professional can offer solutions to serious problems, such as phobias, aggression, or obsessive behavior, while many dog trainers have little or no experience with these issues.

An animal behaviorist observes, interprets, and modifies animal behavior and specializes in resolving problems. He or she studies animal behavior and is concerned with understanding the causes, functions, development, and evolution of behavior. The professional may consult with a veterinarian to rule out any medical issue causing or contributing to the dog's actions and treat problem behaviors using scientific methods, practical solutions, and empathic counseling skills. Working with the owner, the professional may demonstrate techniques to change the bad habit and guides the owner's progress.

When it comes to locating an animal behavior specialist, choose a professional carefully. Like dog trainers and obedience instructors, anyone can call himself or herself a behaviorist. A certified applied animal behaviorist (CAAB) or a board-certified veterinary behaviorist (Dip ACVB) has graduate degrees from an accredited university and has supervised graduate training in animal behavior, psychology, biology, zoology, veterinary medicine, and other related disciplines.

These organizations can refer behaviorists to work with you: the National Association of Animal Behaviorists (NAAB) (www.animalbehaviorists.org), and the International Association of Animal Behavior Consultants, Inc. (IAABC) (www.iaabc.org).

Despite anyone's advanced degrees, you should feel comfortable with the person you select. Rely on recommendations from veterinarians, your local humane society, or other owners. Remember that you can retrain a dog to do anything. You just have to stay determined.

If your dog barks excessively when left alone, he is likely bored and lonely.

How to Manage It

Retraining an aggressive dog isn't for the inexperienced dog owner. While the incidence and frequency of some types of aggression can be lessened, there's no guarantee that an aggressive dog can completely change his personality. Sometimes the only solution is controlling a dog's environment and limiting his exposure to people, places, and situations that trigger aggression.

Seek professional help if you have an aggression problem on your hands. Start by consulting a qualified professional, such as a certified applied animal behaviorist (CAAB) or a board-certified veterinary behaviorist (Dip ACVB). Another option is to contact a certified professional dog trainer (CPDT), but interview the professional before doing any hiring to make sure that the trainer you select has extensive experience with aggressive dogs. These professionals can suggest training strategies that may or may not include obedience classes as well as taking firm control at home.

BARKING (EXCESSIVE)

You expect your dog to bark to express himself: getting attention, saying hello, signaling the approach of a stranger, or asking for play or food. After listening a few times, you know what he wants. It's excessive barking that causes problems.

Some Bostons are naturally barky; some are not. If your boy is an irksome noisemaker, the first step to solving the problem is to understand why he barks in the first place.

Barking traces back to the Boston's wolf ancestors. Young wolves bark to sound an alarm signal when intruders enter their den territory. Couple this with the Boston's spark and enthusiasm, a small part of his terrier heritage, and his insistence on trying to entice his owners into interaction, and the barking can continue indefinitely. Bostons today think that it's their responsibility to protect the family from uninvited guests, but if you actually want the stranger to stop at the front door, don't depend on your Boston to deliver. A stable Boston with a good temperament will bark until the person crosses the threshold of your home but will gladly welcome him once you give your permission. Keep in mind, though, that while the idea of having a watchdog may be appealing, praising this behavior too lavishly will only encourage your dog to bark at anything that pops up in his line of vision. Bostons may also bark when they're left alone for a long period of time and feel bored and lonely, but too much barking often escalates into pitiful howling. For wolves needing to bring the pack together before a hunt, howling works like a charm, but for dogs seeking contact with other pack members, namely the family, this is annoying.

How to Manage It

Before leaving your dog, give him plenty of exercise so that he's too tired to bark. Providing some interactive toys may help too. Fill them with food and give them to your dog as you walk out the door. He'll occupy himself for hours and forget that you've left him behind.

Resist the urge to quiet your dog by saying "It's okay" and petting or cuddling him. This only reinforces this behavior, and he'll think that you agree with the way he's handling the situation. Also, never yell at your Boston while he's barking. This will only reinforce

the barking because he'll think that you're responding to him.

To keep peace in your neighborhood, your dog should learn to quiet down when you ask him to. To teach your dog a command to stop barking:

1. Distract him by throwing an empty soda can with a few pennies in it on the ground.
2. When he's quiet for the briefest moment, say "Enough" and give him a treat. Ask him to sit and stay before giving the reward.

Handle barking this way every time, gradually increasing the length of time he's quiet before you give him a treat. He'll soon learn that "enough" translates to receiving a treat if he's quiet.

Know what barking you will or will not accept and follow up by letting your Boston know in no uncertain terms that too much barking is a big no-no.

CHEWING

Give your Boston a chew toy and he's amused for hours. Leave him to his own devices and he's capable of destroying your best pair of shoes, shredding your bed pillows, and sinking holes in the garden hose. Upping the destruction, he'll think nothing of gnawing on cell phones, wallets, watches, walls, floor, and furniture.

A high activity level, coupled with a fascination for constant play and a need for interaction, can lead to some indoor and outdoor destruction. You wouldn't think that the small Boston could wreak such havoc in the house, but a young adult Boston is an incredibly aggressive chewer. If your dog can fit something in his mouth, he will chew it. The breed is agile and intelligent too. If a Boston wants something badly enough to chew, he will find a way to climb or jump up to reach it. It may take three or four

Rather than trying to discourage your dog from chewing, redirect the behavior to suitable objects such as safe chew toys.

years before the adult Boston loses interest in destructive chewing, but until then, everything is fair game.

How to Manage It

Although some Bostons like to chew more than others, this behavior can be channeled into gnawing on acceptable objects. As soon as you bring your dog home, begin giving him safe toys, like Nylabones, to chew. If he becomes bored with one toy, give him another one. Many Boston owners keep a good supply of toys in every room of the house so that there's no chance for their dogs to find outlets for their busy mouths.

To deter your Boston from chewing, follow these steps:

1. Keep valuable tempting objects up high out of your dog's reach.
2. Keep small children's toys, shoes, and clothes off the floor.
3. Secure electrical wires to the wall and floor.
4. Block off those rooms containing furniture you don't want your dog to chew. If he does take a bite of furniture legs and upholstery, apply a taste deterrent, like a bitter apple spray, that discourages chewing but leaves your possessions undamaged.
5. If you do see your dog chewing one of your treasured objects, don't yell at him. This will only encourage him to seek it out when you're not looking.
6. Offer to trade him a tasty food treat for the object he's chewing. Whatever you do, don't

try to grab it out of his mouth. Once he grasps it in his strong back teeth, there's little chance he'll give it up.

Want to Know More?

Your Boston needs to know some basic cues to help you train him out of certain problem behaviors. For a refresher, see Chapter 4: Training Your Boston Terrier Puppy.

7. Dispose of any object on which your dog chews. Although it's probably useless to you now, by letting your dog continue to chew it, he'll think that it's okay to chew that one and not the replacement you've purchased.

8. For busy chewers, provide plenty of exercise. Chances are your dog is bored.

9. If your dog has a serious chewing problem, keep him crated or in an exercise pen when you must leave the house. Give him plenty of his own toys to play with.

Destructive chewing not only ruins your items but also can cause serious health problems for your dog. An object can become lodged in his throat and he could choke.

DIGGING

From their terrier ancestry, Bostons are born diggers. Although some Bostons are more notorious diggers than others, they still show interest in anything down and dirty. Sure, it's cute to see your Boston pawing at the earth to investigate a wiggly bug, but when it comes to digging up the electrical wires, water valves, and expensive plants and shrubs in your yard, it's time to correct your dog's behavior.

It doesn't matter whether you have dirt, grass, or a rocky outdoor environment. Dogs who like to dig will enjoy scooping out any substance: gravel, sand, muck, or mud. To your dog's way of thinking, there are logical explanations for making your yard resemble craters of the moon. If you leave him alone in the yard for too many hours, he could become bored or lonely and simply be looking for anything to do to keep himself busy. Let's face it: digging and scattering clods of earth everywhere can be fun! In warm weather, he might dig down in the soil to cool off or, on chillier days, warm up by digging down. For those Bostons who detect the odor of rodents underground, unearthing them is the only way to protect the yard from these furry invaders. Digging may also provide an escape route out of the yard or beneath the gate, or something interesting may lie beyond the fence. Tree and plant roots are enticing to Bostons too. Once your dog discovers them buried beneath the earth, he'll return many times to hollow out the base of trees and plants to gnaw and chomp on these goodies. They taste good, feel soothing on his gums, and satisfy the urge to chew. If you've recently planted new landscaping, dogs are often drawn to fresh soil and the odor of chicken and steer manure. It's not out of the ordinary for your Boston to want to investigate this aromatic stuff and plow through it with his paws, looking for food.

Besides ruining your landscaping, sprinklers, and electrical lighting in the yard, vigorous excavation can be dangerous to your dog. If he digs up, chews, and swallows wiring, it can cause intestinal damage. Or he may tear a toenail if it catches on a sharp object.

NYLABONE

To prevent inappropriate digging, never leave your Boston unsupervised in the yard.

How to Manage It

To deter your dog from digging, follow these steps:

1. Don't leave your dog alone for long hours in the yard.
2. Provide plenty of exercise to tire your Boston out and give him interactive food-filled toys while he's out in the yard.
3. Install protective covers around all underground wiring.
4. Erect fencing around flower boxes or prized garden areas to protect them from your dog's digging.
5. Supervise destructive diggers while they're outdoors.
6. Leave a small children's wading pool filled with a little water so that your dog has a place to cool off during hot weather—only with your supervision, of course.
7. Beneath gates and along the fence line, install chicken wire to prevent your dog from digging out.
8. Set aside a specific portion of the yard and build your dog his own digging area. Check the dirt to make sure that it is free

By the Numbers

Just because your dog is an adult and out of the destructive puppy stage doesn't guarantee that he will act perfectly. A dog can develop a problem behavior at any age. As human situations or living conditions change, a dog must adapt. When that proves too difficult, he may respond inappropriately. For example, territorial behavior can appear when puppies mature into adults at one to three years of age.

Regardless of size, a dog who jumps up on people is a nuisance and potentially dangerous. Teach your dog not to jump up unless invited to do so.

It's entirely possible to discourage your dog from inappropriate digging. You just have to dig up the right solutions.

JUMPING UP

At every opportunity, naturally happy Boston Terriers love to make face-to-face contact with you or strangers by jumping up to say hello. In leaps and bounds, all a Boston really wants is someone to acknowledge his presence and to give him attention. And sometimes a springing Boston just wants to hang out on your lap. When you pick up and cuddle your dog, he thinks that he's hit the jackpot. Unfortunately, you can't always stop what you're doing and respond to your dog. Petting him or lifting him up sometimes and not other times does more than just confuse him, it prompts him to jump more. You wouldn't think that a small breed could cause a problem by always leaping up on you, but the behavior can become irritating.

Standing on his back legs, your Boston may only reach your knees if he jumps up on you. While you don't have to worry that this small breed will knock someone over, a sudden 20 pounds (9 kg) of pressure on your body can hurt. Also, your dog can't be expected to discriminate between teenagers who encourage your Boston to leap all over them and your frail elderly neighbor who comes to visit. Your dog also won't understand the difference between your good clothing that may tear and snag from his nails and your everyday grubby threads that are okay to mess up.

Even worse, when your dog jumps up on you he's telling you when to give him attention, rather than letting you make that decision. You're the one who's in charge, not your dog. It's important to establish leadership even with such an innocent-looking act as jumping up.

of pesticides and sharp objects. When he's not looking, bury a few of his favorite toys so that he has something to do in an acceptable space. Take your dog to the digging spot and unearth one of the toys and make a game out of it. Once he sees what you want him to do there, he'll return on his own to check it out.

9. Hire a pet sitter or a dog walker, or ask a friend or neighbor to come in during the day to walk or play with your dog. This will relieve some of his boredom.

How to Manage It

Reinforcing your dog's neediness for constant attention by jumping up or pawing you may lead to separation anxiety or stress when you must leave your dog. To prevent this problem behavior, give your dog attention and affection for good behavior and not for jumping up when he shouldn't.

The best way to stop your dog from jumping is to insist that he keep all four feet on the floor. Yelling, "Get down" or "Off!" at him or pushing him down doesn't work. Neither does stepping on his back feet, or heaven forbid, shoving your knee into his chest or grabbing his paws and squeezing them. Aside from being physically abusive, your dog views these negative responses as attention and will continue to jump to gain it.

To discourage your dog from jumping up on you, follow these steps:

1. If your dog puts his paws on your legs or lap, cross your arms over your chest and look away. Completely ignore him and resist the urge to speak to him. It will take your dog some time to figure out what you expect of him, but if you're consistent, he'll learn what's appropriate
2. If you think your dog is about to jump, cross your arms over your chest and turn your back to him. Don't speak to him.

To teach your dog not to jump up on visitors, follow these steps:

1. When the doorbell rings, tell your dog in a firm but pleasant tone of voice to sit.
2. When he complies, give him a treat and open the door.
3. If your dog moves before you give your chosen release command, return him to the *sit* position.
4. Ask your guest not to communicate with your dog and to cross her arms across her chest and not look at him.

5. If your dog is sitting, have your guest pet your dog or say hello to him in a low-pitched voice. An excited voice and too much fuss over your dog will encourage him to jump again.

Practice these steps several times a day and your dog will wisely comply by keeping all four feet on the ground.

NIPPING

Whether you call it nipping, biting, or mouthing, there's no excuse for your Boston to bare his teeth or touch his teeth to human hands, limbs, or clothing during play or interaction. This bad behavior, no matter how innocent it may seem, often leads to serious injury.

If your Boston excitedly nips at your hand when you hand him a treat or if you both reach for a toy at the same time, it's time to correct him. Adult Boston teeth are strong, and those choppers can penetrate your skin and cause infection if not treated. This bad habit begins with dogs who never learned bite

Training Tidbit

Never give your dog cooked, dried, or sterilized bones to chew. These bones are harder than tooth enamel and can crack teeth. Worse, they can splinter and cause intestinal damage or blockage. Give safe, indestructible toys like the ones made by Nylabone instead. When handing out a new toy, always supervise to make sure that your Boston doesn't tear pieces off and swallow them.

Exercise enriches your Boston's life, decreases his stress levels, and helps eliminate destructiveness and hyperactivity.

inhibition—how much mouth pressure to use without causing pain or harm while playing with their mothers and littermates.

How to Manage It

There are many ways to train your Boston not to nip, but you should never yell, hit, or shake your dog in retaliation. Rather than correct the behavior, these aggressive acts will only escalate your dog's tendency to bite again.

The first step in teaching your dog to have a gentle mouth is to teach the fact that people have sensitive skin. If you've ever seen two pups playing, you'll notice that one dog will bite the other one too hard, prompting a yelp, and the play stops. The offender realizes what he's done and stops. This is how dogs learn to control how hard they bite so that no one gets hurt and playtime continues. This is the same lesson that they can learn from their owners.

For one way to teach your dog not to nip at your hands, follow these steps:

1. Let your dog mouth your hand.
2. If he bites too hard, yelp in a high-pitched tone as if you're hurt, and completely relax your hand, letting it go limp.
3. When your Boston stops in surprise and licks your hands, tell him "Good boy!"
4. Resume playing with your dog. If he bites again, yelp again and repeat.
5. After three bites and yelps, discontinue play and put your dog into his crate and ignore him. This will give him time to unwind and realize that play stops completely if he gets too rough.

Another way to stop your dog from nipping is to give him a time-out by following these steps:

1. If your Boston bites hard, yelp loudly. When he stops, remove your hand and either ignore him for 10 to 20 seconds or leave the room.
2. Return to your dog and resume playtime.
3. If he bites again, yelp and ignore him or walk away.
4. Another variation of this is to put your dog into his crate when he starts to nip and release him 10 to 20 minutes later.

Soon he'll realize that you will not play with him when he bites too hard on your hand. Repeat the procedure for less painful bites until your Boston can control his impulse to touch his teeth to your skin.

To further control your dog's urge to nip, follow these steps:

1. Give him a toy or a chew bone if he tries to gnaw on your hands.
2. If your dog wants to nip while you're petting him with one hand, give him a small food treat from your other hand. This doesn't reward him. It simply shows him that you can touch him without being bitten.
3. If your dog nips at your feet, ankles, or clothing, keep one of his favorite tug toys in your pocket. When he goes for your lower limbs, stop moving, take out the tug toy, and wave it at him. When he grabs it, move again.
4. Provide plenty of exercise for your dog and interesting new toys to distract him. When dogs are bored or overly tired, they turn to nipping.

SEPARATION ANXIETY

As pack animals, many dogs become anxious when they're left alone. Although most

Multi-Dog Tip

Despite the fact that you've purchased dozens of toys for your dogs, if you have more than one dog there's always one toy that both or all of them want. Although they act as if they're fighting over it, they're most likely just playing. If the play-fight escalates to a dangerous level, break it up by verbally distracting them and offering them a treat. Keep your hands away from their mouths, and don't try to take the toy away. Without meaning to, they may grab your hand instead of the toy and accidentally bite you.

Bostons don't mind if you leave them for a reasonable amount of time, some can't handle it. They exhibit signs of separation anxiety by barking, whining, or howling. Highly disruptive and often destructive, these dogs may urinate, defecate, or have diarrhea in the house 5 to 60 minutes after the owner leaves. Frightened and distressed, they engage in destructive chewing or digging and try to escape the yard, house, or crate. They may even eat their own excrement when separated from their owners. These panic-ridden dogs show acute alertness to their owner's every move and will obsessively follow them from room to room. Anticipating their abandonment,

To help your dog deal with separation anxiety, you must teach him to tolerate being left alone by helping him realize you will eventually return to spend quality time with him.

dogs with separation anxiety will pace, drool, pant, or chew and lick their feet excessively.

Bostons who spend their entire lives with the same owner always at home, and especially rescued Bostons who have gone from owner to owner, are particularly vulnerable to separation anxiety. The loss of an important person or group of people in a dog's life can prompt feelings of separation anxiety. For many dogs, a change in their owner's work schedule or daily routine or a sudden departure sets them off. A major change in environment can cause emotional distress. Separation anxiety increases if a dog has insufficient outdoor exercise to tire him out and doesn't know how to amuse himself if you cannot be with him.

How to Manage It

Here's how to manage your dog's separation anxiety:

1. If you spend most of your day at home with your dog, resist the urge to pet and pamper him constantly. It's not that you don't love your dog and want to enjoy his company, but when you leave, your absence hampers his ability to adjust.

2. To help your dog deal with separation anxiety, you must teach him to tolerate being left alone. If your dog exhibits separation anxiety by urinating in the

house during your absence, you first have to rule out any medical or psychological problem that may be causing your dog's incontinence. Urinary tract infections, bladder stones, diabetes, kidney disease, and even some medications can cause urinary accidents. A Boston who occasionally urinates in the house might not be completely housetrained, and a dog who was physically punished for eliminating in the house will do it in the owner's absence. Unrelated to separation anxiety, some male dogs will urinate small amounts on vertical surfaces in the house because they're scent marking to establish their territory around other dogs.

3. For mild cases of separation anxiety, try giving your dog an interactive toy that dispenses food. That will take his mind off your departure and change his anxiety to a pleasant reward if he develops an association between receiving something he loves and being alone. Over time, he'll learn that what he fears predicts something he likes.

4. Providing plenty of outdoor exercise and stimulation helps too, although backyard exercise may not be enough. Include long walks or agility or obedience training to tire him out. Exercise enriches your Boston's life, decreases his stress levels, and helps eliminate destructiveness and hyperactivity.

5. Because dogs with separation anxiety learn to anticipate your every move and begin worrying as soon as they see you pick up your car keys or put on a sweater, teach him that these signs don't always mean that you're leaving. Instead of

leaving, get the keys and your sweater and simply turn on the television and sit down. Repeat several times at intervals.

You can further desensitize your dog's separation anxiety by following these steps:

1. Ignore your Boston ten minutes before you're ready to leave the house and for the first five minutes after your return. This will reduce your dog's stress and excitement surrounding your departure and arrival.

2. Greet your dog calmly in a low-key manner five minutes after your arrival. Your dog will accept your absence easier if you don't make a huge fuss when you leave or return.

3. Reward him with your attention when he's calm and quiet.

Above all, don't scold, hit, or punish your dog for exhibiting fear. He may become more upset, and the problem will only intensify. Remain patient and continue desensitizing him to your departure. Eventually, he will relax when he realizes that you will return to spend quality time with him.

While many dogs can become desensitized to their owners leaving them alone, other dogs may need more help. Here's where contacting a professional canine behaviorist may be the answer. A qualified pet professional can help resolve this serious behavior problem in a safe, nonconfrontational, and positive manner. While this individual will charge a fee for services, it's a small price to pay for a dog's comfort level and the owner's peace of mind.

CHAPTER 11

BOSTON TERRIER SPORTS AND ACTIVITIES

Bright, energetic Boston Terriers love games and new challenges. Your job as your Boston's activities director is to find fun outings you both can appreciate. Trust that whatever you like doing, your dog will too.

From everyday errands to walking and jogging beside your Boston, it's important that he behaves in public. The American Kennel Club's (AKC) Canine Good Citizen® Program has a series of exercises that every dog should know before venturing out. Going camping? If so, take your Boston along for the exercise. He'll love the chance to expand his horizons. But for more organized activities, consider participating in agility, canine freestyle, obedience, or conformation events. If you're searching for a less competitive pastime with your American Gentleman, consider therapy work. Whenever a Boston visits people in nursing homes and children in hospitals, he's sure to bring comfort and smiles all around.

Sometimes you may have to travel, by either plane or automobile, and secure overnight lodging. Boston Terriers are good travelers as long as you plan ahead for their health and safety. If you can't take your dog with you, that's okay. For a long day away, consider taking him to doggy day care, but if you must be gone for longer than that, hire a qualified pet sitter or take your dog to a good boarding kennel. He'll definitely be glad to see you when you return.

ACTIVITIES

It's easy to find physical pursuits for your Boston Terrier. With intelligence and enthusiasm, the breed has a zest for life and is willing to try most new things. But before you set off with your dog camping, walking, jogging, or even participating in the Canine Good Citizen® test and therapy work, there are some provisions you should take for his well-being and safety.

When participating in outdoor sports during warm weather, your Boston needs to stay cool. The breed's flat face restricts the ability to take in air and reduces the efficiency of the dog's cooling system, which is panting. Plan ahead and take precautions anytime your dog is going where the temperature rises above 80°F (25.7°C). It doesn't take much for your dog to suffer from dehydration or heatstroke if overexposed to the heat.

Bring along plenty of drinking water (about 8 ounces [237 ml]) of water per dog during

The bright, energetic Boston loves games and new challenges.

exertion) and a small cooler of ice. If you bring along a crate, place it in a shady area that allows for easy airflow. A wire model is best; avoid using a solid-sided crate because this type can overheat inside. Never, ever leave your dog in a parked car. It can become a furnace in no time.

To cool your dog off outdoors during hot weather, use canine cooling coats or towels soaked in cold water and let your dog stand on them. Or place a canine cooling pad in a crate or exercise pen for the dog to lie on. If your Boston becomes overheated, don't plunge him into ice water. This can actually harm him. Instead, apply ice or a cold wet cloth to the inside of his thighs and beneath his arms, which will bring down his body temperature.

You can also use a spray bottle filled with water to spritz water on his abdomen or into his mouth to lower his body temperature. Always keep an eye on your dog during hot weather for any signs of heat distress, such as severe panting, difficulty breathing, drooling, mild weakness, shaking, and even collapse. Race your dog to the emergency veterinary clinic if you notice any of these signs.

Canine Good Citizen® Test

Boston owners enjoy taking their dogs out on the town, frequenting cafes, and doing errands together. This means that your dog's manners demand perfection. Barking, snapping, lunging at other dogs, or jumping up on strangers will give him a bad reputation and make you think twice about taking him out of the house on future outings.

To avoid missing out on having fun with your dog in public, train him to pass basic obedience requirements and earn the American Kennel Club's Canine Good Citizen (CGC) title. With scant preparation, Boston Terriers usually sail right through the CGC exercises and easily earn their CGC certificates.

Originating in 1989, the Canine Good Citizen certificate program offers a simple noncompetitive test for purebred and mixed-breed dogs of all ages, although the dog must be old enough to have received all immunizations.

The CGC certificate is an important screening device for well-behaved dogs. Many landlords require prospective renters with dogs to possess a CGC certificate, and therapy dog programs require canine candidates to have one as well.

To pass the CGC test, dogs must wear a buckle or slip-type collar, remain on leash, and appear well groomed and in healthy condition. Owners are required to sign a "Responsible Dog Owner's Pledge" before taking the test; the pledge states that the owner agrees to care for the dog and always provide a good home for him.

The AKC test consists of ten steps that your dog must complete:

1. Allow a stranger to approach you and talk to you.
2. Sit politely while a stranger pets him.
3. Allow a stranger, such as a veterinarian or a groomer, to brush him lightly.
4. Walk beside you while you hold a loose leash.
5. Demonstrate his ability to walk through a group of at least three other people without jumping on them or shying away.
6. Obey the *sit*, *lie down*, and *stay* commands.
7. Obey the *come* command.
8. Behave politely without lunging when another dog-and-handler team walks past.
9. React confidently without panicking, barking, or acting aggressively in a distracting situation.
10. Remain calm when held by a stranger while you leave him for three minutes.

For more information about the CGC test, contact the AKC at www.akc.org.

Camping

A trip to the great outdoors with your Boston sounds idyllic, but before leaving home, check that your destination permits dogs. Some parks do not allow dogs or limit them to designated areas. Check leash requirements too. There may

By the Numbers

Boston Terriers aren't natural swimmers and can drown if left unsupervised around water. You can teach yours to enjoy a dip in the pool or lake as early as 12 weeks of age. If fearful around water, your Boston can be gradually introduced to a children's wading pool filled with 3 to 4 inches (7.5 to 10 cm) of water. Graduate to a swimming pool by sitting on the steps with your dog and encouraging him to wade in with you. Don't just throw your Boston in and expect him to swim automatically because he may drown. Make sure that your dog wears a canine life jacket if you take him on a boat ride.

To pass the CGC test, dogs must appear well groomed and in healthy condition.

be restrictions prohibiting dogs off leash. Some states require dogs to remain on a handheld 10-foot (3-m) leash, while other states require dogs on leashes not exceeding 4 (1 m) or 6 feet (2 m).

Protect your dog against fleas, ticks, heartworms, and mosquitoes by administering preventives a month before your departure. Fortunately, a Boston doesn't have a long coat to attract debris, but fleas, ticks, and insects thrive in warm wooded areas and can plague even a short-haired dog.

Take along a canine first-aid kit and know where the nearest veterinarian and emergency veterinary clinic is located before you leave. You never know when your dog may need immediate treatment. Also, make sure your dog's identification tag is up-to-date and he's microchipped. If you and your dog become

separated, whoever finds him will be able to return him to you.

Hiking is an invigorating pastime while camping, but plan ahead if you take your dog with you. Many hikers strap on a doggy backpack in which to carry their dog should he become tired, and they take first-aid canine supplies along with them on the trail. And unless your Boston's tender feet have been conditioned to rough terrain, don't plan to hike far with your dog. Keep checking the pads of his feet in case they tear or become red and swollen.

Bring along plenty of food, treats, and fresh water for your dog, too, as there's no guarantee that you'll find the exact food you feed your dog in a remote area. Don't rely on outdoor water sources, no matter how clear they look. Ponds and streams may contain toxins, bacteria, and parasites that can transmit intestinal distress. Plan to pick up after your dog, so bring along clean-up supplies and properly dispose of the waste.

Don't forget to bring along a few of his favorite toys. In addition to treats, you can use the toys to reward him with when he comes when you call him. This comes in handy if the camping area permits dogs off leash and you want him to return to you. Or if your dog encounters a wild animal you don't want him tangling with, following your command to come back to you may save his life.

Walking and Jogging

Maybe you'd enjoy less adventurous outings with your Boston but still want some exercise. That's okay because you and your dog can always go walking or jogging around your neighborhood or in a safe area nearby. These low-impact activities are a great way to bond with him and give both of you a good cardio workout.

If your dog is already trained to walk on a leash politely beside you instead of pulling at it, the walk or jog will be especially pleasurable. Use a regular 6-foot (2-m) leash or harness when walking your dog. This will give you some control and your dog some leeway. Don't use a retractable leash! If your dog goes out to the end

Hiking Etiquette

Before your Boston explores the great outdoors, make sure that he has some training and knows how to walk politely on leash and to come reliably when you call him. While he doesn't need to heel perfectly at your side if you go hiking, you don't want him yanking on the leash either.

Want to Know More?

For a refresher on teaching your Boston obedience commands, see Chapter 4: Training Your Boston Terrier Puppy and Chapter 9: Boston Terrier Training.

of the leash and an aggressive animal suddenly appears, there's no time to reel him back.

Although jogging burns more calories, don't start off running right away. Your Boston needs time to build up his stamina, so begin by walking for 20 minutes and work up to 30 or 45 minutes. A good walk will stimulate your Boston's mind and help condition the pads of his feet. A Boston isn't a long-distance runner, so don't plan on running a marathon with him.

If you live in a hot climate, walk early in the day or in the evening when the temperature is cooler, and bring along some water for your dog to drink.

Therapy Work

Your Boston's pleasant, easygoing, and soothing nature makes him an ideal candidate for therapy work. Easily recognizable, a Boston helps enhance the human/canine bond by cheering up residents in nursing homes, hospitals, and children's treatment centers. Some dogs do better with children, while others have an affinity for seniors. Some don't mind noisy situations, while others prefer a quieter environment. It helps to know your Boston's talents when choosing the type of therapy work he is capable of performing.

In therapy work, owners visit with their dogs and add companionship, mental stimulation, and interaction. Dogs seem to naturally raise the spirits of people in many therapeutic situations because they provide unconditional love and acceptance. The dogs seem to love the attention as much as the people do.

Many facilities require dogs to have some training and certification before they are accepted. Therapy Dog International (TDI) and the Delta Society offer certification testing, and some therapeutic settings may require a dog to have a Canine Good Citizen certificate. Once your dog has learned basic obedience, he'll need some exposure to wheelchairs, walkers, and canes before he can be accepted into a therapy dog program. Dogs must be at least one year old before visiting and should be bathed and have their nails clipped before each visit. No one wants to snuggle with a dog who smells or has sharp nails.

Therapy dogs must have the ability to leave food, toys, and medications alone when visiting patients and be able to withstand an onslaught of petting and fussing over. Small Bostons may sit on wheelchair patients' laps or may be allowed on a resident's bed.

If your dog can perform a few cute tricks, such as bowing or jumping through an agility hoop, he can provide entertainment to amuse people. When a Boston walks into a hospital or treatment center wearing a costume, he brings a smile to everyone he meets.

The Boston's pleasant, easygoing nature makes him an ideal candidate for therapy work.

Regardless of your dog's skill level, you can find a canine competition to suit you both.

SPORTS

Most Boston owners are perfectly happy to cuddle up with their dogs and enjoy their company around the house. Others, however, enjoy proving their love by spending time training to earn titles and competing in dog events. Regardless of your dog's skill level, you can find a canine competition to suit you both.

For Bostons who are always up for a game and for fast-paced fun, consider getting involved in agility. For more creative types, there's canine freestyle, which teaches your dog one-on-one precision set to music. If you're looking for a regimented sport with practical implications, spending your time training your Boston for competitive obedience is something he'll always use. Or maybe having your dog compete in conformation events is more your style. Whatever you choose to do with your dog only enhances your relationship with him and adds years of enjoyment.

Agility

If speed and accuracy are right up your alley, you'll love participating in agility with your

Training Tidbit

Before training your dog for the show ring, make sure that he's socialized around other dogs, people, new places, and strange noises, and knows how to walk politely on a leash. Reward him with small food treats or his favorite toy when he behaves correctly.

In a conformation show, a dog is evaluated on how closely he conforms to the breed standard.

Boston. An obstacle course for dogs, the goal in this canine fun-filled activity, involves completing a series of exercises without any infractions and within a specified time limit. The sport involves jumping over bars, scaling A-frames, walking an elevated dogwalk, weaving through poles, and zooming through tunnels against the clock. There's camaraderie with other exhibitors, and the dogs' joy is contagious.

A particularly agile and intelligent breed, Bostons excel at this sport because they're able to leap to surprising heights and can turn on a dime. One of the reasons why

Bostons like agility so much is because they think it's a game and they're eager to please you and comply with your directions. Several organizations, including the AKC, the United Kennel Club (UKC), the North American Dog Agility Council (NADAC), and the United States Dog Agility Association (USDAA) sponsor agility trials.

Through the AKC, dogs can earn titles by competing in two types of courses: Standard, which includes a pause box and the obstacles, and Jumpers With Weaves (JWW). The JWW course includes only jumps, tunnels, and weaves. Dogs compete in three levels of competition based on difficulty: Novice with 13 to 15 obstacles, Open with 16 to 18 obstacles, and Excellent with 18 to 20. Dogs new to the sport compete in the Novice class before progressing to Open and finally to Excellent. The MACH (Master Agility Champion) title is the highest agility title.

Sweet Sociable Samuel, owned by Nancy Ames, was the first Boston to earn the AKC agility title and also the first to win a North American Flyball Association (NAFA) flyball dog title in 1990.

Canine Freestyle

If you've ever wanted to dance with your dog, canine freestyle is the sport for you. A choreographed performance set to music between dog and handler, freestyle incorporates basic obedience commands, such as heelwork, *sit*, *down*, and *front*. Routines stress the special and unique bond between dog and handler and include creative moves featuring pivots, kicks, twists, and turns.

Smart, sure-footed Bostons are quick to keep up with their handlers and make natural freestyle performers. They willingly take on advanced maneuvers that include crawl, rollover, spin, bow, sidestep, bounce, back up, and play dead. Simple costumes may be required for both handlers and dogs, but with their tuxedo markings, all most Bostons need is a matching bow tie and cuffs.

The Canine Freestyle Federation, Inc. (CFF), and the World Canine Freestyle Organization, Inc. (WCFO), promote the sport and sponsor various levels of competition. Dogs can enter several divisions and categories to fit their levels of experience.

Freestyle is a multi-faceted activity. You can practice with your dog just for fun in your own home, compete with the freestyle organizations, or take your act on the road to entertain and bring joy to patients in hospital settings in canine therapy.

Conformation (Dog Shows)

No doubt the perfect Boston already rests on your lap. For many owners it doesn't matter what their dogs' ears or bodies looks like, as long as they are active, healthy, and never run out of kisses. Then again, if you want someone impartial to evaluate your dog to see how closely he exemplifies the qualities in the AKC standard for the Boston Terrier, then consider entering him in a dog show. A purebred Boston Terrier who has not been spayed or neutered but is registered with the AKC can participate in AKC conformation shows.

You will need to learn how to show your dog before actually entering one. Locate handling classes where you'll pick up tips on how to train your dog to stand still for the judge's examination and how to trot beside you on a leash around the show ring. Behaving well as a show dog has everything to do with also having a naturally happy attitude and exuding showmanship.

Males are shown separately from females and divided into separate classes for puppies, adolescent dogs, and adults. Adult males and females are further divided into classes of under 15 pounds (7 kg) and over 15 pounds (7 kg), although blacks and brindles compete alongside one another. Dogs must accumulate 15 points to earn their AKC Championship title (CH). Each dog show has the maximum potential of earning a dog five points. The UKC and the Canadian Kennel Club (CKC) also sponsor dog shows, although a dog needs only ten points to become a Canadian Champion of Record.

If you purchased your Boston from a breeder who shows her dogs, she can mentor you and get you started in this fun sport. She can also help evaluate your dog as a show prospect. Children ages 9 to 18 may show their Boston Terriers in Junior Showmanship classes at dog shows. The children's performance is evaluated rather than the dog's conformation.

Obedience

In obedience, dogs are judged on their performance, not their appearance. Formal obedience competitions test your dog's ability to perform specific exercises, such as *sit*, *stay*, *down*, *come*, and *heel*. There's only one chance to complete a routine, and precision counts. All dogs begin with a perfect score of 200, and points are deducted for imperfections. In AKC competition, the top-scoring dog at an obedience trial is awarded a High in Trial (HIT).

Dogs who have never competed before enter the Novice class and can earn a Companion Dog (CD) title. They then proceed to the Open class, where advanced exercises are performed off leash and dogs earn a Companion Dog Excellent (CDX) title.

For his protection and safety during travel, never leave your dog unattended in your car.

Utility classes are the next-highest obedience level, with dogs earning the Utility Dog (UD) and Utility Dog Excellent (UDX) titles. The ultimate obedience title is the Obedience Trial Champion (OTCH).

Obedience training strengthens the bond between dog and owner and can be used at home as well as in a competitive setting.

TRAVELING WITH YOUR BOSTON

If you enjoy traveling but hate the thought of leaving your Boston at home, why not take him along? Bostons are good traveling buddies, and they enjoy getting out to see new surroundings. But whether you're taking a road trip, leaving on a jet plane, or spending the night out of the house, you'll need to plan ahead for your dog's comfort.

There's a lot to pack for a dog, so you may decide to leave him home after all. If so, you have a few options for his caretaking: hire a pet sitter, take him to doggy day care, or take him to a boarding kennel.

By Car

Before hitting the road with your Boston, make sure that he's accustomed to riding in the car. If the only time he rides in the car is when you take him to the veterinarian, a road trip may prove traumatic. Take frequent small trips before your departure. It doesn't hurt to bring treats along and give a small tidbit to your dog as a reward for getting into the car and for rewarding good behavior throughout the journey. However, if your dog gets carsick, hold off on the treats as these may make the condition worse.

Don't forget to secure your dog in the car. The best protection for your Boston in case of an accident is to ride inside a crate securely fastened to the car seat belt. Another safe option is a doggy car seat with a seat belt. If riding loose, it doesn't take much to propel a small dog into the dashboard or through the window.

Make sure that the outside of the crate has emergency information about your dog that includes the name of someone to contact and any medications or health problems your dog may have. He should wear identification with your name and phone number and the name and number of someone at home who can care for your dog in your absence.

Pack along a doggy first-aid kit and a bag of your dog's things so that you can keep everything together in one place. Bring enough food for your entire trip because there's no guarantee that you'll find the same food along the way that your dog is used to eating. A different food may cause intestinal distress. Also, bring plenty of water from home or bottled water for him to drink. Public water sources contain different chemicals that may upset his system and cause diarrhea.

Never leave your dog inside a parked car for any reason. The temperature can heat up quickly and your dog can die. Don't rely on a battery-operated fan or cooling pads either, especially on a hot day. If they fail, your dog will suffer.

Before taking your dog out of the car, give him the *stay* command. Don't let him exit the vehicle until you know it's safe and you have him on leash. The last thing you want is your dog running out into traffic as soon as the door is opened.

Don't feed your Boston before you leave, as some dogs get carsick from the motion of the car. Wait until you reach your destination and feed him then. Pack clean-up materials, and stop every few hours at a clean location

If you can't take your Boston with you while you are away from home, a kennel or pet sitter may be a good option.

so that your dog can walk around and stretch his legs and go to the bathroom. Try not to use areas where other dogs have eliminated. This reduces the chance that your dog will contract an illness.

By Plane

When making your own airline reservation, find out if you can bring your dog along because he'll need a ticket, too. Every airline has different regulations for dogs riding in the passenger section or the baggage compartment when flying. Bostons weighing

10 pounds (4.5 kg) may be allowed to ride in an airline-approved crate that fits under the seat in front of you.

Your dog needs a recent health certificate from your veterinarian, as well as a rabies inoculation. His crate must have a water dish attached to the crate door and absorbent material inside in case he has an accident. Make sure that his identification tag has current information, and bring his leash because you will have to remove him from the crate as you go through security. Again, don't feed your dog before you leave because the stress of travel may upset his stomach.

Lodging for Humans and Pets

Don't leave home without finding a hotel or motel that accepts pets. Be prepared to pay an extra pet charge, and make sure that you and your dog observe good manners. Don't leave your dog unattended in the room as he may bark or destroy the room.

Clean up any mess your dog leaves behind, and dispose of it properly. Bring plenty of bottled water for him, and don't let him drink from the toilet or give him any water from the sink. Your Boston will appreciate his favorite blanket and a few toys from home, too.

If You Have to Leave Your Boston Behind

If you decide to leave your Boston at home, you may want to ask a trusted neighbor, friend, or family member to care for him while you are away. Your dog will be able to stay in familiar surroundings, remain on his regular diet, and sleep in his own bed. If they can visit with him during the day

and perhaps even stay overnight, he will have the best of both worlds. Regardless of where you leave your Boston, you should feel comfortable with the people looking after him and know that he is in the best of hands during your absence.

Pet Sitters

If you don't know someone who can watch your dog, you may need to hire a professional pet sitter. Ask your veterinarian, friends, neighbors with dogs, trainers, or groomers for recommendations. You can also check with Pet Sitters International (PSI) or the National Association of Professional Pet Sitters for reliable pet sitters (NAPPS). Be sure to leave the number where you'll be staying and the name and phone number of a friend who can assist with your dog if necessary.

Doggy Day Care

If you won't be away from home overnight, another option is to leave your dog at doggy day care. Your Boston will have personal attention, and if he's comfortable interacting with other dogs, he'll have the opportunity to play and romp with them. Tour the facility before taking your dog, and make sure that it's clean and well organized.

Boarding Kennels

If interacting with other dogs is not your Boston's thing, then a boarding kennel may suit his needs. Visit prospective kennels before booking your dog, and check that they are clean and free of debris and well disinfected. The kennel should be licensed, with personnel remaining on the premises at all times in case there's an emergency. Your dog should have a safe and completely fenced-in area. A run that is indoor–outdoor and fully heated and air-conditioned is ideal.

Multi-Dog Tip

If you take two Bostons out for a walk, don't be surprised if one tries to walk ahead of the other one. Some Bostons have a competitive streak and want to outdo their housemate. Try using a dog leash coupler, which attaches to a regular leash. This stops one from pulling ahead of the other and prevents both from becoming tangled up.

PART III

SENIOR YEARS

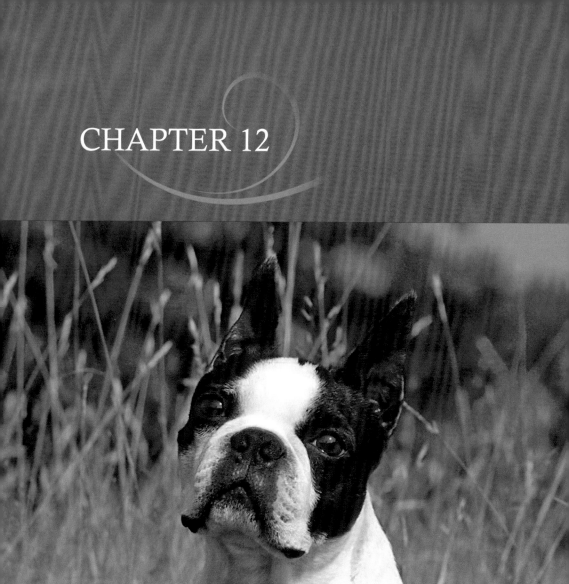

CHAPTER 12

FINDING YOUR BOSTON TERRIER SENIOR

With eyes clouded over, his once-black muzzle now filled with gray and white hairs, an elderly Boston waits in a breed rescue facility hoping his family will come back and pick him up. Sadly, that will never happen. His owners lost their home and can no longer afford to take care of him. People have come to look at him since he was taken to rescue, but no one seems to want a senior dog who has trouble hearing and who can see only out of one eye. Potential caretakers reject him, thinking that he comes with health problems they can't handle, or that he didn't make a good companion in the first place, but this simply isn't the case.

Although Bostons are considered seniors beginning at around 8 years of age, they may often live to 14 or 15 if they are well cared for. When adopted any time prior to that, they still have a lot of love to give and never run out of kisses. Some oldsters may look ancient, but down deep they're young at heart and will act like puppies forever.

THE TRUTH ABOUT SURRENDERED DOGS

Many senior dogs, along with countless other dogs of all ages, are not given up because they are bad dogs with behavioral problems. They may in fact have been rescued from their situations due to animal abuse or neglect. Others are simply the victims of circumstances beyond their control, such as when their owners undergo changes in their lives that make it difficult or impossible to continue caring for them.

There can be many reasons good dogs end up in shelters. In the past, treasured pets were carefully handed down to other family members when an elderly owner died. Today not everyone makes plans for their pet's care after they pass away; as a result, the pets are abandoned because there is no one who can give them a permanent home. Many pets are surrendered because of an owner's lack of knowledge about the breed. You may see a Boston on a television commercial and think that he looks cool and decide to go out and buy one, failing to realize that this breed comes with a lively personality and, like other dogs, will need training. You may also be surprised that this little dog requires daily attention and exercise and doesn't have the couch potato personality you expected. Or you may discover that the sound of a Boston snoring while he's asleep is more than you bargained for. Not researching a breed before bringing home your new dog is unfair to him and to you.

Some people may develop medical problems that prohibit keeping a pet, such as allergies or physical disabilities. Sometimes the owner moves into an apartment building that doesn't allow pets. Many dogs started out as gifts to adults or children who eventually lost interest in them. People give up older dogs for similar reasons, but the most common explanations include discovering that they do not have enough time to take care of an aging dog who now has special needs, or that they can't afford the expense of treating a prolonged illness or degenerative condition.

For these reasons, it's important to understand that whether you are planning to buy a puppy or adopt an adult, you are committing to caring for him for his entire lifetime—even if he's in his golden years. Anything short of that is doing him a huge disservice and causing him unnecessary pain and sadness.

WHY ADOPTING A SENIOR IS A GOOD IDEA

Adopting a senior Boston Terrier after other people have given him up can be intensely satisfying. There's a big emotional return for making the investment to help save a life. At shelters and breed rescues, older dogs are often the last to be adopted and the first on the list to be euthanized.

Senior Bostons are gentle, loving creatures who are easy keepers.

You may discover that a senior Boston suits your lifestyle perfectly. Most adult dogs are past the chewing, digging, and destructive periods and are only interested in having a warm bed to sleep in along with some human companionship. Perfect for owners with neighbors who dislike barking dogs, a geriatric Boston is no longer interested in protecting his territory and barking at strangers—he may sleep so soundly that he may not even hear odd noises. He may also be less likely to run out the door if it's accidentally left open or to sneak out of the yard seeking adventure. A senior Boston who spends most of his day lazing in the sun is also an excellent choice for someone who is home only in the evenings or someone who doesn't have the energy or physical ability to run after a puppy all day long. While some people are hesitant to adopt a senior dog because they think he will have a lot of health concerns to deal with, the fact is that dogs can suffer from illnesses at any age. Older Bostons have no more health issues than their younger counterparts.

Senior Bostons are gentle, loving creatures who are easy keepers. They make a great match for an elderly person who yearns for a canine companion but may hold back because they're

By the Numbers

Homeless Boston Terriers between 8 or 9 years of age wait longer for new homes than younger dogs. That's because most people think seniors are too old to adopt and don't have many years left. With a life span of up to 14 or 15 years, senior Bostons can enjoy many good times with their families.

Multi-Dog Tip

If you adopt a senior dog, consider adopting a second one, too. Both will bond with one another and keep each other company. Because they are in the same stage of life, you can keep them both on the same schedule and manage them easily.

concerned about what might happen in their own lives in the coming years. While a puppy or young dog can be a 15-year responsibility, which is not appropriate for someone with certain long-term future plans, providing a loving home for a Boston in his golden years is a shorter commitment that benefits both parties. Older dogs are content to sit calmly and wait for attention, while puppies require constant interaction. They will also be comfortable being left alone for longer periods of time. Plus, you don't have to worry about dog-proofing your house and putting all of your fragile items out of reach.

Adopting a Boston Terrier in his golden years sets a good example for children. It teaches them the basic values of compassion, caring, and respect for the elderly, especially if you need to provide special care and nurturing. Older Bostons are companionable but lack the intensity of a puppy's nonstop energy level, so they're perfect for children who aren't accustomed to dogs and may be somewhat fearful of them. Senior dogs are calm, slow-moving, and less likely to frighten them or knock them over. While parents should always supervise any dog around a child, an older, quieter dog can provide loving companionship as well as a wonderful learning opportunity.

WHAT YOU SHOULD KNOW BEFORE GETTING YOUR SENIOR

You can expect to pay a nominal amount to adopt an elderly Boston. Rescue groups of affiliated clubs charge different fees, depending on the cost of veterinary care in their respective areas. While most volunteer organizations are nonprofit, they do have to pay the expenses of food and veterinary bills themselves. Often there's a reduced fee for a senior or none at all.

If you decide to adopt a senior Boston Terrier, know which qualities you're looking for and those that you can't accept. Also carefully consider what the dog's needs will be. For example, a home with many stairs may not be a good match for a blind or arthritic dog who may find this kind of an environment difficult to maneuver and hazardous to him. Or if a dog requires special medical treatments that you can't afford to provide or don't have the heart to give, that may not be the best match for you either. While you may want to desperately help a Boston in need, there's no sense in adopting a dog only to return him when things don't work out later on.

Your adopted senior will need some time to adjust to his new surroundings.

Training Tidbit

If you adopt a senior who is blind, show him where the food and water dishes are and don't move them. Don't move the furniture either. Once your dog knows where things are, he will remember the route and adapt surprisingly well.

When you're interviewed by shelter or breed rescue coordinators, be honest with what you can handle and what you can't. Ask questions about the dogs you're considering adopting. The coordinators assess the dogs' personalities and have some idea what they're like. If you don't find a dog you care for, wait for the one you want. You'll be more likely to keep him if you are satisfied.

Chances are he's had more than one home already or has possibly even been abandoned once or twice. Bounced around from place to place, it's normal for an adopted pet to feel wary about trusting strangers and forming new friendships. Some older Bostons are slightly depressed from the abrupt changes in their surroundings and need to feel comfortable with their new home and family on their own terms. When you are ready to adopt, set aside several weeks so you can spend more time to establish a bond with your Boston. If he's physically able, take him out for regular walks and car rides to visit friends or see new sights. Introduce him to the neighbors so he has a chance to socialize and be familiar with them. All these activities will add to his self-esteem and help build his confidence.

Give your dog at least a month to settle in. An older pet deserves happiness and love in a good home as much as a younger one does, and this takes time. Your devotion and affection will be returned tenfold. Know that he will be forever grateful to you for rescuing him from a bad environment and certain death.

Trial Run: Try Fostering First

If you're unsure whether you want to bring a Boston Terrier who's in the autumn of his life into your home, consider fostering him first. Breed rescue groups appreciate placing their wards into foster care because this not only provides a newly abandoned pet with a comfortable temporary home environment but also offers adoption coordinators an opportunity to evaluate the dog for permanent placement.

Although every organization sets different requirements for foster families, you'll be responsible for providing basic needs, including feeding, grooming, housing, and medical care. Some groups cover expenses; some do not. Depending upon the dog's needs and the availability of new adoptive homes, the length of time the dog remains with you varies. By caring for an elderly Boston until he finds permanent placement, you'll have some idea about whether a senior is a better fit for your family than a puppy or a middle-aged dog.

CHAPTER 13

CARE OF YOUR BOSTON TERRIER SENIOR

Where did the time go? It seems only yesterday that you brought your Boston Terrier puppy home. Now he's an esteemed elder and aging gracefully. He's had a long, wonderful life, thanks to his parents and the good genes they've passed along, coupled with the excellent care you've given him all these years.

Now the time has come to change some of his routines to make his mature years as comfortable for him as possible. His diet may need some tweaking, and keeping up with grooming is now more important than ever before. To catch health issue before they become more serious, your Boston should visit the veterinarian twice a year and have a senior checkup. Don't neglect his mental state either.

One way to keep your older Boston healthy is to continue to play with him, provide regular exercise, and train him to master new behaviors. Bear in mind that you may need to adapt the level of play and exercise to match his slower movements, reduced energy level, and declining eyesight and hearing, but your efforts will pay off. By paying attention to his changing needs, your Boston's senior years will be the best time of all.

WHEN IS A BOSTON TERRIER A SENIOR?

Dogs are living longer than ever. Veterinarians at Tufts University consider most small dogs to reach senior citizen status at about 10 to 12 years of age, while most large dogs are considered seniors at about 6 to 8 years of age. But if your Boston is 12 years or older, don't say goodbye just yet. With good care, the breed's life span can be as long as 15 years, and like people, dogs age differently. Lots of Bostons act like puppies well into their golden years, while others begin to look and act like oldsters at about age 8.

Fortunately, advances in nutrition and veterinary care are helping Bostons live a longer and healthier life. You play a large part in your dog's longevity, too, because there are many things you can do to enhance his daily routines and make life easier for him.

Signs of Aging

On his twelfth birthday, you may not see any changes in your dog's appearance or behavior. Then one day you'll look at his face and notice a few more white hairs around his cheeks and mouth, or realize that he sleeps a little longer in the morning or takes longer naps in the afternoon.

You may observe other signs of aging as well. Perhaps your Boston has arthritis and doesn't move as fast as he once did, or he shows hesitation or stiffness when getting up or lying down. His coat may be drier and look somewhat thinner, or his eating habits may be different. Perhaps he always gobbled his food before, but lately it seems to take him longer to finish. Or, if he was picky in the past, he may now attack the bowl before you put it down. His weight may not be the same either. He may look thinner than he should or keep putting on the pounds and lose his boyish physique.

Although Bostons act like puppies well into their golden years, they are considered seniors at about age 8.

Bathroom habits change for older Bostons, too. They may need to urinate more frequently and, despite being housetrained, can accidentally eliminate in the house. As time goes by, vision and hearing diminish as well, and your dog may not be able to see or hear you. The ability to hear high-pitched sounds usually disappears first, so lower the tone of your voice when you call him. Likewise, because your dog will not realize that his bark is shriller or his whine is ten times louder than it once was, louder vocalizations may occur. If loss of hearing occurs, petting your dog often will help him connect with you; keep in mind that because he can't hear you he may think that you've quit talking to him or paying attention to him.

Many senior dogs develop separation anxiety and may bark, whine, or become destructive when you leave them alone for even a few minutes. Sensitivity to noise, especially to thunderstorms, is another sign of old age, as is confusion, lack of attentiveness, disorientation, roaming in circles, barking at nothing, and acting withdrawn. Their painful joints may bring on uncharacteristic aggression or they may growl if you reach out to pet them. Older dogs don't like change either. Growing old is certainly no picnic.

FEEDING SENIORS

Just as Boston pups and canine athletes have special nutritional requirements, so do older dogs. Maintaining a quality diet and optimal body condition are just as important as they ever were. Feeding your senior dog correctly and maintaining a healthy weight are the most important things you can do to increase your Boston's quality of life.

Don't think that being overweight is acceptable just because a dog is reaching his senior years. Too much weight increases pressure on the joints, makes your dog work harder to move around, and predisposes him to diabetes and other medical problems.

What to Feed a Senior

Your senior Boston needs a well-balanced diet that is lower in calories and fat and high in fiber. Seniors need a nutritious diet, but that doesn't mean more calories. In fact, a 1-year-old, 20-pound (9 kg) Boston needs 764 calories a day, while a 12-year-old 20-pound (9 kg) Boston needs only 538 calories a day.

As dogs age, their metabolism slows down, burns fewer calories, and stores more fat. They actually benefit from eating a diet with less fat and fewer calories. Older dogs tend to lose muscle mass, even with exercise, which means they lose protein. This impairs their immune system and decreases the body's ability to respond to stress, trauma, or infectious disease.

Older dogs require as much as 50 percent more protein than younger dogs, and the protein should consist of high-quality ingredients. This may mean feeding your dog his regular food, but a lesser amount so that he doesn't become overweight. Or you may need to feed a specially formulated senior diet. Most commercial senior recipes contain 18 percent protein. If your dog has kidney problems, a diet containing about 14 percent protein is usually recommended because it reduces the kidney's workload.

Many senior recipes contain 10 to 12 percent fat. For dogs who tend to develop constipation, a diet higher in fiber is usually recommended—about 3 to 5 percent. Some Boston owners choose to bulk up their dog's meal with steamed or grated vegetables. Fiber is essential in your senior's diet to prevent problems with constipation.

If your senior Boston is healthy, has no medical problems, is not overweight, and remains fairly active, you can probably continue feeding him an adult formula.

Feeding Schedule

As your Boston enters his senior years, his feeding schedule isn't much different from what it was in his younger years. When senior dogs are engaged in daily activities, they should look forward to their meals and will expect them at regular times.

How Many Times a Day

Continue the good habit of feeding your senior Boston Terrier twice a day. If he seems extra-hungry toward the middle of the day, you can give him a small amount of some steamed or grated vegetables for an additional meal, but keep this meal small so he still has room for dinner.

When to Feed

As you did when he was younger, feed your dog a morning and an evening meal. Try to

Multi-Dog Tip

As Bostons age, their social relationship with other pets in the home may change. They may feel the need to protect themselves and could become aggressive toward their housemates. Or a younger dog may sense the older dog's frailties and try to seize the opportunity to become the leader. To maintain the older dog's leadership, always support him by putting his food bowl down first, letting him out of the house first, and greeting him first in the morning.

Dealing With Picky Eaters

Some dogs become more finicky in their eating habits as they age. For picky Bostons, try warming food slightly in the microwave, which also helps increase the aroma. Test it so it's not too hot, and stir it to evenly distribute any hot pockets. Ask your veterinarian what you can add to your dog's present diet to encourage him to eat. Some Boston owners add a little water from canned tuna, a small amount of salt-free chicken broth, some canned food, or cooked chicken.

If you're feeding your picky eater a commercial diet, consider switching to a homemade diet. Cooked salmon (without any bones, of course) and cooked sweet potatoes, for example, can spark just about any dog's interest in food. When you take your Boston to the veterinarian for his semi-annual examination, discuss what recipe you should feed him.

provide them at the same time intervals so your dog doesn't have to wait too long between meals. For example, if you feed your dog his breakfast at 6 am, his dinner time should be around 6 pm. That way he doesn't have to wait longer than 12 hours between meals.

GROOMING

Grooming your senior Boston isn't just about beauty. Keeping his skin and coat in good condition with regular bathing and brushing protects him from the environmental perils of cold wet weather and parasites such as fleas and ticks.

In older dogs, the circulation and muscle tone beneath the skin weaken, and the dog has a harder time warding off disease and illness. While grooming isn't going to turn back the clock and transform your senior into a puppy again, it does help support the skin.

Grooming your senior for a few minutes every day also soothes his need for physical contact and attention from you. A bath every other week or a daily brushing session helps to energize him and lets him know that you still care about him. This special bonding time contributes to your Boston's overall sense of well-being, which stimulates good health.

How to Make Grooming Comfortable

It's important to maintain a regular grooming routine as your dog ages. In less than an hour, you can brush and bathe your Boston and trim his nails. This small commitment of time helps maintain his overall health and eliminates pesky skin problems.

When it comes to giving your senior Boston a bath, it helps to remember that he's not as agile as he once was. His joints may be sore and he may feel some pain when you lift him up to place him in the sink or tub. To reduce discomfort, lift him with two hands by supporting his body beneath the abdomen above the groin and across his chest slightly below his front legs. For a better alternative, consider giving him a shower. Use a hand-held attachment to wet him down and to rinse off the soap. Whether you bathe or shower your dog, take special care to thoroughly dry him so he doesn't become chilled.

Keeping your senior Boston's nails trimmed is critical. Nails that are too long throw off his balance, affect his gait, and cause muscle strain. His nails should not touch the ground when

It's important to maintain a regular grooming routine as your dog ages.

just getting old and nothing can be done. Some behavior changes are signs of medical disorders that can be managed.

Preventive Care: Senior Checkups

Your older Boston Terrier should have a veterinary checkup twice a year. Where you may have turned down having blood work done when your dog was younger, it's a necessity now. A thorough blood panel can detect kidney failure, diabetes, liver failure, and other problems.

A senior's immune system is less effective now, so it's even more important to protect your dog from infectious diseases. If your Boston is mostly indoors and doesn't vacation with you or play with other dogs in the neighborhood, he may not need vaccinations. Because this topic is controversial, discuss this issue with your veterinarian.

Stay on the alert for any bouts of vomiting or diarrhea. These problems will debilitate a senior dog quickly and can also be a sign of more serious problems. If you have put off taking your younger dog to visit the veterinarian to wait out these symptoms, don't do so with a senior. Err on the side of caution and have the veterinarian check for anything new or unusual in your dog's condition or behavior.

Dogs hide their illness, and it's not always easy to tell when they're not up to par. A few reasons to take your senior to the veterinarian include:

- Bad breath or bleeding gums—may be a sign of gum disease, oral cancer, infections, kidney disease, or diabetes.
- Coughing and excessive panting—may indicate heart disease.
- Hair loss or itchy skin—may be dietary or environmental, but a mild condition can worsen quickly.

he is standing still. If you do it yourself, try using an electric rotary grinder rather than nail clippers. The grinder's variable speed makes it easier to shave off a little at a time, while clippers carry the risk of cutting too much nail off and causing it to bleed.

To make your dog more comfortable during nail trimming, don't put him up on a table. Instead, lay a blanket on the floor or the couch, and when your Boston cuddles up on the blanket, begin trimming his nails. Give him a treat after you've completed each nail; if he seems nervous, reassure him with a soft tone.

HEALTH CARE

Veterinarians recommend beginning geriatric health screening at age 7, followed by semi-annual visits. Observe any changes in your dog's health or behavior and report them to the veterinarian. Don't assume that your dog is

- Increased water intake or bathroom accidents—may indicate underlying conditions.
- Sudden blindness, hearing loss, or head tilting/staggering—may have several causes, including cataracts or diabetes.

Your veterinarian will perform a thorough hands-on physical exam and the following routine laboratory tests on your senior dog during his checkup:

- Complete blood count—measures the number of red blood cells, white blood cells, and platelets in the blood. This information helps the veterinarian to diagnose anemia, infections, and leukemia. This helps monitor your pet's response to some treatments.
- Urinalysis—helps detect the presence of one or more substances that normally don't appear in urine, such as protein, sugar, white blood cells, or blood. Will help the veterinarian diagnose urinary-tract infections, diabetes, dehydration, kidney problems, and other conditions.
- Blood chemistry panel—measures electrolytes, enzymes, and chemical elements such as calcium and phosphorus. This provides information about how the kidneys, pancreas, and liver are functioning.
- Parasite evaluation—a fecal sample reveals difficulties with digestion, internal bleeding, and pancreatic disorders.

These regular laboratory tests provide important health information in the event that your senior dog requires emergency surgery. Also, as his senses (sight, hearing, taste, touch, and smell) begin to dull, it's important to maintain regular veterinary care because your doctor's examination can catch something that you may miss.

SENIOR ILLNESSES

Just because your dog is getting older, don't assume that nothing can be done to help him. Many behavior changes are signs of other medical disorders, and many therapies are available to comfort your Boston and help ease pain and manage his symptoms.

Arthritis

Osteoarthritis, or degenerative joint diseases (DJD), is a progressive debilitating disorder that affects up to 20 percent of older dogs. Although it can be found in any joint, it most often occurs in the hips. Dogs with arthritis are stiff and slow to rise when they

Your older Boston Terrier should have a veterinary checkup twice a year.

first get up in the morning or after a nap and vigorous exercise.

To treat arthritis, control the pain, increase mobility, and slow down the destructive process in the joint and encourage cartilage repair, many veterinarians recommend using drugs and nonsteroidal anti-inflammatory medications (similar to ibuprofen for people).

Other ways to treat canine arthritis include acupuncture, water therapy, massage, and supplements such as chondroitin, glucosamine, and omega-3 fatty acids (fish oil). These therapies provide pain relief by reducing swelling in the joints and improving circulation and mobility. The Journal of the American Veterinary Medical Association reports that dogs who receive omega-3 fatty acids (fish oil) for the treatment of arthritis or degenerative joint disease have an improved ability to rise from a resting position and play by 6 weeks after beginning supplementation, with improved ability to walk by 12 weeks.

To provide some relief from arthritis or stiffness in the joints, keep your dog warm and comfortable. Older dogs tend to chill easily, so protect your Boston from any cold or drafty areas, especially where he sleeps. A crate with full sides will keep him warmer than a wire crate, as will a heated dog blanket. A memory foam dog bed also helps cushion pressure points that can cause muscle and joint stiffness.

To support your Boston when he climbs up or down stairs, gets in and out of the car, or walks across floors, have him wear an ergonomic canine support harness. A fabric handle at the top of the harness helps you lift and restore his balance. Or place a fabric sling close to his rear legs and tie it loosely at the top to help lift his rear end when necessary. If your Boston has a tendency to slip on slick surfaces, try applying an all-natural rosin spray to the pads of his feet to give him more traction.

Athletes use it to improve their grip for sweaty hands. Your dog will appreciate slipper socks with nonskid material on the bottom to help keep him from slipping and falling.

To help your dog climb into the car or onto the bed or couch more easily, construct inexpensive steps or a ramp, or purchase one already made from a pet supply store. Just make sure that it is sturdy enough, and be sure to supervise your dog when he uses it so he doesn't tumble off the platform.

Canine Cognitive Dysfunction Syndrome

Similar to Alzheimer's disease, which disturbs people, canine cognitive dysfunction syndrome (CDS) is caused by physical and chemical changes that affect brain function in older dogs. It is often associated with the depletion of dopamine, a neurotransmitter or chemical in the brain that reduces the activity of nerve cells.

Some Bostons with CDS may show physical signs or exhibit behavioral changes that are not a normal part of aging as early as eight years of age. The symptoms include aimless wandering, pacing, disorientation, confusion about familiar places (such as getting stuck in a corner or lost in the yard), forgetting about housetraining, eating, or drinking water, or an inability to recognize favorite people. They may stare into space or withdraw from family members.

Dogs with CDS also experience a decline in physical functioning. They may lose their memory and suffer a decrease in their awareness and their senses of sight and hearing. These changes cause sleep disturbances, making them restless at night but sleepy throughout the day.

To diagnose CDS, a veterinarian will perform a physical examination, note the dog's health history, and perform routine diagnostic tests.

These may include a serum chemistry blood profile, complete blood count, urinalysis, and an electrocardiogram. A brief neurological examination, including an assessment of cranial nerves, an X-ray, and an ultrasound may also be used to rule out any medical conditions that might affect behavior.

Other health problems that may cause the same symptoms as CDS are kidney, thyroid, or adrenal gland disease. Some signs of CDS may be subtle and not readily apparent during an examination.

Once your veterinarian confirms a CDS diagnosis, he or he may prescribe the drug L-Deprenyl (Anipryl®). Although this drug may help slow the process and improve the symptoms of CDS, it may produce side effects. Discuss the pros and cons of giving this medication to your Boston Terrier.

Some veterinarians may also recommend choline, a natural vitamin supplement, to help increase mental alertness. You can find choline supplements for dogs at pet supply stores that have a natural or organic food and supplement section. Other remedies that may help improve cognitive dysfunction include dietary supplements and environmental enrichment through training, exercise, and grooming. Diets containing antioxidants (mixed tocopherols, vitamin C, beta-carotene, carotenoids, and flavonoids), mitochondrial cofactors (coenzyme Q10), and omega-3 fatty acids (EPA, DHA) have also been shown to help improve cognitive ability in older dogs.

Congestive Heart Failure

The heart of a dog diagnosed with congestive heart failure cannot pump blood effectively, and fluid can back up into the lungs or abdomen. Bostons with congestive heart failure often cough and have shortness of breath, difficulty in breathing, fatigue, or weight loss.

To diagnose this problem, your veterinarian will listen to the dog's heart with a stethoscope, looking for heart murmurs or sounds of moisture buildup in the chest. He or she may perform other tests, including a chest X-ray, an electrocardiogram (ECG), or an echocardiogram.

Bacterial infections, heartworm disease, sudden injury, heatstroke, degenerated heart valve tissue, and high blood pressure can cause congestive heart disease.

Medications are available to treat congestive heart failure, and the veterinarian will recommend feeding a diet low in salt and high in nutrients. With the proper treatment, dogs with heart disease can live a normal life for months or even years.

Cushing's Disease (Hyperadrenocorticism)

Common in Boston Terriers five years and older, Cushing's disease is caused when the adrenal glands, which are found on top of the upper part of the kidneys, produce too much cortisol in the body. Cortisol is a corticosteroid

By the Numbers

Veterinary researchers at the University of California School of Veterinary Medicine report that 62 percent of 11- to 16-year-old dogs showed at least one sign of cognitive dysfunction syndrome (CDS), with 100 percent of dogs 16 years of age and older affected. A pet owner survey claims that nearly half of dogs 8 years and older exhibited one symptom associated with CDS.

Certain behavior changes in seniors may be signs of a medical disorder, so have your dog examined by your vet if you notice anything unusual.

hormone involved in metabolism. A tumor can lead to too much cortisol and eventually Cushing's disease.

Signs of this disease include excessive thirst and urination. Because it thins the muscles of the abdomen, causing enlargement of the liver, dogs with Cushing's disease have a rounded, pot-bellied appearance. Excess cortisone increases appetite and thirst, which results in weight gain. A skin rash, weakness, sluggishness, and wounds that heal slowly are other signs. Coats may also develop a rust or brown color and the hair may become sparse, especially on the outside of both legs. The hair on the head and legs usually remains the same.

The veterinarian can diagnose Cushing's disease by performing a series of blood tests to measure levels of cortisol. Medications are available to decrease the amount of cortisol in the body but they must be closely monitored. Some have more side effects than others. If Cushing's disease is left untreated, it often progresses to life-threatening conditions such as congestive heart failure, liver failure, diabetes, and neurological disorders. While none of the medications restore normal adrenal function, they provide some relief, and dogs with this disease may live a few more quality years.

Eye Problems

Boston Terriers are prone to developing more than 20 different eye diseases, with cataracts being the most common.

Cataracts

According to a study conducted by the Boston Terrier Club of America in 2000, about 9 percent of Bostons have cataracts late in life.

A cataract is opacity in the lens of the eye. The lens is clear and transmits and focuses light onto the retina in the back of the eye. A cataract in the lens blocks the transmission of light to the retina. Depending upon the severity of the disorder, the opacity may be small and look like white flecks in the eye. Most likely this will not disturb the dog's vision, unless the cataracts progress into a more solid-looking milky gray cast. The thicker and denser they become, the more likely they will lead to blindness.

Most cataracts are genetically transmitted types. They may also develop after a trauma to the eye, and also from diabetes. They may occur in old age, as does nuclear sclerosis, a normal aging change that occurs in the lens and does not cause blindness. If you notice any cloudiness in your dog's eye, take him to the veterinarian for an examination. Mature or complete cataracts or another condition that causes cloudiness in the eye can be diagnosed by dilating the eye and examining it with magnification and a strong light source. The veterinarian may refer you to a veterinary ophthalmologist who can detect small cataracts. This specialist can perform a more thorough examination using high-tech equipment and can suggest ways to manage the condition.

While there is no medical treatment to reverse, prevent, or shrink cataracts, a dog may be a candidate for cataract surgery. Surgically removing the lens and replacing it with an acrylic lens may help restore vision loss caused by cataracts.

For dogs with vision problems, there are a few things you can do to make life easier. Keep everything in its place, as now's not the time to rearrange the furniture. By this time your dog knows where everything is located in the house and can find his way around. Don't leave objects lying around on the floor because your dog may trip and fall over them. Create familiar paths such as carpet runners on slippery floors inside the house and outdoor carpeting or gravel walks outdoors, so your dog can feel with his paws where he's headed. Block off dangerous places, such as stairways and open doors and windows, and prevent access to the swimming pool. Make sure that your yard is securely fenced. Most dogs with limited eyesight function well in familiar settings.

Glaucoma

Glaucoma is a painful buildup of pressure inside the eye. It is the seventh most common health problem in Bostons over seven years of age. According to a study conducted by the Boston Terrier Club of America, glaucoma affects about 1 percent of Boston Terriers.

A cause of blindness, glaucoma develops when the small drainage sites within the eye begin to narrow or become blocked. The condition is inherited or can occur from a complication of another eye disease, injury, tumors, or infections.

The symptoms of glaucoma are readily apparent. The whites of the infected eye will turn red and the pupil will be dilated. The increased pressure inside the eye will cause squinting, drainage, and swelling of the eye. Not every dog shows the same symptoms of glaucoma. Some may experience pain or rub their eyes with their paws or on the ground; some may show no signs.

A veterinary ophthalmologist can test the pressure in the eye with a tonometer, a blunt-tipped instrument that gently touches the

Training Tidbit

If your Boston is losing his hearing, try substituting your verbal cues for hand signals. You don't need to know American Sign Language to communicate with your dog nonverbally. Keep the commands simple, and make sure that you have your Boston's attention. Follow up compliance by giving your dog a food treat, a hug, or petting.

cornea and provides a digital measure of the pressure in the eye.

Treatment includes reducing the pressure to decrease the pain and to prevent the glaucoma from advancing. Medication can help remove fluid from the eye or to reduce fluid production. Surgery or laser therapy may also help. In severe cases where the vision is lost, the entire eye may be removed so a dog will not suffer any more pain. If glaucoma is detected early enough, blindness may be preventable.

TRAINING

Like people, dogs need mental and physical exercise to stay alert and healthy into old age. It's simply not true that you can't teach an old Boston some new tricks. In some ways, training an older dog may be even easier than training a puppy.

While a senior may have a slower learning curve, he already knows the meaning of "no" and is calmer and less excitable than a youngster. An older dog has a longer attention span. He's more keyed into accepting the handler's leadership and understands dominance, so he may retain lessons faster.

How to Make Training Easier

Whether you adopted an older dog from a shelter or rescue and don't know what previous training he has had, or you're introducing new behaviors to your long-time canine companion, you'll need patience.

Just as with training younger dogs, keep training sessions short. You can accomplish more in three five-minute sessions than you will in one long fifteen-minute session. Use food treats, toys, praise, or petting to reward good behavior and ignore the bad. Keep all training lessons positive, upbeat, and fun so

Want to Know More?

For a refresher on training your dog, see Chapter 9, Boston Terrier Training.

your dog looks forward to working with you.

Don't assume that your older dog can't hear you and that you have to repeat the commands over and over. Saying, "Sit, sit, sit," trains your dog to ignore you the first few times you tell him to do something. Give the command once, and reward your dog when he complies. Train the behavior you do want and ignore the behavior you don't want.

To help keep your older Boston's mind sharp, as well as provide him with some fun, give him an interactive chew or food puzzle toy, like the ones made by Nylabone. Stuff the food puzzle toy with your dog's favorite treats, such as peanut butter, cheese, cooked oatmeal, or hot dog pieces. He'll have to figure out how to get the food out by pawing, shaking, rolling, nibbling, or licking the toy. Chewing and licking has a calming effect on dogs, and getting at the goodies takes time and patience. Expanding his problem-solving skills enhances the training you do with him.

If your dog has forgotten his housetraining lessons, don't reprimand or punish him. No matter how much your older dog wants to please you, he may be physically unable to do so. Clean him up and go back to housetraining basics. Supervise him as if he were a puppy by taking him outside more frequently—when he awakens from a nap, right after every meal, and every two hours or so. Expect bathroom accidents and plan for cleanup.

Don't hesitate to consult with a certified professional dog trainer (CPDT) if you need help training your senior or for some new fun ways to teach your dog.

CHAPTER 14

END-OF-LIFE ISSUES

No matter how long you share your life with your Boston Terrier, it's never enough time. When your Boston was a young pup you couldn't imagine the day when he might suffer from a terminal illness and you would have to care for him and eventually make the decision to end his life.

There's nothing more painful than grieving for a dog you've happily shared your life with. Explaining death to children is never easy, but remembering the fun times with your Boston always helps.

WHEN IS IT TIME?

When the time comes to say goodbye to your dog, you may wonder whether you are doing the right thing. If so, try to think about his present quality of life. Is he enjoying his meals? A good game? Going for a walk? Being petted by the family? Is he handling bathroom issues without seeming to be embarrassed? Is he in pain?

If your dog cannot maintain the quality of life he once enjoyed, it may be time to consider euthanasia. Sometimes you might not notice that your dog is suffering. The will to survive is strong and prevents a dog from showing any signs of pain.

HOSPICE AND EUTHANASIA

Depending upon your dog's condition, you may be able to care for him at the end of his life in your home and provide comfort until he decides to take his last breath. Sometimes that's not possible and you are faced with the unpleasant decision of ending his life.

Only you know when the time is right to say goodbye to your dog. While well-meaning friends and relatives feel free to tell you what you should do, the responsibility for this choice solely rests on your shoulders. It's even more difficult when two people share the responsibility of caring for a dog.

To help you make the decision easier, ask yourself the following questions:

By the Numbers

With proper care, the life span of a Boston Terrier can be as long as 15 years.

- Does my Boston suffer from a terminal illness? If so, ask your veterinarian what to expect and ask yourself whether you're capable of caring for your dog.
- Is he suffering pain that can't be alleviated by medication? No doubt you wouldn't want your dog to suffer in pain.
- If treatment is available, will it improve your dog's quality of life or only maintain a poor quality? Surely you don't want to put your dog through additional pain with treatment if it's not effective.
- Can you honestly afford end-of-life treatment? This can be very expensive, with little relief for your dog.
- Has your dog lost all of his bodily functions? If he can no longer stand up, lie down, defecate or urinate normally, his quality of life is greatly diminished.
- Does your dog still have an appetite? The ability to sustain himself is a basic need. When a dog no longer chooses that option, this is a signal that he's close to the end.

The memories you have of your senior Boston can help comfort you during this difficult time.

Want to Know More?

Some veterinary hospitals and organizations offer hospice care, which allows pets to be kept comfortable in their own homes during their last days and gives family members time to come to terms with their impending loss. If you are interested in learning more about veterinary home hospice care, ask your vet or contact your closest veterinary school. The American Association of Human-Animal Bond Veterinarians (AAH-ABV) offers information on its website at http://aah-abv.org.

• For whom are you extending your dog's life? For him or for yourself? Be honest when answering this question.

Whatever you decide, know that your dog is grateful for everything you have ever done for him and that he doesn't blame you for any hard decisions you must make.

GRIEF

Everyone experiences loss differently, and there's no right or wrong way to deal with grief. In the past, whenever you felt sad your dog instinctively knew the best time to comfort you. He'd come to you, jump up on your knees or lap, and look at you with those big brown eyes, only now he's not there.

Explaining Pet Loss to Children

It's hard enough to deal with your own feelings of loss over your beloved dog, but explaining the death of a pet to children is even harder. While it may seem easier to protect little ones from grief by minimizing

their pain, a better option is to teach them how to cope with the reality.

If your dog is terminally ill and death is pending, discuss this with your children as soon as possible. Kids want to know first and foremost that their grief is normal and that it's all right to feel sad. Let them know that it is the pet's death and not something they did or didn't do that caused your tears or unhappiness.

Explain that death means that the dog's body will stop working and it is not the same as sleeping. Avoid using the common phrase for euthanasia, "put to sleep," so children will not experience anxiety when it's time for them to go to bed. Children shouldn't be told that the dog has "passed away," "left us," or "gone on." These phrases translate to the dog's going on a trip and coming back and give the impression that he may return or is simply lost. Choose instead to tell children that the dog is suffering with a disease that

◎ Training Tidbit

After a lifetime of positive training, you've established a strong bond with your dog. When aging and illness begin to take their toll, this relationship will help you to observe the tell-tale behavior changes that will require you to assess his quality-of-life issues. This bond will also reassure you that your dog knows you love him, and that he will trust you to make the right decisions for him, sometimes even letting you know he's ready to leave.

Because dogs feel the loss of other canine companions, provide your surviving pet with lots of extra love, attention, and patience.

can't be cured and is extremely ill or that there has been an accident. Don't blame the veterinarian because children should trust the doctor and not develop a fear of health caregivers.

If possible, prepare children ahead of time and discuss the veterinarian's diagnosis and your dog's quality of life. If children are old enough, think about letting them be present during the procedure if they so choose. Witnessing a peaceful death is less traumatic to children than a fantasy about what might happen. Encourage children to see the dog after euthanization to remove the mystery about death.

Allow children to express their feelings and share their sadness. If they don't bring it up, ask what they are thinking about their departed dog. This lets them know that he hasn't been forgotten and that it's okay to remember him.

Whatever you do, don't run out and buy another Boston Terrier—or any other dog for that matter—to replace the one you just lost. This sends the message that a dog is replaceable. While you may want to get another dog, let some time pass so that everyone in the family can adjust to the loss and take the time to grieve.

MEMORIALIZING YOUR BOSTON

Coping with the loss of your Boston is heart wrenching, but sometimes if you can find a few ways to create a memorial to your dog it may help ease the pain. Some Boston owners use social networking to post a message on a website grief forum list, or create a Facebook page or a website to remember their special companion. This gives friends you may not regularly communicate with the opportunity to comfort you long distance. Sometimes they will remember special times they shared with your dog that you may have forgotten.

If you have a favorite photograph of your dog, commission a professional portrait or work of art. Some owners plant a memorial tree or purchase a garden memorial or stone engraved with the name of their Boston and place it in their dog's favorite spot in the yard.

Now may be a good time to gather up all of the photographs you've even taken of your dog and put them together in a colorful scrapbook.

This walk down memory lane gives you the opportunity to recall the special times you shared with your dog.

For owners who feel comfortable expressing their thoughts on paper, writing a poem, a song, or a story about their dog or writing a letter to him may provide peace. Artists find solace by creating a special work of art in their dog's memory.

Donating to an animal rescue group, your local shelter, or the Boston Terrier Club of America in your dog's name pays your Boston's memory forward as it helps other canines.

Other owners use a portion of their dog's ashes to create a special piece of jewelry or retain them in a special container as keepsakes.

These are just a few ways to remember your dog. But perhaps you won't be able to do anything until the pain subsides a bit. That's alright. Your dog knows how much you loved him while he was alive. Give yourself time to treasure your memories in the way that works best for you.

HELPING OTHER PETS DEAL WITH LOSS

Dogs are bonded to one another in a household and know when one is missing. They feel the loss of other canine companions and may act depressed. This is the perfect time to give your surviving dog a lot of extra attention and love. Provide a few minutes of extra exercise and playtime and perhaps a few extra treats.

Multi-Dog Tip

When one dog passes on, his canine companion may feel the loss in much the same way that humans do. He may seem depressed, lose his appetite, sleep more, or generally seem lost without a partner. The remaining dog may sense your grief as well, which may double his sadness. Here's where time, patience, and providing extra love and attention will heal.

50 FUN FACTS EVERY BOSTON TERRIER OWNER SHOULD KNOW

1. The Boston Terrier's seal color only glows red when in the sun or bright light.

2. The Boston reaches his full height at 9 or 10 months of age. Over the next three years, he will lose that puppy look and round out to develop a more mature appearance as his muscle tone develops.

3. Sweet Sociable Samuel, owned by Nancy Ames, was the first Boston to earn the AKC Agility title and also the first to win a NAFA Flyball dog title (1990).

4. The normal body temperature for a Boston Terrier is about 100° to 102°F (38° to 39°C) and a normal pulse rate at rest is about 60 to 120 beats per minute.

5. Boston Terriers are prone to developing more than 20 different eye diseases, with cataracts being the most common.

6. The Boston is a brachycephalic breed. This means he has a flat face and a short, compacted muzzle.

7. The breed's hometown is Boston, Massachusetts. In 1979, the Boston Terrier was named the official state dog.

8. The breed dates back to 1870, with Robert C. Hooper of Boston purchasing an imported dog named Judge. That dog became known as Hooper's Judge and was the ancestor of the modern-day Boston Terrier.

9. Hooper's Judge was a cross between an English Bulldog and the now-extinct white English Terrier, who weighed about 32 pounds (15 kg).

10. Original works of art from the late 19th century through the mid-20th century depicting Boston Terriers are highly sought after by collectors.

11. Oil paintings, watercolors, pastels, and prints of Boston Terriers can run into thousands of dollars if signed by artists Lucy Dawson or Reuben Binks.

12. In 1976, the Boston Terrier was named America's Bicentennial Dog.

13. Until the 1940s, Boston Terriers weighed 25 to 35 pounds (11 to 16 kg).

14. The combination that was originally used to develop the Boston Terrier is the same combination (Bulldog-and-terrier cross) used to create the American Pit Bull Terrier and other fighting breeds.

15. The Boston temperament lies somewhere in the middle of mellow and more stubborn Bulldog temperaments to the feistier, terrier attitude.

16. The Boston's thin coat requires additional protection from cold weather.

17. Boston puppies are big chewers and need plenty of stimulating, hard, chew toys.

18. Most Bostons are good with children who are taught to behave properly around dogs.

19. The breed is active, busy, and lively, and not likely to be a couch potato.

20. Bostons love to play tug or any game with people, especially retrieving a ball as often as the owner will throw it.

21. Bostons don't enjoy being left home alone for long hours.

22. Male Bostons tend to be more dependent and develop a special attachment to one family member.

23. Two Bostons enjoy one another's company but will vie for their owner's individual attention.

24. It may take Boston puppies two or three years to get over destructive chewing.

25. Bostons are sensitive dogs and seem to know what you are thinking.

26. As long as they receive some exercise every day, Bostons adapt to most lifestyles and enjoy living in the country or the city.

27. When raised together, Bostons and cats may get along well. Introduced later in life, however, this may not be so.

28. Bostons are motivated by food and toys, which helps during training.

29. According to the Boston Terrier standard, the dog must not appear spindly or coarse. A blocky or chunky appearance is considered a fault.

30. The ideal Boston Terrier must be a compact dog with a large, square head. The head is one of the most important hallmarks of the breed.

31. Ideal ears on the Boston should be small and carried erect, set up high on the head. Today, most people showing their dogs will leave the ears natural and uncropped.

32. Bostons are a generally healthy and sturdy breed, with only a few genetic illnesses.

33. Bostons are capable of following a scent and can participate in AKC tracking events.

34. Health-care facilities welcome well-behaved and qualified Bostons as therapy dogs.

35. Bostons will enjoy water activities if you introduce them gradually and playfully, making them a positive experience.

36. Bostons are prone to reverse sneezing, which occurs when air is sucked in during a sneeze instead of blown out. After a minute or two, it will end on its own or you can gently stroke your dog's throat to help him swallow.

37. Stress hormones, which are triggered by changes in light and temperature, illness, or dietary insufficiencies, affect shedding in Bostons.

38. You can use your hand to loosen dead hair in a Boston's coat. This massage helps distribute the oils in the coat and makes it healthy.

39. Remove tear stains on the face by wiping the area daily with a damp washcloth.

40. Besides using a toothbrush to brush your dog's teeth every day, you can wrap a small washcloth around your finger and rub your dog's teeth and gums to keep them clean.

41. The Boston Terrier Club of America works in conjunction with 25 affiliate breed clubs throughout the United States.

42. The Breed Standard of the Boston Terrier was originally written by the Boston Terrier Club of America and approved by the American Kennel Club in 1900. It has been revised a few times; most recently in 1990.

43. Created in 1891, the Boston Terrier Club of America was one of the first dog breed clubs in America.

44. The Boston Terrier breed was first recognized by AKC in 1893.

45. From 1905 to 1935, the breed was ranked first or second among the most popular breeds registered by the American Kennel Club.

46. In recent years the breed has hovered in the top 20 breed rankings, moving from 21st place in 1996 to 19th in 2009.

47. Although the breed was known throughout the United States, people believed that the best dogs were in Boston.

48. In the early 1900s, a Boston puppy from top stock sold for $100 to $150, which was a lot of money in those days!

49. President Warren G. Harding, Bing Crosby, and jazzman Louis Armstrong each had a Boston Terrier. Silent-film star Pola Negri took her Boston, Patsy, with her everywhere.

50. The Boston Terrier is a highly intelligent breed and can understand the meaning of 50 or more words.

ASSOCIATIONS AND ORGANIZATIONS

Breed Clubs

American Kennel Club (AKC)
5580 Centerview Drive
Raleigh, NC 27606
Telephone: (919) 233-9767
Fax: (919) 233-3627
E-Mail: info@akc.org
www.akc.org

Boston Terrier Club of America
www.bostonterrierclubofamerica.org

Boston Terrier Club of Canada
www.bostonterrierclubofcanada.com

Canadian Kennel Club (CKC)
89 Skyway Avenue, Suite 100
Etobicoke, Ontario M9W 6R4
Canada
Telephone: (416) 675-5511
Fax: (416) 675-6506
E-Mail: information@ckc.ca
www.ckc.ca

Federation Cynologique Internationale (FCI)
Secretariat General de la FCI
Place Albert 1er, 13
B–6530 Thuin
Belqique
www.fci.be

The Kennel Club
1 Clarges Street
London W1J 8AB
England
Telephone: 0870 606 6750
Fax: 0207 518 1058
www.the-kennel-club.org.uk

United Kennel Club (UKC)
100 E. Kilgore Road
Kalamazoo, MI 49002-5584
Telephone: (269) 343-9020
Fax: (269) 343-7037
E-Mail: pbickell@ukcdogs.com
www.ukcdogs.com

Pet Sitters

National Association of Professional Pet Sitters
15000 Commerce Parkway, Suite C
Mt. Laurel, NJ 08054
Telephone: (856) 439-0324
Fax: (856) 439-0525
E-Mail: napps@ahint.com
www.petsitters.org

Pet Sitters International
201 East King Street
King, NC 27021-9161
Telephone: (336) 983-9222
Fax: (336) 983-5266
E-Mail: info@petsit.com
www.petsit.com

Rescue Organizations and Animal Welfare Groups

American Humane Association (AHA)
63 Inverness Drive East
Englewood, CO 80112
Telephone: (303) 792-9900
Fax: 792-5333
www.americanhumane.org

American Society for the Prevention of Cruelty to Animals (ASPCA)
424 E. 92nd Street
New York, NY 10128-6804
Telephone: (212) 876-7700
www.aspca.org

The Humane Society of the United States (HSUS)
2100 L Street, NW
Washington, DC 20037
Telephone: (202) 452-1100
www.hsus.org

Royal Society for the Prevention of Cruelty to Animals (RSPCA)
RSPCA Enquiries Service
Wilberforce Way, Southwater,
Horsham, West Sussex RH13 9RS
United Kingdom
Telephone: 0870 3335 999
Fax: 0870 7530 284
www.rspca.org.uk

Sports

International Agility Link (IAL)
Global Administrator: Steve Drinkwater
E-Mail: yunde@powerup.au
www.agilityclick.com/~ial

The World Canine Freestyle Organization, Inc.
P.O. Box 350122
Brooklyn, NY 11235
Telephone: (718) 332-8336
Fax: (718) 646-2686
E-Mail: WCFODOGS@aol.com
www.worldcaninefreestyle.org

Therapy

Delta Society
875 124th Ave, NE, Suite 101
Bellevue, WA 98005
Telephone: (425) 679-5500
Fax: (425) 679-5539
E-Mail: info@DeltaSociety.org
www.deltasociety.org

Therapy Dogs, Inc.
P.O. Box 20227
Cheyenne, WY 82003
Telephone: (877) 843-7364
Fax: (307) 638-2079
E-Mail: therapydogsinc@qwestoffice.net
www.therapydogs.com

Therapy Dogs International (TDI)
88 Bartley Road
Flanders, NJ 07836
Telephone: (973) 252-9800
Fax: (973) 252-7171
E-Mail: tdi@gti.net
www.tdi-dog.org

Training

Association of Pet Dog Trainers (APDT)
150 Executive Center Drive, Box 35
Greenville, SC 29615
Telephone: (800) PET-DOGS
Fax: (864) 331-0767
E-Mail: information@apdt.com
www.apdt.com

International Association of Animal Behavior Consultants (IAABC)
565 Callery Road
Cranberry Township, PA 16066
E-Mail: info@iaabc.org
www.iaabc.org

National Association of Dog Obedience Instructors (NADOI)
PMB 369
729 Grapevine Hwy.
Hurst, TX 76054-2085
www.nadoi.org

Veterinary and Health Resources

Academy of Veterinary Homeopathy (AVH)
P.O. Box 9280
Wilmington, DE 19809
Telephone: (866) 652-1590
Fax: (866) 652-1590
www.theavh.org

American Academy of Veterinary Acupuncture (AAVA)
P.O. Box 1058
Glastonbury, CT 06033
Telephone: (860) 632-9911
Fax: (860) 659-8772
www.aava.org

American Animal Hospital Association (AAHA)
12575 W. Bayaud Ave.
Lakewood, CO 80228
Telephone: (303) 986-2800
Fax: (303) 986-1700
E-Mail: info@aahanet.org
www.aahanet.org/index.cfm

American College of Veterinary Internal Medicine (ACVIM)
1997 Wadsworth Blvd., Suite A
Lakewood, CO 80214-5293
Telephone: (800) 245-9081
Fax: (303) 231-0880
E-Mail: ACVIM@ACVIM.org
www.acvim.org

American College of Veterinary Ophthalmologists (ACVO)
P.O. Box 1311
Meridian, ID 83860
Telephone: (208) 466-7624
Fax: (208) 466-7693
E-Mail: office09@acvo.com
www.acvo.com

American Holistic Veterinary Medical Association (AHVMA)
2218 Old Emmorton Road
Bel Air, MD 21015
Telephone: (410) 569-0795
Fax: (410) 569-2346
E-Mail: office@ahvma.org
www.ahvma.org

American Veterinary Medical Association (AVMA)
1931 North Meacham Road, Suite 100
Schaumburg, IL 60173-4360
Telephone: (847) 925-8070
Fax: (847) 925-1329
E-Mail: avmainfo@avma.org
www.avma.org

ASPCA Animal Poison Control Center
Telephone: (888) 426-4435
www.aspca.org

British Veterinary Association (BVA)
7 Mansfield Street
London W1G 9NQ
England
Telephone: 0207 636 6541
Fax: 0207 908 6349
E-Mail: bvahq@bva.co.uk
www.bva.co.uk

Canine Eye Registration Foundation (CERF)
VMDB/CERF
1717 Philo Rd.
P.O. Box 3007
Urbana, IL 61803-3007
Telephone: (217) 693-4800
Fax: (217) 693-4801
E-Mail: CERF@vmbd.org
www.vmdb.org

Orthopedic Foundation for Animals (OFA)
2300 NE Nifong Blvd.
Columbus, MO 65201-3856
Telephone: (573) 442-0418
Fax: (573) 875-5073
E-Mail: ofa@offa.org
www.offa.org

**US Food and Drug
Administration Center for
Veterinary Medicine (CVM)**
7519 Standish Place
HFV-12
Rockville, MD 20855-0001
Telephone: (240) 276-9300 or
(888) INFO-FDA
http://www.fda.gov/cvm

PUBLICATIONS

BOOKS

Anderson, Teoti. *The Super
Simple Guide to Housetraining.*
Neptune City: TFH
Publications, 2004.

Anne, Jonna, with Mary Straus.
*The Healthy Dog Cookbook: 50
Nutritious and Delicious Recipes
Your Dog Will Love.* UK: Ivy
Press Limited, 2008.

Dainty, Suellen. *50 Games to
Play With Your Dog.* UK: Ivy
Press Limited, 2007.

Libby, Tracy. *The Boston
Terrier.* Neptune City: TFH
Publications, 2005.

Morgan, Diane. *Good
Dogkeeping.* Neptune City: TFH
Publications, 2005.

MAGAZINES

AKC Family Dog
American Kennel Club
260 Madison Avenue
New York, NY 10016
Telephone: (800) 490-5675
E-Mail: familydog@akc.org
www.akc.org/pubs/familydog

AKC Gazette
American Kennel Club
260 Madison Avenue
New York, NY 10016
Telephone: (800) 533-7323
E-Mail: gazette@akc.org
www.akc.org/pubs/gazette

Dog & Kennel
Pet Publishing, Inc.
7-L Dundas Circle
Greensboro, NC 27407
Telephone: (336) 292-4272
Fax: (336) 292-4272
E-Mail: info@petpublishing.com
www.dogandkennel.com

Dogs Monthly
Ascot House
High Street, Ascot,
Berkshire SL5 7JG
United Kingdom
Telephone: 0870 730 8433
Fax: 0870 730 8431
E-Mail: admin@rtc-associates.
freeserve.co.uk
www.corsini.co.uk/dogsmonthly

WEBSITES

Nylabone
www.nylabone.com

TFH Publications, Inc.
www.tfh.com

PHOTO CREDITS

ABOUT THE AUTHOR

Elaine Waldorf Gewirtz, a lifelong dog owner, is the author of 13 books and nearly a hundred magazine articles about dogs. She's a multiple recipient of the prestigious Maxwell Award for writing excellence from the Dog Writers Association of America, the ASPCA Humane Issues Award, and the Wiley/Ellsworth S. Howell Award. While she was growing up, her family bred Boston Terriers, and Elaine's first Boston as an adult was her beloved Daisy. She and her husband live in Westlake Village, California, with their four-footed best friends.

VETERINARY ADVISOR

Wayne Hunthausen, D.V.M., consulting veterinary editor and pet behavior consultant, is the director of Animal Behavior Consultations in the Kansas City area and currently serves on the Practitioner Board for *Veterinary Medicine* and the Behavior Advisory Board for *Veterinary Forum*.

BREED ADVISOR

Carl E. Gomes, breed advisor, has been involved in the sport of dogs since he was a teenager. His first acquisition was a Boston Terrier. He started showing in 1968 and was granted a Professional Handlers License in 1973, courtesy of the American Kennel Club. He is currently licensed to judge Best In Show, the Non-Sporting Group, and several breeds in other groups.

   Carl is also Chairman of Judges Education for the Boston Terrier Club of America. He is responsible for the training and development of future judges of the breed and the dissemination of information, with the intent to promote and protect the interests of the breed. His judging assignments, which include the Westminster Kennel Club and the AKC Eukanuba Invitational, have also taken him to several states and foreign countries. He has been a member of several National Breed Clubs and is currently a Delegate to the American Kennel Club, representing the Pacific Coast Boston Terrier Club, based in Los Angeles, California.